Nutshell Series

of

WEST PUBLISHING COMPANY

P.O. Box 3526

St. Paul, Minnesota 55165

October, 1983

Accounting—Law and, 1984, approximately 392 pages, by E. McGruder Faris, Professor of Law, Stetson University.

Administrative Law and Process, 2nd Ed., 1981, 445 pages, by Ernest Gellhorn, Dean and Professor of Law, Case Western Reserve University and Barry B. Boyer, Professor of Law, SUNY, Buffalo.

Admiralty, 1983, 400 pages, by Frank L. Maraist, Professor of Law, Louisiana State University.

Agency-Partnership, 1977, 364 pages, by Roscoe T. Steffen, Late Professor of Law, University of Chicago.

American Indian Law, 1981, 288 pages, by William C. Canby, Jr., former Professor of Law, Arizona State University.

Antitrust Law and Economics, 2nd Ed., 1981, 425 pages, by Ernest Gellhorn, Dean and Professor of Law, Case Western Reserve University.

Banking and Financial Institutions, 1984, approximately 406 pages, by William A. Lovett, Professor of Law, Tulane University.

Church-State Relations—Law of, 1981, 305 pages, by Leonard F. Manning, Late Professor of Law, Fordham University.

Civil Procedure, 1979, 271 pages, by Mary Kay Kane, Professor of Law, University of California, Hastings College of the Law.

Civil Rights, 1978, 279 pages, by Norman Vieira, Professor of Law, Southern Illinois University.

Commercial Paper, 3rd Ed., 1982, 404 pages, by Charles M. Weber, Professor of Business Law, University of Arizona and Richard E. Speidel, Professor of Law, Northwestern University.

Community Property, 1982, 423 pages, by Robert L. Mennell, Professor of Law, Hamline University.

Comparative Legal Traditions, 1982, 402 pages, by Mary Ann Glendon, Professor of Law, Boston College, Michael Wallace Gordon, Professor of Law, University of Florida and Christopher Osakwe, Professor of Law, Tulane University.

Conflicts, 1982, 469 pages, by David D. Siegel, Professor of Law, Albany Law School, Union University.

Constitutional Analysis, 1979, 388 pages, by Jerre S. Williams, Professor of Law Emeritus, University of Texas.

Constitutional Power—Federal and State, 1974, 411 pages, by David E. Engdahl, Professor of Law, University of Puget Sound.

Consumer Law, 2nd Ed., 1981, 418 pages, by David G. Epstein, Professor of Law, University of Texas and Steve H. Nickles, Professor of Law, University of Minnesota.

Contract Remedies, 1981, 323 pages, by Jane M. Friedman, Professor of Law, Wayne State University.

Contracts, 2nd Ed., 1983, approximately 410 pages, by Gordon D. Schaber, Dean and Professor of Law, McGeorge School of Law and Claude D. Rohwer, Professor of Law, McGeorge School of Law.

Corporations—Law of, 1980, 379 pages, by Robert W. Hamilton, Professor of Law, University of Texas.

Corrections and Prisoners' Rights—Law of, 2nd Ed., 1983, 384 pages, by Sheldon Krantz, Dean and Professor of Law, University of San Diego.

Criminal Law, 1975, 302 pages, by Arnold H. Loewy, Professor of Law, University of North Carolina.

Criminal Procedure—Constitutional Limitations, 3rd Ed., 1980, 438 pages, by Jerold H. Israel, Professor of Law, University of Michigan and Wayne R. LaFave, Professor of Law, University of Illinois.

Debtor-Creditor Law, 2nd Ed., 1980, 324 pages, by David G. Epstein, Professor of Law, University of Texas.

Employment Discrimination—Federal Law of, 2nd Ed., 1981, 402 pages, by Mack A. Player, Professor of Law, University of Georgia.

Energy Law, 1981, 338 pages, by Joseph P. Tomain, Professor of Law, Drake University.

Environmental Law, 1983, 343 pages by Roger W. Findley, Professor of Law, University of Illinois and Daniel A. Farber, Professor of Law, University of Minnesota.

Estate Planning—Introduction to, 3rd Ed., 1983, 370 pages, by Robert J. Lynn, Professor of Law, Ohio State University.

Evidence, Federal Rules of, 1981, 428 pages, by Michael H. Graham, Professor of Law, University of Illinois.

Evidence, State and Federal Rules, 2nd Ed., 1981, 514 pages, by Paul F. Rothstein, Professor of Law, Georgetown University.

Family Law, 1977, 400 pages, by Harry D. Krause, Professor of Law, University of Illinois.

Federal Estate and Gift Taxation, 3rd Ed., 1983, 509 pages, by John K. McNulty, Professor of Law, University of California, Berkeley.

Federal Income Taxation of Individuals, 3rd Ed., 1983, 487 pages, by John K. McNulty, Professor of Law, University of California, Berkeley.

Federal Income Taxation of Corporations and Stockholders, 2nd Ed., 1981, 362 pages, by Jonathan Soboloff, Late Professor of Law, Georgetown University and Peter P. Weidenbruch, Jr., Professor of Law, Georgetown University.

Federal Jurisdiction, 2nd Ed., 1981, 258 pages, by David P. Currie, Professor of Law, University of Chicago.

Future Interests, 1981, 361 pages, by Lawrence W. Waggoner, Professor of Law, University of Michigan.

Government Contracts, 1979, 423 pages, by W. Noel Keyes, Professor of Law, Pepperdine University.

NUTSHELL SERIES

Historical Introduction to Anglo-American Law, 2nd Ed., 1973, 280 pages, by Frederick G. Kempin, Jr., Professor of Business Law, Wharton School of Finance and Commerce, University of Pennsylvania.

Immigration Law and Procedure, 1984, approximately 240 pages, by David Weissbrodt, Professor of Law, University of Minnesota.

Injunctions, 1974, 264 pages, by John F. Dobbyn, Professor of Law, Villanova University.

Insurance Law, 1981, 281 pages, by John F. Dobbyn, Professor of Law, Villanova University.

Intellectual Property—Patents, Trademarks and Copyright, 1983, approximately 410 pages, by Arthur R. Mil-ler, Professor of Law, Harvard University, and Michael H. Davis, Professor of Law, University of Tennessee.

International Business Transactions, 2nd Ed., 1984, approximately 490 pages, by Donald T. Wilson, Professor of Law, Loyola University, Los Angeles.

Introduction to the Study and Practice of Law, 1983, 418 pages, by Kenney F. Hegland, Professor of Law, University of Arizona.

Judicial Process, 1980, 292 pages, by William L. Reynolds, Professor of Law, University of Maryland.

Jurisdiction, 4th Ed., 1980, 232 pages, by Albert A. Ehrenzweig, Late Professor of Law, University of California, Berkeley, David W. Louisell, Late Professor of Law, University of California, Berkeley and Geoffrey C. Hazard, Jr., Professor of Law, Yale Law School.

Juvenile Courts, 3rd Ed., 1984, approximately 260 pages, by Sanford J. Fox, Professor of Law, Boston College.

Labor Arbitration Law and Practice, 1979, 358 pages, by Dennis R. Nolan, Professor of Law, University of South Carolina.

Labor Law, 1979, 403 pages, by Douglas L. Leslie, Professor of Law, University of Virginia.

Land Use, 1978, 316 pages, by Robert R. Wright, Professor of Law, University of Arkansas, Little Rock and Susan Webber, Professor of Law, University of Arkansas, Little Rock.

Landlord and Tenant Law, 1979, 319 pages, by David S. Hill, Professor of Law, University of Colorado.

Law Study and Law Examinations—Introduction to, 1971, 389 pages, by Stanley V. Kinyon, Late Professor of Law, University of Minnesota.

Legal Interviewing and Counseling, 1976, 353 pages, by Thomas L. Shaffer, Professor of Law, Washington and Lee University.

Legal Research, 3rd Ed., 1978, 415 pages, by Morris L. Cohen, Professor of Law and Law Librarian, Yale University.

Legal Writing, 1982, 294 pages, by Dr. Lynn B. Squires, University of Washington School of Law and Marjorie Dick Rombauer, Professor of Law, University of Washington.

Legislative Law and Process, 1975, 279 pages, by Jack Davies, Professor of Law, William Mitchell College of Law.

Local Government Law, 2nd Ed., 1983, 404 pages, by David J. McCarthy, Jr., Professor of Law, Georgetown University.

Mass Communications Law, 2nd Ed., 1983, 473 pages, by Harvey L. Zuckman, Professor of Law, Catholic University and Martin J. Gaynes, Lecturer in Law, Temple University.

Medical Malpractice—The Law of, 1977, 340 pages, by Joseph H. King, Professor of Law, University of Tennessee.

Military Law, 1980, 378 pages, by Charles A. Shanor, Professor of Law, Emory University and Timothy P. Terrell, Professor of Law, Emory University.

Oil and Gas, 1983, 443 pages, by John S. Lowe, Professor of Law, University of Tulsa.

Personal Property, 1983, 322 pages, by Barlow Burke, Jr., Professor of Law, American University.

Post-Conviction Remedies, 1978, 360 pages, by Robert Popper, Professor of Law, University of Missouri, Kansas City.

Presidential Power, 1977, 328 pages, by Arthur Selwyn Miller, Professor of Law Emeritus, George Washington University.

Procedure Before Trial, 1972, 258 pages, by Delmar Karlen, Professor of Law, College of William and Mary.

Products Liability, 2nd Ed., 1981, 341 pages, by Dix W. Noel, Late Professor of Law, University of Tennessee and Jerry J. Phillips, Professor of Law, University of Tennessee.

Professional Responsibility, 1980, 399 pages, by Robert H. Aronson, Professor of Law, University of Washington, and Donald T. Weckstein, Professor of Law, University of San Diego.

Real Estate Finance, 1979, 292 pages, by Jon W. Bruce, Professor of Law, Vanderbilt University.

Real Property, 2nd Ed., 1981, 448 pages, by Roger H. Bernhardt, Professor of Law, Golden Gate University.

Regulated Industries, 1982, 394 pages, by Ernest Gellhorn, Dean and Professor of Law, Case Western Reserve University, and Richard J. Pierce, Professor of Law, Tulane University.

Remedies, 1977, 364 pages, by John F. O'Connell, Professor of Law, Western State University College of Law, Fullerton.

Res Judicata, 1976, 310 pages, by Robert C. Casad, Professor of Law, University of Kansas.

Sales, 2nd Ed., 1981, 370 pages, by John M. Stockton, Professor of Business Law, Wharton School of Finance and Commerce, University of Pennsylvania.

Secured Transactions, 2nd Ed., 1981, 391 pages, by Henry J. Bailey, Professor of Law Emeritus, Willamette University.

Securities Regulation, 2nd Ed., 1982, 322 pages, by David L. Ratner, Dean and Professor of Law, University of San Francisco.

Sex Discrimination, 1982, 399 pages, by Claire Sherman Thomas, Lecturer, University of Washington, Women's Studies Department.

Titles—The Calculus of Interests, 1968, 277 pages, by Oval A. Phipps, Late Professor of Law, St. Louis University.

NUTSHELL SERIES

Torts—Injuries to Persons and Property, 1977, 434 pages, by Edward J. Kionka, Professor of Law, Southern Illinois University.

Torts—Injuries to Family, Social and Trade Relations, 1979, 358 pages, by Wex S. Malone, Professor of Law Emeritus, Louisiana State University.

Trial Advocacy, 1979, 402 pages, by Paul B. Bergman, Adjunct Professor of Law, University of California, Los Angeles.

Trial and Practice Skills, 1978, 346 pages, by Kenney F. Hegland, Professor of Law, University of Arizona.

Trial, The First—Where Do I Sit? What Do I Say?, 1982, 396 pages, by Steven H. Goldberg, Professor of Law, University of Minnesota.

Unfair Trade Practices, 1982, 444 pages, by Charles R. McManis, Professor of Law, Washington University, St. Louis.

Uniform Commercial Code, 1975, 507 pages, by Bradford Stone, Professor of Law, Detroit College of Law.

Uniform Probate Code, 1978, 425 pages, by Lawrence H. Averill, Jr., Dean and Professor of Law, University of Arkansas, Little Rock.

Welfare Law—Structure and Entitlement, 1979, 455 pages, by Arthur B. LaFrance, Dean and Professor of Law, Lewis and Clark College, Northwestern School of Law.

Wills and Trusts, 1979, 392 pages, by Robert L. Mennell, Professor of Law, Hamline University.

Workers' Compensation and Employee Protection Laws, 1984, approximately 243 pages, by Jack B. Hood, Professor of Law, Cumberland School of Law, Samford University and Benjamin A. Hardy, Professor of Law, Cumberland School of Law, Samford University.

*

Hornbook Series

and

Basic Legal Texts

of

WEST PUBLISHING COMPANY

P.O. Box 3526

St. Paul, Minnesota 55165

October, 1983

Administrative Law, Davis' Text on, 3rd Ed., 1972, 617 pages, by Kenneth Culp Davis, Professor of Law, University of San Diego.

Agency, Seavey's Hornbook on, 1964, 329 pages, by Warren A. Seavey, Late Professor of Law, Harvard University.

Agency and Partnership, Reuschlein & Gregory's Hornbook on the Law of, 1979 with 1981 Pocket Part, 625 pages, by Harold Gill Reuschlein, Professor of Law, St. Mary's University and William A. Gregory, Professor of Law, Southern Illinois University.

Antitrust, Sullivan's Hornbook on the Law of, 1977, 886 pages, by Lawrence A. Sullivan, Professor of Law, University of California, Berkeley.

Common Law Pleading, Koffler and Reppy's Hornbook on, 1969, 663 pages, by Joseph H. Koffler, Professor of Law, New York Law School and Alison Reppy, Late Dean and Professor of Law, New York Law School.

Common Law Pleading, Shipman's Hornbook on, 3rd Ed., 1923, 644 pages, by Henry W. Ballentine, Late Professor of Law, University of California, Berkeley.

Conflict of Laws, Scoles and Hay's Hornbook on, Student Ed., 1982, 1085 pages, by Eugene F. Scoles, Professor of Law,

University of Illinois and Peter Hay, Dean and Professor of Law, University of Illinois.

Constitutional Law, Nowak, Rotunda and Young's Hornbook on, 2nd Ed., Student Ed., 1983, 1172 pages, by John E. Nowak, Professor of Law, University of Illinois, Ronald D. Rotunda, Professor of Law, University of Illinois, and J. Nelson Young, Professor of Law, University of North Carolina.

Contracts, Calamari and Perillo's Hornbook on, 2nd Ed., 1977, 878 pages, by John D. Calamari, Professor of Law, Fordham University and Joseph M. Perillo, Professor of Law, Fordham University.

Contracts, Corbin's One Volume Student Ed., 1952, 1224 pages, by Arthur L. Corbin, Late Professor of Law, Yale University.

Contracts, Simpson's Hornbook on, 2nd Ed., 1965, 510 pages, by Laurence P. Simpson, Late Professor of Law, New York University.

Corporate Taxation, Kahn's Handbook on, 3rd Ed., Student Ed., Soft cover, 1981 with 1983 Supplement, 614 pages, by Douglas A. Kahn, Professor of Law, University of Michigan.

Corporations, Henn and Alexander's Hornbook on, 3rd Ed., Student Ed., 1983, 1371 pages, by Harry G. Henn, Professor of Law, Cornell University and John R. Alexander, Member, New York and Hawaii Bars.

Criminal Law, LaFave and Scott's Hornbook on, 1972, 763 pages, by Wayne R. LaFave, Professor of Law, University of Illinois, and Austin Scott, Jr., Late Professor of Law, University of Colorado.

Damages, McCormick's Hornbook on, 1935, 811 pages, by Charles T. McCormick, Late Dean and Professor of Law, University of Texas.

Domestic Relations, Clark's Hornbook on, 1968, 754 pages, by Homer H. Clark, Jr., Professor of Law, University of Colorado.

Environmental Law, Rodgers' Hornbook on, 1977, 956 pages, by William H. Rodgers, Jr., Professor of Law, University of Washington.

HORNBOOKS & BASIC TEXTS

Estate and Gift Taxes, Lowndes, Kramer and McCord's Hornbook on, 3rd Ed., 1974, 1099 pages, by Charles L. B. Lowndes, Late Professor of Law, Duke University, Robert Kramer, Professor of Law Emeritus, George Washington University, and John H. McCord, Professor of Law, University of Illinois.

Evidence, Lilly's Introduction to, 1978, 486 pages, by Graham C. Lilly, Professor of Law, University of Virginia.

Evidence, McCormick's Hornbook on, 3rd Ed., Student Ed., 1984, approximately 1028 pages, General Editor, Edward W. Cleary, Professor of Law Emeritus, Arizona State University.

Federal Courts, Wright's Hornbook on, 4th Ed., Student Ed., 1983, 870 pages, by Charles Alan Wright, Professor of Law, University of Texas.

Federal Income Taxation of Individuals, Posin's Hornbook on, Student Ed., 1983, 491 pages, by Daniel Q. Posin, Jr., Professor of Law, Hofstra University.

Future Interest, Simes' Hornbook on, 2nd Ed., 1966, 355 pages, by Lewis M. Simes, Late Professor of Law, University of Michigan.

Insurance, Keeton's Basic Text on, 1971, 712 pages, by Robert E. Keeton, Professor of Law Emeritus, Harvard University.

Labor Law, Gorman's Basic Text on, 1976, 914 pages, by Robert A. Gorman, Professor of Law, University of Pennsylvania.

Law Problems, Ballentine's, 5th Ed., 1975, 767 pages, General Editor, William E. Burby, Late Professor of Law, University of Southern California.

Legal Writing Style, Weihofen's, 2nd Ed., 1980, 332 pages, by Henry Weihofen, Professor of Law Emeritus, University of New Mexico.

Local Government Law, Reynolds' Hornbook on, 1982, 860 pages, by Osborne M. Reynolds, Professor of Law, University of Oklahoma.

New York Practice, Siegel's Hornbook on, 1978, with 1981–82 Pocket Part, 1011 pages, by David D. Siegel, Professor of Law, Albany Law School of Union University.

Oil and Gas, Hemingway's Hornbook on, 2nd Ed., Student Ed., 1983, 543 pages, by Richard W. Hemingway, Professor of Law, University of Oklahoma.

Poor, Law of the, LaFrance, Schroeder, Bennett and Boyd's Hornbook on, 1973, 558 pages, by Arthur B. LaFrance, Dean and Professor of Law, Lewis and Clark College, Northwestern School of Law, Milton R. Schroeder, Professor of Law, Arizona State University, Robert W. Bennett, Professor of Law, Northwestern University and William E. Boyd, Professor of Law, University of Arizona.

Property, Boyer's Survey of, 3rd Ed., 1981, 766 pages, by Ralph E. Boyer, Professor of Law, University of Miami.

Property, Law of, Cunningham, Whitman and Stoebuck's Hornbook on, Student Ed., 1984, approximately 808 pages, by Roger A. Cunningham, Professor of Law, University of Michigan, Dale A. Whitman, Dean and Professor of Law, University of Missouri–Columbia and William B. Stoebuck, Professor of Law, University of Washington.

Real Estate Finance Law, Osborne, Nelson and Whitman's Hornbook on, (successor to Hornbook on Mortgages), 1979, 885 pages, by George E. Osborne, Late Professor of Law, Stanford University, Grant S. Nelson, Professor of Law, University of Missouri, Columbia and Dale A. Whitman, Dean and Professor of Law, University of Missouri, Columbia.

Real Property, Burby's Hornbook on, 3rd Ed., 1965, 490 pages, by William E. Burby, Late Professor of Law, University of Southern California.

Real Property, Moynihan's Introduction to, 1962, 254 pages, by Cornelius J. Moynihan, Professor of Law, Suffolk University.

Remedies, Dobb's Hornbook on, 1973, 1067 pages, by Dan B. Dobbs, Professor of Law, University of Arizona.

Sales, Nordstrom's Hornbook on, 1970, 600 pages, by Robert J. Nordstrom, former Professor of Law, Ohio State University.

Secured Transactions under the U.C.C., Henson's Hornbook on, 2nd Ed., 1979, with 1979 Pocket Part, 504 pages, by Ray D. Henson, Professor of Law, University of California, Hastings College of the Law.

Torts, Prosser and Keeton's Hornbook on, 5th Ed., Student Ed., 1984, approximately 1052 pages, by William L. Prosser, Late Dean and Professor of Law, University of California, Berkeley, Page Keeton, Professor of Law, University of Texas, Dan B. Dobbs, Professor of Law University of Arizona, Robert E. Keeton, Professor Law Emeritus, Harvard University and David G. Owen, Professor of Law, University of South Carolina.

Trial Advocacy, Jeans' Handbook on, Student Ed., Soft cover, 1975, by James W. Jeans, Professor of Law, University of Missouri, Kansas City.

Trusts, Bogert's Hornbook on, 5th Ed., 1973, 726 pages, by George G. Bogert, Late Professor of Law, University of Chicago and George T. Bogert, Attorney, Chicago, Illinois.

Urban Planning and Land Development Control, Hagman's Hornbook on, 1971, 706 pages, by Donald G. Hagman, Late Professor of Law, University of California, Los Angeles.

Uniform Commercial Code, White and Summers' Hornbook on, 2nd Ed., 1980, 1250 pages, by James J. White, Professor of Law, University of Michigan and Robert S. Summers, Professor of Law, Cornell University.

Wills, Atkinson's Hornbook on, 2nd Ed., 1953, 975 pages, by Thomas E. Atkinson, Late Professor of Law, New York University.

Advisory Board

THE LAW

OF

JUVENILE COURTS

IN A NUTSHELL

By

SANFORD J. FOX

Professor of Law, Boston College Law School

THIRD EDITION

ST. PAUL, MINN.

WEST PUBLISHING CO.

1984

Library of Congress Cataloging in Publication Data

Fox, Sanford J.
The law of juvenile courts in a nutshell.

(Nutshell series)
Includes index.
1. Juvenile courts—United States. I. Title.
II. Series.

| KF9795.F68 | 1983 | 345.73'081 | 83–21876 |
| | | 347.30581 | |

ISBN 0–314–79306–2

Fox Juv.Cts. in a Nutshell 3rd Ed.

To

Diana, Michael and Gregory

PREFACE

This third edition includes two new sections, on Child Abuse Reporting Laws and Termination of Parental Rights. In addition, new cases from the Supreme Court and from state courts have been included in the text to update the state of judicial opinion. Recent statutory material, especially from Florida and Washington where new juvenile codes have been enacted, serves to keep current the legislative activity in juvenile court law. Reference continues to be made to the Model Act and to the Standards for Juvenile Justice produced by the American Bar Association and the Institute for Judicial Administration.

SANFORD J. FOX

November, 1983

OUTLINE

		Page
PREFACE		XVIII
TABLE OF CASES		XXIII

CHAPTER I. THE COURT AND ITS PHILOSOPHY

Section
1.	The Juvenile Court Image	1
2.	The Juvenile Court in the Judicial Structure	8
3.	Traditional Views	12
4.	Critique of the Tradition	15
5.	The Quest for Philosophy	17

CHAPTER II. JURISDICTION

6.	In General	21
7.	Venue	23
8.	Lower Age Limits	27
9.	The Presumption of Incapacity	30
10.	Maximum Age	33
11.	Children's Criminal Conduct	37
12.	Noncriminal Misbehavior: Status Offenders	41
13.	Need for Treatment	45
14.	Traffic Offenses	48

OUTLINE

Section   **Page**

15. Neglect and Abuse ---------------------- 51
16. Child Abuse and Neglect Reporting Laws   59
17. Termination of Parental Rights --------- 61
18. Concurrent or Exclusive Jurisdiction ---- 64
19. Double Jeopardy ----------------------- 68
20. Family Courts ------------------------- 73
21. Personal Jurisdiction and Problems of Notice ------------------------------------- 75

CHAPTER III. THE ROLES OF LAW ENFORCEMENT AGENTS

22. Surveillance of Juveniles and Parents --- 80
23. Arrests ------------------------------- 85
24. Detention for Investigation ------------ 99
25. Entrapment --------------------------- 104
26. Post Arrest Duties: Detention and Notice   107
27. Questioning the Child ----------------- 114
    27.1   Voluntariness --------------------- 115
    27.2   Miranda ------------------------- 117
    27.3   The Role of the Attorney --------- 122
    27.4   Compliance With Statutes --------- 125
    27.5   Parens Patriae Interrogations ----- 127
28. Searches ----------------------------- 129
29. Lineups and Other Identifications ------- 136

CHAPTER IV. COMMENCING THE JUDICIAL PROCESS

30. Intake and Diversion ------------------ 141
31. Detention Hearings and the Right to Bail   146

OUTLINE

Section   **Page**

32. The Petition ------------------------------ 153
33. The Plea ---------------------------------- 159
34. The Right to Counsel --------------------- 162
35. Discovery --------------------------------- 169

CHAPTER V. FACT–FINDING HEARINGS

36. In General ------------------------------- 174
37. An Impartial Judge --------------------- 178
38. Trial by Jury --------------------------- 181
39. Public and Speedy Trials --------------- 184
40. Burden of Proof ----------------------- 188
41. Recording the Proceedings ------------- 191
42. Rules of Evidence: In General --------- 192
43. Constitutional Exclusions ------------- 194
44. Impeachment -------------------------- 197
45. Accomplice Testimony ------------------ 200
46. Privileges --------------------------- 201
47. Hearsay ----------------------------- 203
48. Findings ---------------------------- 206
49. Dismissing the Petition --------------- 208
50. Protective Orders -------------------- 209

CHAPTER VI. DISPOSITIONS

51. Separate From Jurisdictional Findings --- 211
52. Disposition Authority ------------------ 214
53. Right to Counsel ---------------------- 217
54. Procedural Requirements -------------- 218
55. The Social Study --------------------- 220
56. Probation --------------------------- 225

OUTLINE

Section   **Page**

57. Institutions _____ 231
58. Cruel and Unusual Punishment and the Right to Treatment _____ 241

CHAPTER VII. WAIVER FOR CRIMINAL TRIAL

59. In General _____ 249
60. Age and Offense _____ 251
61. The Hearing _____ 252
62. Criteria for Waiver _____ 257
63. Statement of Reasons for Waiver _____ 261
64. Proof of Delinquency _____ 263
65. Appeal From Waiver _____ 265

CHAPTER VIII. APPEALS

66. The Right to Appeal _____ 268
67. Final Orders _____ 269
68. The Record on Appeal _____ 270
69. Notice and Timing _____ 272

Index _____ 275

TABLE OF CASES

A., In re, 44

A., In re Dianna, 181

A., In re Patricia, 35

A. A., In re, 40, 56

A. A. A., In re, 219

A. C., In re, 168

A. D. R., In re, 119

A. F., In re, 214

A. H., In re, 218

A___ N___, In re, 214

A Juvenile, Commonwealth v., 119, 197

Aaron, In re, 191

Abrams, People v., 65

Adams v. Williams, 101

Alexander, In re, 199

Alexander v. Deddens, 164

Alexander v. State, 188

Allgood, People v., 266

Alsager v. District Court, 53, 54

Anderson, In re, 33, 111

Anthony, State v., 249

Appeal No. 179, In re, 235

Appeal No. 245, In re, 87, 120, 121

Appeal No. 544, In re, 160

Appeal of (see name of party)

Arbeiter, State v., 148

Armentrout, In re, 56

Armour, People v., 23

Arnold v. State, 123

A–S v. Murphy, 45

Aye v. State, 267

B., In re Carlos, 139, 140

B., In re Clarence, 184

TABLE OF CASES

B., In re James, 216

B., In re Michael John, 32

B., In re Preston, 226

B.F. v. State, 270

Baby X, In re, 28

Bailey v. Commonwealth, 78

Baker v. Hamilton, 234

Baker v. Smith, 150

Baldwin v. Lewis, 171

Bambrick, State ex rel. Wilson v., 166

Bartley, In re, 236

Belding, In re, 270

Benbow v. State, 31

Bendler v. Percy, 37

Bensinger, U.S. ex rel. Bombacino v., 262, 264

Bergman v. Nelson, 187

Berkley v. State, 157

Bills, State ex rel. T.J.H. v., 262

B.L.M., In re, 231

Black, In re, 28, 55

Black, State ex rel. Leis v., 66

Blackwell v. State, 67

Blackwolf, In re, 23

Blakes, In re, 237

Blondheim v. State, 44, 233

B.M.C., In re, 132

Boardman, State v., 12

Bolan, State v., 122

Bolden, In re, 270

Bombacino, U.S. ex rel. v. Bensinger, 262, 264

Boone v. Danforth, 234

Bordone v. F., 228

Bowers, People v., 263

Boykin v. Alabama, 161, 257

Braswell, In re, 36

Braver, U.S. v., 106

Breed v. Jones, 3, 28, 50, 68, 70, 71, 72, 174, 250, 251, 255, 263, 264

Bridges v. State, 161

TABLE OF CASES

Brisendine, People v., 99

Brown, In re, 268

Brown v. Baldwin, 33

Brown v. Illinois, 121, 127, 139

Browning, People v., 259

Bullard, In re, 254

Burke, In re, 272

Bykofsky v. Middletown, 40

C., In re, 74

C., In re Ellery, 233

C., In re Michael, 220

C.A.J. v. State, 206

Calandra, U.S. v., 195

Calendine, State ex rel. Harris v., 44

Camp v. Howe, 199

Carey, People ex rel. v. White, 183

Carlo, In re, 115

Carmichael, State v., 255

Carrillo v. State, 159

Carson, In re, 157

Carter, In re, 193, 196, 197

Cato, People v., 213

Chatman, In re, 162

Cissna v. State, 203

City Court, State ex rel. Maier v., 166, 176

Clemons v. State, 256

Cochise County etc., In re Appeal in, 55, 59

Cohen, People ex rel. Silbert v., 240

Coleman v. Alabama, 151, 152, 153

Collins, In re, 191

Commonwealth v. _____ (see opposing party)

Conques v. Fuselier, 90

Cox, State v., 198

Croft, Commonwealth v., 269

Crouse, Ex parte, 241

C.T.F., In the Interest of, 186

Cuomo, U.S. v., 187

TABLE OF CASES

D., In re Aline, 235, 236

D., In re Garth, 116, 117

D., In re William, 189

D.A.B. v. State, 167

Dalton, People v., 34

D.A.M., In re, 196

Daugaard v. People, 58

Davis, In re, 31

Davis v. Alaska, 173, 198, 199

Davis v. Mississippi, 139

Decoster, In re, 72

Deitz, State ex rel. Oregonian Publishing Co. v., 185

Dell, In re, 92

DeMarce, U.S. v., 126

Dennis, In re, 157

Department of Health and Rehabilitative Services v. Crowell, 232

D.F., In re, 242

D.H., State v., 31

DiIorio, In re, 271

District of Columbia v. B.J.R., 42, 47

Division of Family Services v. J.F., 58

D.J., In re, 270

D.J.B., In re, 223

D.L.C. v. State, 132

D.L.E., In re v. State, 78

D.M.D., In re, 154

D.M.L., In re, 41

Doe, In re, 41, 187, 256, 265

Doe v. Staples, 60

Doe v. State, 135, 162

Doe, U.S. v., 36

Donaldson, In re, 135

Dorsey v. State, 65

Douglas v. California, 165

Dow, In re, 30

D.P. v. State, 158

D.S.H., In re, 156

TABLE OF CASES

Dudley, In re, 205
D.W.D. v. State, 201

Eastmond, State v., 95
Edwards, In re, 56, 79, 165, 192
EE, In the Matter of Roger, 123
Ellis, People v., 35
E.P. v. State, 228
E.T.C., In re, 119
Evangelista, State v., 265
Ex parte (see name of party)
Ex rel (see name of party)

F., In re Anthony, 158
F., In re Drexel, 269
F., In re Theodore, 162
F., In re Thomas A., 40
F., In re William, 168
F., People ex rel. Arthur v. Hill, 239
Fare v. Michael C., 118, 123
Farms, In re, 197
Ferguson v. Commonwealth, 37
F.G., In re, 168
Finch v. State, 230
Fisher, In re, 181
Flowers, People v., 134
Forrest, In re, 172
F.R.W., In re, 257
Franklin, Commonwealth v., 254
Franks v. State, 230

G., In re Benny, 72
G., In re Henry, 84
G., in re Kevin, 205
G., In re Lee, 196
G., In re Lynette, 98, 102, 139
G., In the Matter of Mark, 203
G.A.T., In re, 78
Gage, In the Matter of, 120
Gagnon v. Scarpelli, 166, 230, 241

TABLE OF CASES

Gallegos v. Colorado, 115

Gandy v. Panama City, Florida, 110

Garcia, In re, 157

Gaskins, Commonwealth v., 119

Gault, In re, 76, 77, 108, 116, 118, 164, 165, 167, 174, 175, 191, 194, 196, 202, 211, 219, 253, 268

Geboy v. Gray, 168

George v. State, 87

Gerstein v. Pugh, 86, 150, 151, 152, 153, 166

Gesicki v. Oswald, 43

Getty, People v., 232

Gilbert v. Commonwealth, 205

Giminez, People v., 151

Giordenello v. U.S., 92

Glenford's, In the Matter of, 66

Godfrey v. State, 30

Gonsalves v. Devine, 169

Gonzalez, In re, 190

Gonzalez-Gonzalez, U.S. v., 187

Graham v. Ridge, 266

Greene, In re, 34

Griffin v. California, 196

Grosso, U.S. v., 95

Guggenheim, People ex rel. v. Mucci, 152

Gustafson v. Florida, 98

H., In re Arlene, 235

H., In re Frank, 144

H., In re James Edward, 34

H., In re Wade, 193

Haley v. Ohio, 115

Halverson, State v., 255

Hamilton v. Commonwealth, 266

Hampton v. U.S., 106

Hanrahan v. Felt, 172

Hanson, In re, 58

Hardy, State v., 119, 128

Harling v. U.S., 127

Harris, In re, 205

Harris v. New York, 117, 195

TABLE OF CASES

Harris, State ex rel. v. Calendine, 44
Hartsfield, In re, 90
Harvey, In re, 101, 102
Haskins v. Carter, 183
Hathaway, State v., 202
Haziel v. U.S., 168, 256
Henry v. U.S., 87
Hernandez v. State, 252
Herron, In re, 78
Hershman, State ex rel. Johnson v., 237
Hill, People ex rel. Arthur F. v., 239
H.M.L. v. State, 215
Holley, In re, 137
Hoppe, In re, 26
Howe, In re, 156
Huff v. Walker, 90, 130
Huffman v. Missouri, 254
Hughes v. State, 204
Hutchins, People v., 140

I__ B__ v. State, 273
In re (see name of party)
In the Interest of (see name of party)
In the Matter of (see name of party)

J., In re Anthony, 121
J., In re Robin, 160
J., In re Terrance, 216
J. v. Superior Court, 271
J.A., In the Interest of, 135
Jackson, In re, 86
Jackson v. State, 137
Jackson, State v., 188
Jamison, State v., 214
J.B. v. State, 225
J.B., Jr., In re, 96, 131
J.D., In re, 193
J.D.H., In re, 24, 26
J.E.C., In re, 260
JGL, In re, 164

XXIX

TABLE OF CASES

J.H., State v., 187
J.J., In re, 71
J.J., In the Matter of, 214
J.K., In re, 237
J.M., In re, 43
J.M., State ex rel. v. Taylor, 160, 169
Johnson, Application of, 36
Johnson, In re, 54
Johnson v. City of Opelousas, 41
Johnson v. People, 213
Johnson v. State, 199
Johnson, State ex rel. v. Hershman, 237
Jones, In re, 186
Jones v. State, 50
Jones, People ex rel. v. Jones, 58
J.P., In re, 43, 85
Judges of Family Court, People ex rel. Thomas v., 72
Juvenile Department, State ex rel. v. W., 39

K., In re, 177, 197
K., In re James, 161
Kalvin, Matter of, 34
Katz v. U.S., 92
Keller v. State ex rel. Epperson, 230
Kent v. U.S., 170, 217, 223, 224, 250, 251, 252, 253, 254, 261, 262
Kenyon, People v., 75
Kern v. State, 256
King v. State, 252
King, U.S. v., 183
Kirby v. Illinois, 137, 138
Klopfer v. North Carolina, 184
K.M.S. v. State, 29

L., In re James, 96
L., In the Matter of, 186
L., Charles v. Schupf, 113
L. v. Superior Court, 257
Lamb v. Brown, 35
Landeros v. Flood, 59

TABLE OF CASES

Landry v. State, 196
Lang, In re, 102
Lassiter v. Department of Social Services, 61
Lauring, People ex rel. v. Mucci, 152
L.B., In re, 120
Leach v. Superior Court, 256
Lee v. County Court, 202
Lego v. Twomey, 121
Leis, State ex rel. v. Black, 66
LePage, State v., 266
Lewis, State ex rel. Morrow v., 149
Little v. State, 31
L.J., In re, 175
Logan v. State, 66
Long v. Robinson, 12
Longley, People v., 157
Luckett, U.S. v., 88

M., In re, 104, 130
M., In re Eduardo, 121
M., In re Edward, 216
M., In re John, 40
M., In re Lavette, 84
M., In re Michael, 161
M., In re Ricardo, 226
M., In re Robert, 193
McCloud, In re, 181
McGurren v. S.T., 58
McKeiver v. Pennsylvania, 118, 178, 181, 182, 183, 185
McMaster, In re, 193
Maegher, State v., 68
Maier, State ex rel. v. City Court, 166, 176, 177
Maloney, State v., 128
Maricopa County, Juvenile Action No. J-72918-S, In re, 190
Maricopa County, Juvenile Action No. J-73355, In re, 257
Maricopa County, Juvenile Action No. J-74449A, In re, 190
Maricopa County, Juvenile Action No. J-75755, In re, 158
Maricopa County, Juvenile Action No. J-77286, In re, 230
Marschall v. City of Carson, 86
Marshall, State v., 72

TABLE OF CASES

Martarella v. Kelley, 242

Martin, Commonwealth v., 251

Massiah v. U.S., 124

Mathews v. Commonwealth, 262

Mathews, State v., 199

M.D.A., In re, 232

M.D.J., In re, 180

M.E.B. v. State, 27

Meek, In re, 219

Mempa v. Rhay, 218

Meyer, In re, 78

M.G.S., In re, 161

Michigan v. Koenig, 23

Miguel v. State, 33

Miller v. Quatsoe, 37

Miller v. State, 31

Miller, U.S. v., 105

Mills, State v., 52

Minor v. State, 87

Minor Boy v. State, 94

Miranda v. Arizona, 116, 117, 118, 119, 120, 121, 122, 124, 125, 126, 128, 139, 165, 195

Mitchell v. State, 128

M.J.E., In re, 215

M.K.H. v. State, 125

M.L., In re, 214

Montgomery, People v., 173

Montgomery County, In re Appeal for, 269, 270

Moore v. Haugh, 234

Moore v. State, 208

Mora, State v., 135

Morales v. Turman, 233, 243, 246, 248

Moreno v. State, 267

Morgan, In re, 241

Morris v. D'Amario, 153

Morris, People v., 110

Morrissey v. Brewer, 240, 241

Morros, State ex rel. v. Lewis, 149

Moss v. Weaver, 150, 151, 152, 153, 166

XXXII

M.P.S., In re, 202
M.S., In re, 233
Mucci, People ex rel. Guggenheim v., 152
Mucci, People ex rel. Lauring v., 152
Mullen, State v., 106
Murcray, In re, 78
Murphy, In re, 256
Murphy, People v., 125
Murray, U.S. ex rel. v. Owens, 233
M.W., In re, 23, 24
Myricks, In re, 167

N., In re, 268
N., In re Arthur, 190
Naimie, In re, 54
Naves v. State, 166
Nelson v. Heynes, 242
Noble, In re, 196, 197

O., Matter of Robert, 119
Oliver, In re, 184
O'Neill, State v., 102
Oregonian Publishing Co., State ex rel. v. Deiz, 185
Oswald v. Gesicki, 43
Owens, U.S. ex rel. Murray v., 233

P., In re, 51
P., In re Carlos, 216
P., In re Michael, 117
Parnes, State v., 199
Pendergraft v. Superior Court, 102
People v. _____ (see opposing party)
People ex rel. (see name of party)
People, In re Robert, 59
Pereira, In re, 188
Piland v. Clark County Juvenile Court, 186
Pima County, In re Appeal in, 87, 96, 179, 259, 271
Pima County, Juvenile Action, In the Matter of, 71
Pima Cty., Juvenile Action No. J–46735, In re Appeal in, 57
P.L.V., People v., 269

Porter v. State, 32
Potter, In re, 189
Potts, In re, 179
Powell v. Greg, 207
P.R. v. State, 228
P–S–M v. State, 189
Pyle, Commonwealth v., 254

R., In re, 223
R., In re Celia, 212
R., In re Donald, 272
R., In re Gladys, 32
R., In re Reynaldo, 47
R., In the Matter of John, 160
R. v. Burton, 123
R. v. Superior Court, 179
R.A.H., In re, 122
R.D. v. State, 204
R., Donald v. Whitmer, 150
Ramey, People v., 99
Ramsey, U.S. v., 116
Ransom, Commonwealth v., 205
Reasoner v. State, 167, 272
Reed v. Duter, 166
Reed v. State, 79
Reeves v. Warden, 134
Reis, In re, 180
Reist v. Bay County Circuit Judge, 57
R.E.J., In re, 123
Rhodes v. State, 65
Richardson, In re, 232
Richardson, State v., 140
Rising Sun, People v., 266
Risner v. Commonwealth, 262
R.J.C., In re, 264
R.L.P., In re, 272
R.L.R., In re, 208
R.L.R. v. State, 181, 186
R.N., In re, 207
Roberts, Commonwealth v., 254, 262

TABLE OF CASES

Robinson v. California, 244
Robinson v. State, 181
Robinson, U.S. v., 98
Rodriguez v. State, 169
Roe v. Conn, 52, 53, 54
Roskov, Commonwealth v., 77
Ross, State, v., 192
R.P., In the Interest of, 78
RR, In the Matter of Leon, 63
Rundle, U.S. ex rel. Turner v., 253
Rusecki v. State, 205, 206
Russell, U.S. v., 105
R.W. v. State, 122

S., Ex parte, 208
S., In re, 59, 131
S., In re Anthony, 144
S., In re Gregory, 54
S., In re Herman, 136
S., In re Julius, 200
S., In the Matter of Martin, 87
Salas, In re, 260, 262
Sanchez v. Department of Family and Children Services, 270
Sanders, In the Interest of, 63
Santosky v. Kramer, 61, 62, 191
Saunders v. People, 104
Schoos, People v., 52, 53
D., Scott, People v., 135
Scoville, State v., 34
S.D., In re, 57
S.E.B., In re, 83
Sedberry v. State, 58
Senn v. State, 29
S.H., In re, 119
Shadwick v. City of Tampa, 92
Shaver, U.S. v., 237
Shepherd, State v., 265
Silbert, People ex rel. v. Cohen, 240
Simmons, In re, 122
Singleton, U.S. v., 140

TABLE OF CASES

Sippy, In re, 202
S.J.C., In re, 200, 201
Slack, In re, 262
S.M.G., State v., 210
Smith, In re, 46, 219
Smith v. Daily Mail Publishing Co., 185
Smith v. State, 98
Smithers, State v., 132
Sorrels v. Steele, 157
Spalding, In re, 43, 166
Spencer, In re, 138
Staley, In re, 175
Stangel, State v., 33
Stanley, In re, 169
State v. _____ (see opposing party)
State ex rel. (see name of party)
Steel v. State, 266
Stein, State v., 134
Strode v. Brorby, 222
Stokes v. Commonwealth, 70
Superior Court, People v., 182
Swisher v. Brady, 71

T., In re, 116, 121
T., In re Carl, 137
T., In re Guardianship of Vera, 63
T., In re Robert, 132
T.A.F., In re, 272
Taylor, People v., 36
Taylor, State ex rel. J.M. v., 160, 169
Terry v. Ohio, 100, 102
Theriault v. State, 125
Thomas, People v., 249
Thomas, People ex rel. v. Judges of Family Court, 72
Thomas v. State, 65
Thompson, State v., 264
Times and Democrat, State ex rel. The, 185
T.J.H., State ex rel. v. Bills, 262
T.K. v. State, 151
Tolliver v. Judges of Family Court, 72

Tucker, In re, 93
Turner v. Commonwealth, 254
Turner, State v., 189
Turner, U.S. ex rel. v. Rundle, 253
Tyler v. State, 219

United States v. _____ (see opposing party)
United States ex rel. (see name of party)
Unsworth, In re, 188

V., In re Cynthia, 55
V., In re Michael, 104, 132
V., Ivan v. New York, 188
Vega v. Bell, 66, 254
Virgin Islands v. Brodhurst, 186
V.R.S., In re, 112

W., In re, 40
W., In re Gary, 184
W., In re Terry, 203
W., State ex rel. Juvenile Department v., 39
Wachlin, In re, 54
Wade, U.S. v., 137, 138
Waldron, In re, 41
Walker, In re, 43
Walker v. Florida, 110
Walker's Case, 29
Walls v. State, 25, 26, 105, 106
Wasson, People v., 200
Watchman, State v., 36
Waterman, In re, 267
Watkins, In re, 265
Watson, U.S. v., 95, 99
Watts, U.S. v., 108
Welch, State v., 161
W.F. v. State, 36
Whatley, State v., 118, 121
White, People ex rel. Carey v., 183
White, State v., 124
Whittenburg, In re, 158

TABLE OF CASES

Whitter, State v., 110
Wilkinson, In re, 213
Williams, In re, 97, 201, 272
Williams, People v., 259
Williams v. State, 77
Wilson, State ex rel. v. Bambrick, 166
Winship, In re, 188
W.J., In re, 194
Woodward v. Wainwright, 67
Wooten, In re, 213
Wright, State v., 128
W.W.M., In re, 77

Y., In the Matter of Hime, 63
Young, State v., 136, 195

Z., In re Joe, 172
Zepeda, People v., 126, 127

THE LAW
OF
JUVENILE COURTS
IN A NUTSHELL

THIRD EDITION

*

THE
LAW OF JUVENILE COURTS
IN A NUTSHELL

CHAPTER I

THE COURT AND ITS PHILOSOPHY

§ 1. The Juvenile Court Image

There was a time when the core of a juvenile court could be defined by projecting a picture of the judge, a wise and mature man, conversing "man to man" with a young boy in trouble on account of some minor misbehavior; the dialogue has the adult speak concerning the evils of the path the youngster had embarked on, and then persuade him that America had far more satisfying things to offer his future than a life of crime. The boy perhaps chastised, but certainly enlightened and inspired, departs to err no more.

In the rare case where further guidance and instruction is required, the boy is placed in a state training school where other kindly adults provide the support and guidance called for. This is essentially the outline of a juvenile court proceeding which was popularly entertained and the experience described by a prominent juvenile court judge as late as 1945, see Schramm, *The Judge Meets the Boy and His Family*, Nat.Prob.Assoc. 1945 Yearbook pp. 182–194; similar descriptions are commonplace in the juvenile court literature of earlier days.

To what extent this *tableau* represented more an idealized image than a typical juvenile court proceeding no one can ever know. But it is clear that in the space of the past four decades virtually all of this traditional picture has disappeared from both the lay and professional conception of an ideal juvenile court. The actors in the drama as well as the plot have undergone dramatic change; both judge and child, are far more likely to be female, the children, and to a lesser degree the judge are from racial minority groups. The judge's maturity and wisdom are expressed not to the child, but to a lawyer—the child's defense counsel, or the state's prosecutor—and the script proceeds not in homolies on virtue and citizenship, but more in terms of the scope of the hearsay rule, an issue of statutory interpretation or the sweep of constitutional requirements. The subject of the discussion is often murder, rape, robbery and assault. To the child, whose entire time in court is likely to be no more than 15 minutes, the experience is largely incomprehensible and hardly designed to advance his capacity to escape the social, economic and educational poverty looming in his future. All participants are acutely aware, in fact, that the best the child can get from his day in court is merely a "record," while the worst is a sentence to an institution that is functionally indistinguishable from an adult prison. As the Chief Justice of the United States has recently remarked concerning juvenile court hearings: "Thus in terms of potential consequences, there is little to distinguish an adjudicatory hearing such as was held in this case from a traditional criminal prosecution." Breed v. Jones, 421 U.S. 519, at 531, 95 S.Ct. 1779, at 1786 (1975). Whether this evolution is good or bad, sensible or nonsensical social policy, is a question best reserved for discussion of juvenile justice philosophy (see § 4).

In addition to this more or less evolutionary definition, there are several other conceptions of a juvenile court. None is any better than another and all should be kept in mind as the over-all context in which the legal issues discussed subsequently in this book arise. There is, for example, a definition in terms of bricks and mortar. That is, the juvenile court is sometimes in a building all of its own, there being no other functions going on within the place. Or it may be housed together with a juvenile detention facility. But most often neither of these is the case and the business of the juvenile court is usually carried on in a courthouse in which other sorts of trials and appeals also take place. Juvenile proceedings normally do not, however, share the same courtrooms or other facilities, such as waiting rooms, staff offices or judges' chambers, with other tribunals in the building. It is probably true, in fact, that the effort to separate the juvenile justice system from adult criminal justice has achieved its most notable success in the provision of specialized physical facilities for the juvenile court to do its work. It is certainly difficult, for example, to see a similar degree of success in the physical separation of children from adults when it is time to lock a door behind them; the most recent (1982) comprehensive survey of jails in this country estimates that "more than 300,000 juveniles would have been held in jail at some time during the 12-month period." U. S. Bureau of Justice Statistics, *Bulletin* 2 (Feb. 1983.) Ms. Sarri annotates such a computation with the irony: "This, in the last quarter of the century that opened with the founding of the juvenile court, which was to remove children from jails and the adult criminal system." Sarri, Under Lock and Key: Juveniles in Jails and Detention

5 (1974). Strictly speaking, this is an accurate historic observation. It would, however, be a serious mistake to assume that the founding of the juvenile court was entirely a matter of promoting the welfare of youthful offenders. The court was a far more complex reform which involved supporting a diversity of groups and interests, many of which had little to do with benevolent attitudes towards delinquents. See Fox, *Juvenile Justice Reform: An Historical Perspective,* 22 Stan.L.Rev. 1187 (1970); Garlock, *"Wayward" Children and the Law: The Genesis of the Status Offense Jurisdiction of the Juvenile Court,* 13 Ga.L.Rev. 341 (1979).

Making reference to the complexity of the juvenile court's background serves to introduce another way of conceiving of a juvenile court. The juvenile court is a part, a subsystem if you like, of several other systems. Most obviously, it is part of the law enforcement system and interacts on a daily basis with the police and other agencies primarily concerned with controlling criminal behavior. With almost the same frequency and intimacy, the juvenile court is the single most important enforcement agency in the educational system, dealing with truancy and disruptive behavior in school. In seeking to obtain social work counselling, medical help or psychiatric treatment for delinquents, the court is also part of the health care and social service delivery systems.

Finally, it is part of the social services system that protects abused and neglected children.

It is most often the case that each of these systems sees the problem of delinquency or child protection in a different light. The police, for example, may be wholly unsympathetic with recommendations of a court psychologist about what to do with a particular youngster. Those who provide helping services for delinquents and their families, on the other hand, may see the whole ritual of arrest and prosecution as being distinctly counterproductive to the effort to make their clients independent and self-respecting. This clash of interests and philosophies is often reflected in juvenile court proceedings and helps to account for some of the legal policies pursued in the court which are examined later in this book.

The juvenile court is also a part of the judicial system and has, therefore, certain hierarchical characteristics in that system. It may be established, for example, as a special branch or session of some other court (a Superior Court, a District Court, etc.) whose main task it is to try regular criminal or civil cases, or it may be a special and independent court which has no other business to pursue except juvenile matters (see § 2). The juvenile court is also one from which appeals may be taken to another trial court for a completely new and duplicative adjudication, or the appeal may lie to an appellate court only on is-

sues of law (see § 64). The definition may in
other words, be in terms of the juvenile court's
relationships in the larger judicial framework.
It should be noted, however, that many of the
most important functions of the court might well
be lodged elsewhere, as has been done in Scotland
where most of the intake screening and disposition work has been taken out of courts and vested
in a specially created system of lay persons. See
Fox, *Juvenile Justice Reform: Innovations in
Scotland*, 12 Amer.Crim.L.Rev. 61 (1974); Martin, Fox & Murray, *Children Out of Court* (1981).

An additional source of definition and conception relates to the geographical area over which
the court has authority, e.g. the juvenile court
may be a county court, or a city court, or a court
governing a territory specially laid out by the
legislature for this purpose; or it may be a court
with statewide jurisdiction. Jurisdiction can also
be a matter of the subject matter of the juvenile
court as well as its geography; this is a still additional means of defining it. Thus, it is a court
that deals with delinquency, neglect, child abuse,
paternity, truancy, etc. In this respect, it is a
court that hears cases of parents and of children
who have not completed adolescence.

It is possible to attempt to develop a conception
of a juvenile court by calling attention to its
unique procedural features, although in the actual trial of cases there is only the absence of a

jury which distinguishes delinquency hearings from criminal trials. These hearings are only a small part of juvenile court delinquency business, however, since most children appearing in court plead guilty to the charges against them. The procedural uniqueness lies elsewhere. For example, in pre-trial issues such as pleading, detention and case screening, and in post-trial concerns such as procedures for reaching a disposition decision and the nature of the dispositional choices available, there are things which tend to distinguish the juvenile court from other courts.

Finally, the juvenile court might be distinguished by its philosophy, namely, that the court's central purpose is to provide for the welfare and healthy development of all children who come before it, including those who are charged with violating the criminal law. But whether this is, or should be, the philosophy of juvenile justice is a subject of some vigorous current controversy which is discussed later in § 4.

§ 2. The Juvenile Court in the Judicial Structure

At the beginning of 1972 there were 3,455 courts hearing juvenile cases in the United States, according to the Law Enforcement Assistance Administration's National Survey of Court Organization, 1973. This represented approximately 20% of the nation's courts of original jurisdiction. Nearly half (48%) of these juvenile courts were empowered to hear litigation of every sort, being courts of general jurisdiction. The remaining 52% were courts of limited jurisdiction, with power to try only specially designated and less serious sorts of disputes. Since that report was compiled, however, both Florida and Iowa have both taken jurisdiction over juvenile cases away from their courts of limited jurisdiction (these courts were abolished completely in Florida) and vested power over juvenile causes in their courts of general jurisdiction. It may be, therefore, that there is coming about a majority acceptance of the long-standing recommendation from authorities such as the late Dean Roscoe Pound to the effect that juvenile cases be tried by a specialist judge who is part of the trial court of general jurisdiction.

On a state by state basis, however, there are at present only 17 states and the District of Columbia which have assigned juvenile jurisdiction exclusively to their trial courts of general jurisdiction. In five other states juvenile jurisdiction is also vested in general jurisdiction courts, but not exclusively; in some counties of these states juvenile cases are heard by either a full time juvenile court or by the court of limited jurisdiction. In courts of general jurisdiction judges are assigned to hear juvenile cases on a rotating basis, usually for a period of one year.

Courts which spend all of their time on juvenile and family cases are found in eight states. This means that there is a judge and staff who are specialists in these cases. Even in courts of general jurisdiction there is a non-rotating staff, so that except for the judge, personnel such as probation officers and clerical staff are also specialists in juvenile affairs.

In another six states juvenile cases are heard exclusively by a court of limited jurisdiction. The remaining 16 states present a mixed picture of where authority to try juvenile cases is vested. In Massachusetts, for example, there are four full time·juvenile courts in the state's largest metropolitan areas while in other parts of the state these cases are heard by more than 60 separate courts of limited jurisdiction.

The 1973 LEAA report also presents a suggestive picture of the degree of specialization in juvenile cases which exists among the nation's judiciary. Perhaps "non-specialization" better describes the results of this government survey since it shows that among all the courts of limited and special jurisdiction in the country, only a bare 2% of these courts spend more than three-fourths of their available judge-time on juvenile cases. When account is taken that this figure includes full time juvenile courts, the extremely tangential nature of juvenile cases in the judicial business of limited jurisdiction courts is all the more outstanding. Thus, at the other end of the scale, fully 89% of these courts report that less than one tenth of their judge time is devoted to hearing juvenile cases. In the courts of general jurisdiction the figures are still more extreme, with the number of these courts which distribute more than three-fourths of their judge time to juvenile cases amounting to .0005 of the total number of courts (2 out of 3,630). It appears, therefore, that where authority to try juvenile cases is assigned to a court which also has jurisdiction to hear other cases, it is extremely rare that these cases occupy more than a very small percentage of the courts' judicial manpower. Only in the country's full time juvenile and family courts, whose precise number cannot be ascertained from the LEAA document, is there a judicial specialization in juvenile problems.

Where there is a full time court hearing juvenile cases, it may hear related matters of family affairs as well, such as offenses between family members or adoptions, as well as the delinquency, neglect and child abuse cases. These juvenile or family courts may sit in a territorial jurisdiction of the state that is specially created for these purposes, as in Connecticut, or they may be assigned to the established counties of the state, as in New York. Where these specialist courts are found only in some parts of the state, it is usually in the larger population centers, as in Massachusetts.

Unless a state constitution itself provides for a juvenile or family court, as in N.Y.Const. art. 6,

§ 13, there is no constitutional right to be tried in a special juvenile court, or pursuant to special juvenile procedures. The legislature may, therefore, create these courts or procedures on such terms as it decides, withholding certain criminal conduct for trial in the regular criminal court, for example. S. v. Boardman, 267 A.2d 592 (Del. Super.1970). There may, however, be a denial of constitutionally required equal protection of the laws in a state scheme which denies juvenile treatment to children in certain localities of the state, Long v. Robinson, 316 F.Supp. 22 (D.C.Md. 1970), affirmed in 436 F.2d 1116 (4th Cir. 1971).

The juvenile and family courts identified in this section are not, of course, the only courts which try children's cases. Section 18, below, discusses when there is parallel authority (concurrent jurisdiction) in some other court and how the choice between courts is made in such situations, while section 59, below, introduces the subject of juvenile courts relinquishing (waiving) their jurisdiction over children who commit crimes in certain cases so that they may be tried in a criminal court.

§ 3. Traditional Views

A reading of juvenile justice literature from the early decades of the 19th century to the present day indicates a continuous philosophic tradition relating to the goals of the system. The tradition is a pattern woven of several threads. In its earliest forms, American juvenile justice emphasized the separation of young offenders from adult criminals by the construction of specialized juvenile institutions, first known as Houses of Refuge. This theme of separation from the criminal process was perpetuated and strengthened by the arrival of juvenile courts at the turn of the twentieth century.

Consistent, too, is the dualistic thread of child welfare. On the one hand, the managers and other officials of the 19th century's juvenile correctional institutions, joined by judges who wrote opinions upholding the legality of their enterprises, proclaimed that their programs were designed solely to educate their young charges—at first in morality and religion, then as the century progressed, with more of an emphasis on agricultural and vocational skills. This child welfare goal evolved in a more personal and individualistic direction as the 20th century celebrated the powers of psychotherapy to diagnose and correct misbehavior; religion and education became treatment and rehabilitation. But there was also a second and somewhat negative side to child welfare, apparent in the disclaimer that any of the action taken against juvenile offenders constituted, or even implied, punishment for their criminal conduct, a position that derived support from two sources. One was the manifest separation of juvenile justice from criminal justice; the latter was punitive, the former had to be something else. Judicial and correctional institutions for delinquents could also be proclaimed as non-punitive by pointing out that these same institutions were being appropriately used to deal with neglected and dependent children for whose welfare only caring and protective policies could be invoked; it being all of a piece, care and protection was the policy for delinquents as well.

The ethical dimension of traditional juvenile court philosophy clustered about the view that there was virtue in being kind to children. Kindness in this context consisted of sparing them from the law's retribution and in providing each child with a helping hand finely tuned to his particular circumstances. Individualized treatment became a slogan which itself conveyed a powerful ethical appeal. The broad official discretion needed to produce individualization consequently became a basic feature not only of juvenile justice but of the criminal process as well.

The philosophy of kindness to errant children rested, therefore, on the separation of juvenile from criminal justice, on individualization flowing from legislative grants of discretionary powers to judges and corrections officials, and on a characterization of the whole enterprise as non-punitive.

§ 4. Critique of the Tradition

Juvenile justice philosophy has not been immune to the 20th century's pressures of change. The period following World War II, especially the development of what came to be known as the Civil Rights Movement and the War on Poverty, inevitably affected the outlook of a system whose coercive powers reached large numbers of minority and poor children. The arrival, moreover, of new technologies in the form of mind controlling drugs, behavior modification programs of various sorts and direct electronic influence on brain functions put a new ethical light on efforts to provide treatment and rehabilitation. An era of judicial activism, under the controversial leadership of the Supreme Court, also opened juvenile justice to the scrutiny of constitutional values. The administration of justice generally became contaminated by the pervasive distrust of the candor and competence of public officials brought to crisis proportions by the war in Vietnam and symbolized by the Watergate affair.

These and other features of our times, however, served to widen cracks that were inherent in the philosophic structure, not to undermine an otherwise sturdy jurisprudence. The separation from adults, for example, was never as complete as juvenile court zealots would have us believe. Young offenders whose criminality was serious or chronic were, from the beginning, excluded from juvenile correctional facilities and assigned to adult prisons. As to exclusion from juvenile court, this century has developed several legal techniques, such as waiver, whereby the juveniles whose crimes are of major proportions are tried in the regular criminal court. That large numbers of juveniles are detained in adult jails—as many as three hundred thousand according to some authorities, makes it more than clear that juvenile justice still has at least one foot in the criminal process.

The concepts of the tradition were as faulty as the factual premises it relied on. Even if children had been completely removed from the punitive adult system, it was simply bad logic to conclude that there were not punitive elements in the children's system. Buried too by the promotional rhetoric of education and treatment was any reference or analysis of the coercion which characterized these efforts and which has a prominent place in any sound conception of punishment. The idea of coerced treatment which must not be viewed as punitive was a frail one to start with, not an indisputable principle whose implementation was subverted by penny-pinching legislatures or an uncaring public.

Individualization and the discretion it requires have also received their share of criticism: the former on grounds that we lack the resources and knowledge to accomplish it with any meaningful number of children, and the latter as a result of the revelation of abuse and discrimination. Here, too, however, the problems are conceptual and the sorry experience juvenile justice has had stems as much from a weakness of principle as from faulty implementation. If enforcement of criminal law is a prominent value of the system, then justice can never be completely individualized since the law's commands are addressed to everyone and their violation cannot be totally ignored in the face of individual needs without diluting the command to the status of a request. In a system of law enforcement, uncontrolled discretion conflicts sharply with the need to have a system of laws and not of men. The sanctions that are applicable for penal law violation, for children as well as adults, are so potent that they can in each case be applied justly only by resort to generally acceptable rules and policies, not idiosyncratically—at least under a government that is more responsible than tyrannical.

§ 5. The Quest for Philosophy

As the remainder of this book will detail, in recent years the juvenile court has rapidly become a court of law—or so it would seem from reading statutes and judicial opinions. The Supreme Court has, except in regard to jury trials, answered affirmatively every question put to it concerning the applicability of constitutional rules of criminal procedure to juvenile court delinquen-

cy proceedings. Where the Court has not spoken
to a procedural issue, other tribunals have generally aligned juvenile law with the law governing the adult criminal process—in the requirements for a valid plea of guilty, for the specificity
of the charge against a child, for revoking his
probation, etc.   Juvenile court statutes have
sometimes gone further, providing an unwaivable
right to counsel or greatly circumscribing sentencing discretion, for example. It would appear,
therefore, that juvenile courts have simply become criminal courts for under-age criminals and
have acquired the ponderous jurisprudence of responsibility, deterrence, rehabilitation, incapaci-
tation and the like which applies to the criminal
process.   There are, however, two objections to
accepting this conclusion, one factual and one
normative.

As to the first, the legalization of the juvenile
delinquency process is more apparent than real.
In order for children effectively to have legal
rights they have to have lawyers, and in light of
the relative poverty of most juvenile court children, these must be publicly paid lawyers. While
there has, of course, been an increase in the
amount of legal talent available in juvenile
courts, it has been far less than has been necessary for each child to have a well prepared ad-
vocate on his side. Children who are both poor
and criminal do not have the public purse opened

very widely for them. In addition to this, however, the still prominent position of the traditional treatment philosophy significantly tempers the assertion of rights in all but cases involving major crime where the likelihood is high that punishment—by anyone's definition—is in the cards. In the vast majority of cases the concept of a legal defense against help is as irrational here as it would be if a defense contractor ordered its lawyers to defend it against a million dollar government subsidy. In the juvenile court setting the subsidy (rehabilitation, treatment, welfare, etc.) is, of course, an empty promise; but its ideological pressure for the legal system to compromise its adversary characteristics remains potent.

The second objection to the evolution of the juvenile court system into a mini-criminal court is that for the bulk of children such a development is entirely inappropriate. Those who commit minor offenses and those who commit no crimes at all find themselves unjustly in a punitive system not because their conduct deserves punishment or because protection of the public demands punishment, but solely because coercive court powers are inherently punitive. They are the fleas staring down the barrel of an elephant gun. For the status offenders, proposals in recognition of the inappropriateness of punishment, i.e. that they be taken out of juvenile court jurisdiction, are currently receiving wide support from many quarters, although these same proposals are also being vigorously denounced by organizations of juvenile court judges and other elements of the rehabilitation industry. A similar proposal is in order for minor juvenile offenders for whom nothing more is required than a solemn reaffirmation of the law's requirements. Only an effort to breathe life back into the defunct idea that there is wisdom in rehabilitative treatment, applied early in the life of children who manifest the symptom of illegal conduct, would require more coercive power than this. It appears to be time to explore alternatives to juvenile court for this purpose. See, for example, the report on the working of the Scottish system of children's hearings in Martin, Fox & Murray, *Children Out of Court* (1981).

CHAPTER II

JURISDICTION

§ 6. In General

The term *jurisdiction* occurs frequently in legislation, judicial opinions and other writings concerning juvenile courts. It has, however, a variety of meanings and it is the purpose of this section to identify the most common uses of an otherwise confusing word.

Following an adjudicatory hearing, it is sometimes said that jurisdiction has been established, meaning that the conduct charged has been satisfactorily proved. As used in another sense, *jurisdiction* refers to the authority acquired over a particular person by virtue of written notice of the proceedings having been served on him. The law relating to this is discussed below in section 32. In still a third sense, *jurisdiction* may mean the geographic limits of a particular court's power, as when a juvenile court has jurisdiction within the city, or county boundaries. It is possible, of course, for there to be one sort of jurisdiction but not another, as would occur when a delinquent act is committed within the geographic jurisdiction of the court, but there is no jurisdiction over the delinquent child on account of his not having received the appropriate notice.

Jurisdiction may also be used in describing a relationship which the juvenile court has with other courts. Thus, the jurisdiction may be denominated *exclusive*, meaning that no other court has power to hear cases assigned by law to a juvenile court; or the jurisdiction may be *concurrent*, meaning that the power is shared with another court. These two sorts of jurisdiction are discussed in section 18. Another kind of jurisdictional relationship is involved when it is said that the juvenile court has *original* jurisdiction, meaning that its cases are being heard in a court for the first time, as contrasted to cases that are heard within the *appellate* jurisdiction of a court which involves review of another court's decision.

A common usage of *jurisdiction* is when it refers to the kinds of cases which a juvenile court is empowered to hear. The court invariably has jurisdiction to hear cases in which it is alleged that a child is delinquent, or neglected; it may have jurisdiction to hear claims that the child is "unruly" or "in need of supervision," or that the parents are "unfit" in which case it may have jurisdiction to terminate their parental rights. The juvenile court may also have authority to hear cases where it is alleged that an adult has contributed to the delinquency of a minor. Family courts usually have all of this jurisdiction plus a wider authority over disputes arising within the family unit, such as where one member of the family commits a crime against another. Whether a juvenile court has jurisdiction in this sense over a particular piece of litigation may involve the interplay of the laws from several different sources. In re Blackwolf, 158 Mont. 523, 493 P. 2d 1293 (1972) (jurisdiction of state juvenile court over Indian children); Michigan v. Koenig, 300 Minn. 432, 220 N.W.2d 825 (1974) (jurisdiction of juvenile court to extradite child to another state).

Finally, there is a variant use of the term found when a court decides whether the failure to follow a particular prescribed procedure is *jurisdictional*, meaning that the proceedings in which the failure occurred are void. In re M.W., 523 S.W.2d 513 (Tex.Civ.App.1975) (failure to provide notice to child is jurisdictional); People v. Armour, 15 Ill.App.3d 529, 305 N.E.2d 47 (1973) (failure to hold hearing within prescribed time is not).

§ 7. Venue

When there is more than one court within a state which might hear a case, each with similar jurisdictional powers, identifying which is the proper court for any particular case is a matter of *venue*. As section 2 has indicated, every state has several courts which exercise jurisdiction in juvenile cases so that the question of proper venue is an ever-present one.

Suppose, for example, that young X steals a car in County One. He lives in County Two. The police in County Three who hear about the theft, arrest him there. If there is a juvenile court in all three counties, which one is the proper one to hear the case? Where is the venue? Both statutes and constitutions supply the answer.

Pursuant to some statutes, the juvenile court in County Three would have authority to try X. Ill.Juv.Ct.Act § 702–6(1) (venue is where the child resides, where the law violation takes place, or where he is found); Mo.Rev.Stat.1969 § 211.-031 (venue where child resides or is physically present). Under the Missouri venue law, the place where the offense was committed is of no significance. In re M.W., 504 S.W.2d 189 (Mo. App.1973).

The emphasis on venue where the child resides is based on the belief that "in most cases it will be the county of his residence where his roots will be found—parents, school, church, friends and acquaintances—and where will be the greatest interest in bringing about his rehabilitation and improvement, if it can be accomplished." In re J.D.H., 508 S.W.2d 497, 500 (Mo.1974). With the recent decline in the belief of rehabilitation, one would expect venue provisions to emphasize the need to hold trials at the location of the crime, as does the Maryland law, Md.Ann.Code § 3–805 (b) ("the proceedings shall be brought in the county where the alleged delinquent act occurred . . ."). The new H.E.W. model proposes the same rule, subject to commencing the case where the child resides, if he consents. Model Fam.Ct. Act § 11(a). The venue provisions of the recent Maine law simply provides that the criminal rules are to be followed. Me.Rev.Stat.Ann. tit. 15 § 3102. The New York law is similar in requiring delinquency cases to commence in the county where the delinquent act occurred; it grants the court, however, discretion to transfer the case to another county. N.Y.Fam.Ct.Act § 717. Transfer provisions such as this are common. When the transfer occurs may be important. If it is after the hearing has commenced and there is "any further adjudicatory action" by the court to which the case is transferred, it has been suggested that there would be a violation of the prohibition against double jeopardy. Walls v. S., 326 So.2d 322, 325 (Miss.1976). This difficulty can be avoided if the transfer authority does not arise until after there has been a finding of delinquency, as is provided in Texas. Tex.Fam.Code § 51.-07(a). In none of the transfer statutes is there any guidance to the judge in exercising his discretion; there is a similar uncontrolled discretion when the statute gives to the police or the prosecutor the choice of bringing the proceeding where the child resides or where the act occurred, as is the case where the law simply says it may be commenced in one place or the other. Tex. Fam.Code § 51.06(a). Such statutes are more likely to serve administrative convenience rather than any substantive end of justice. Where, however, the court in a county where the child is arrested would not be the proper venue, the police cannot hand him over to the police of the proper county; the child must be released to his parents or brought to the local juvenile court which can then formally turn him over to proper authorities. In re J.D.H., 508 S.W.2d 497 (Mo.1974). If no objection is raised to the venue, any error is waived. In re Hoppe, 237 Or. 179, 390 P.2d 937 (1964).

Parts of state constitutions may be important in determining venue. It is frequent, for example, for these constitutions to require that persons be tried for crimes in the place where the crime was alleged to have been committed. No court appears to have held this requirement applicable to delinquency cases. Where the juvenile court has relinquished (waived, see § 59) its jurisdiction and the child is tried in a regular criminal court, however, this rule for criminal venue does come into play. Walls v. State, supra.

On the other hand, there may be a constitutional provision which states that in civil cases the venue must be in the place where the defendant resides. This has been reconciled with legislation which permits a child to be tried in a juvenue court sitting where the delinquency occurred by finding the trial which results in a delinquency finding to be only the equivalent of an arraignment in criminal prosecutions; the "case" to which the constitution speaks is the disposition hearing. The constitution is, therefore, satisfied so long as the disposition is made where the child resides, M.E.B. v. S., 230 Ga. 154, 195 S.E.2d 891 (1973).

§ 8. Lower Age Limits

As a system of law for children, juvenile court statutes must obviously draw a line between childhood and adulthood. Accordingly, all of these acts contain a maximum age limit, beyond which it is no longer legally possible for a person to be delinquent or neglected. This law relating to this upper limit of juvenile court jurisdiction is discussed below in § 10.

The authority of juvenile courts is similarly uniform in regard to the absence of any lower age limit for dealing with neglected and abused children. The statutes generally declare a child to be neglected, for example, if his is under a certain age—usually 18—and meets the statutory

definition of neglect (discussed below in § 15).
The legal system for protecting children from
mistreatment by parents and for insuring that
they are provided at least the minimal conditions
for healthy development is, therefore, applicable
from the moment they are born. In re Baby X,
97 Mich.App. 111, 293 N.W.2d 736 (1980) (newborn with symptoms of narcotics withdrawal);
In re Black, 273 Pa.Super. 536, 417 A.2d 1178
(1980) (2 older children had died from improper
care).

Strangely enough, most juvenile court acts do
not contain any lower age limits in their defini-
tions of delinquent children, despite the fact that
the philosophy and policies arising here are mark-
edly different from those occurring in neglect
and abuse proceedings. The problem arises from
the typical legislation which defines a delinquent
child as any person under the age of 18 who commits a delinquent act. Were protection and
healthy development all that were involved there
would be no anomaly. But, as Chief Justice Burger has recently pointed out, a delinquency proceeding "is designed 'to vindicate [the] very vital
interest in enforcement of criminal laws.'" Breed
v. Jones, 421 U.S. 519, 531, 95 S.Ct. 1779, 1786
(1975). One must ask, therefore, what sense it
makes to pursue this law enforcement goal
against very young children. A toddler who is
too young to distinguish "mine" from "thine"

hardly threatens social interests in private property when he makes away with a playmate's toy.

The common law refused to impose criminal liability on children under the age of seven, granting them an absolute immunity regardless of the harm that might have been produced by their conduct. Walker's Case, 5 N.Y. City-Hall Recorder 137 (N.Y.1820); Senn v. S., 53 Ala.App. 297, 299 So.2d 343 (1975).

Some states have raised the criminal immunity age as high as 12, but this has been interpreted as not to impair the delinquency jurisdiction of juvenile courts over children who are below the statutory age of criminal responsibility. K.M.S. v. S., 129 Ga.App. 683, 200 S.E.2d 916 (1973).

Among the minority of states which put some lower age limit to delinquency jurisdiction, this common law age is sometimes used. Mass.Gen. Laws c. 119 § 52. North Carolina puts the minimum age at 6. N.C.Gen.Laws § 7A–523. Others, such as the Texas Family Code § 51.02(1) (A) have raised the minimum to 10. This minority view recognizes that child welfare and protection is *not* the sole, or even dominant, aim of the delinquency laws. The prominence of *public* protection and notions of moral responsibility in the evaluation of juvenile justice has not, however, led to the inclusion of a minimum age for delinquency in many of the recent juvenile codes, e.g., Iowa (1979); Louisiana (1979); Maine (1978); Nebraska (1981); Washington (1979). It has been held that raising the minimum age of criminal responsibility to 13 does not prevent adjudicating a younger child to be a delinquent. In re Dow, 75 Ill.App.3d 1002, 31 Ill.Dec. 39, 393 N.E. 2d 1346 (1979).

Juvenile court legislation generally follows the pattern just described for delinquency in regard to its jurisdictional age limits for "status offenses." Where a child might be adjudicated delinquent at age 3 or 4, for example, he could also be declared "unruly" or "in need of supervision" with a similar disregard to his immaturity. Here there is no common law absolute immunity below 7 and it is perhaps this which accounts for the exception to the pattern, such as in the N.Y. Family Court Act § 712(b), which has no bottom limit for PINS, although there is a minimum age of 7 for delinquents in the N.Y. law.

§ 9. The Presumption of Incapacity

Along with the common law rule that children under the age of 7 had an absolute immunity to criminal liability went a companion rule that youngsters between 7 and 14 were *presumed* to lack criminal capacity. They could be convicted only if the state could prove beyond a reasonable doubt that they knew right from wrong. Godfrey v. S., 31 Ala. 323 (1858). It has sometimes also been required that this proof show knowledge of the "nature and legality" of what the child did. Benbow v. S., 128 Ala. 1, 29 So. 553 (1910). In a criminal prosecution of a child nearly 14 rebuttal of the presumed incapacity need not be beyond a reasonable doubt. Little v. S., 261 Ark. 859, 554 S.W.2d 312 (1977).

Efforts at applying this so-called infancy defense in delinquency proceedings have mostly failed. In re Davis, 17 Md.App. 98, 299 A.2d 856 (1973); S. v. D.H., 340 So.2d 1163 (Fla.1976). Courts rejecting this defense have reasoned that the common law rule, although preserved in penal law codification, was designed to protect young children from the rigors and penalties of the criminal process; and since the juvenile court scheme is, itself, precisely that sort of protection, it should be assumed that when the legislature enacted a juvenile court law it intended the presumption of incapacity not to apply. Until 1970 this view prevailed uniformly, except for a period of time in Texas when that state's juvenile court law had been considered penal in nature. Miller v. S., 82 Tex.Cr.R. 495, 200 S.W. 389 (1918). See Fox, *Responsibility in the Juvenile Court*, 11 Wm. and Mary L.Rev. 659 (1970).

Since 1970, however, the Supreme Court of California, has required the state to rebut the presumption in juvenile court in order to establish delinquency. In re Gladys R., 1 Cal.3d 855, 83 Cal.Rptr. 671, 464 P.2d 127 (1970). A mere admission by a 9 year old that he knew it was wrong to break into cars and steal is not sufficient to satisfy this requirement. In re Michael John B., 44 Cal.App.3d 443, 118 Cal.Rptr. 685 (1975). These courts have found no evidence of an implied repeal of the presumption of incapacity, codified in California, especially in light of the fundamental protection the presumption accords children accused of criminal conduct. The California court has also pointed out that although some children may not be found delinquent by virtue of the presumption, they might well be subject to the authority of a juvenile court's other types of jurisdiction.

The proof that a child know right from wrong may be closely related to proof of one of the essential elements of a crime, i.e. the mental element or *mens rea*. To decide that a child took someone else's property by mistake, and therefore lacked the intent to deprive another of his property (the *mens rea* of theft), is virtually the same thing as concluding that he did not know his conduct was wrong. Thus a court may reject the applicability of the infancy defense to delinquency proceedings, but still refuse to find a child delinquent on account of a failure to establish the *mens rea* which is also a failure to rebut the presumption. Porter v. S., 327 So.2d 820

(Fla.App.1976) (no proof of intent for theft). Even when a child is charged with reckless conduct a result is reached which is similar to what would obtain through application of the presumption when proof is required that he knew he was taking too great a risk. In re Anderson, 14 Or. App. 391, 513 P.2d 514 (1973).

§ 10. Maximum Age

When a child reached the age of fourteen the common law treated him as an adult for purposes of criminal responsibility. Under the juvenile court acts the upper age limit for juvenile court jurisdiction is both considerably higher and considerably more flexible.

Unlike the general lack of lower age limits, the statutes are uniform in setting *some* upper limit to the court's jurisdiction. The most frequent provision has that jurisdiction terminate when the juvenile reaches his eighteenth birthday. A few states use sixteen, seventeen or nineteen for this purpose. In order to determine age the common laws rules which declare that fractions of a day do not count and a person attains his next year on the day before his birthday have been invoked. See Brown v. Baldwin, 356 F.Supp. 831 (E.D.Mo.1973) (birthday rule applies); S. v. Stangel, 284 N.W.2d 4 (Minn.1979), contra. That the child falls within the jurisdictional age limits is a fact which the state must prove, Miguel

v. S., 500 S.W.2d 680 (Tex.Civ.App.1973), although controversy exists over whether proof of age is necessary to establish the jurisdiction of the court. See Matter of Kalvin, 99 Misc.2d 996, 417 N.Y.S.2d 826 (Fam.Ct.1979) (age is jurisdictional); In re Greene, 76 Ill.2d 204, 28 Ill.Dec. 525, 390 N.E.2d 884 (1979) (age is not). How the age may be proved has sometimes been troublesome. If, for example, age is an element of the criminal offense (indecent liberties with a child by a person over 16) the rule that an offense cannot be established by an extrajudicial confession alone requires some corroboration of the accused's admission of his age. People v. Dalton, 93 Ill.App.3d 264, 48 Ill.Dec. 795, 417 N.E.2d 197 (1981). However, a court may accept as proof of a child's age the birth date set forth in a probation report on the theory that that hearsay statement is admissible as a business record. In re James Edward H., 121 Cal. App.3d 268, 175 Cal.Rptr. 141 (1981). Despite the fact that the drawing of an age line between juvenile and criminal court involves an irreducible degree of arbitrariness, this has not induced a holding that a denial of equal protection of the laws is involved. S. v. Scoville, 113 N.H. 161, 304 A.2d 366 (1973).

In some of the juvenile court statutes there was a differing upper age limit for males and females, both in regard to delinquency and status offenses. Although these were for a long time upheld by courts, the most recent decisions have found an unconstitutional denial of Equal Protection in the age differences. Lamb v. Brown, 456 F.2d 18 (10th Cir. 1972) (criminal violations); In re Patricia A., 31 N.Y.2d 83, 335 N.Y. S.2d 33, 286 N.E.2d 432 (1972) (status offenses). In Illinois a new constitutional provision prohibiting denial of equal protection on account of sex has been held to invalidate the juvenile court act's sex discrimination. P. v. Ellis, 57 Ill.2d 127, 311 N.E.2d 98 (1974). The *Ellis* opinion noted that Texas was the only state whose statutes continued to draw an age distinction between boys and girls regarding eligibility for juvenile court treatment. The Texas Family Code § 51.02(1) now has a uniform age limit for both sexes.

The Juvenile Justice Standards, Juvenile Delinquency and Sanctions, 2.1(A), recommend that age at the time of the offense be the crucial determinant for jurisdiction. Traditional juvenile court legislation does not usually specify whether that or some other event fixes the age for jurisdictional purposes. More recently enacted statutes, however, take the same position as the Standards. Both recent legislation and the Standards also concur in providing for juvenile court jurisdiction to extend beyond the upper limit if the offense was committed within the specified ages. Thus, although the upper age is 16, a child who commits an offense while 15 years old may be proceeded against in juvenile court so long as he is under 18, according to § 51.02(1)(B) of the Texas Family Code. The Standards extend this to when the child is "not more than twenty years of age at the time juvenile court delinquency proceedings are initiated." 2.1(B). The rule is similar in the federal courts. U. S. v. Doe, 631 F.2d 110 (9th Cir. 1980) and several states. W.F. v. S., 144 Ga.App. 523, 241 S.E.2d 631 (1978); P. v. Taylor, 76 Ill.2d 289, 29 Ill.Dec. 103, 391 N.E. 2d 366 (1979). There would be obvious objections to a juvenile court trial for a person in his thirties, or older, even if the offense with which he is charged was committed while he was a young adolescent within the upper limits of the age jurisdiction. Application of Johnson, 178 F. Supp. 155 (D.C.N.J.1957) (age 27 is beyond juvenile jurisdiction). Nonetheless, some statutes do have a seemingly open ended juvenile court jurisdiction for any person who committed an act of delinquency while under the jurisdictional limit. In re Braswell, 294 So.2d 896 (La.App.1974).

Where the legislation is not clear whether it is age at the time of the offense, or some other time, many courts have held that it is a subsequent event, such as the time of the indictment, which determines whether the juvenile court's exclusive jurisdiction has expired. S. v. Watchman, 20 Or.App. 709, 533 P.2d 361 (1975); Bendler v. Percy, 481 F.Supp. 813 (E.D.Wis.1979) (Wisconsin rule that age at time charges are filed controls is constitutionally permissible). The possibility for prosecutorial abuse in these circumstances—delaying the proceedings until the child becomes too old for juvenile court—is obvious and courts have sometimes noted that in upholding a criminal prosecution in these circumstances that "the institution of the prosecution proceeded with due dispatch." Ferguson v. Commonwealth, 512 S.W.2d 501, 505 (Ky.App. 1974). Where there has been purposeful delay in order for juvenile court authority to expire, a federal court has required that the child must be given a hearing, analogous to a waiver hearing (see § 59) before the criminal prosecution can proceed. Miller v. Quatsoe, 348 F.Supp. 764 (E.D. Wis.1972).

§ 11. Children's Criminal Conduct

With some exceptions which will be set forth in this section, it is generally true that a child may be adjudged delinquent if he violates state or local criminal law. The Massachusetts statute is an example, without any exceptions, of the scope of this jurisdiction. Mass.Gen.Laws.Ann. c. 119, § 52 defines a delinquent child as "a child between seven and seventeen who violates any city ordinance or town by-law or who commits any offense against a law of the commonwealth."

Several states also include violation of federal law as a basis for finding a child delinquent, and some of these, such as Iowa, Louisiana and Oregon go still further and define delinquency as encompassing violation of the laws of another state, if the act occurred in the other state. In light of the fact that the penal laws among the states are far from being uniform, it is distinctly possible that an exercise of such a broad jurisdiction would find a child being declared delinquent in state X for violation of the law of state Y which occurred when the child was in Y, even if the same conduct is *not* a criminal violation under the laws of state X where the child is tried. This is an anomaly in a legal system which includes a principle that one state does not normally undertake to enforce the criminal laws of another state. Such a broad jurisdiction is difficult to explain as anything but an excessive preoccupation with the idea that a criminal act—any criminal act—is a symptom of the child's need for help which any juvenile court that happens to catch him is prepared and obliged to provide. Although there is no rule permitting prosecution of adults for out-of-state crimes, the legislature may extend delinquency jurisdiction in this manner without violating the Equal Protection guarantee of the Fourteenth amendment.

State ex rel. Juvenile Department v. W., 34 Or. App. 437, 578 P.2d 824 (1978).

In contrast to this extremely wide jurisdiction, are statutes which define delinquency as conduct which violates something *less than* the whole of the state's penal law. There are several ways in which states carve out these exceptions to the generalization that delinquency can be found wherever there is crime. One approach is to except from the juvenile court's jurisdiction the most serious offenses. This is accomplished either by naming the particular crimes—murder, rape, etc.—or by identifying them according to how they are punished—usually any offense punishable by death, or by life imprisonment. The consequence of statutory exceptions of this sort is to place the child within the jurisdiction of the regular criminal court if he is charged with one of the excepted crimes.

At the other end of the scale of seriousness, it is sometimes provided that juvenile courts have no jurisdiction over minor traffic offenses by children (see § 14), or fish and game law violations, leaving these children, too, in the jurisdiction of the court which normally deals with such misconduct. A variation on the approach of confining juvenile courts to serious offenses by children is to limit delinquency to offenses that are punishable by incarceration. Tex.Fam.Code § 51.03(a) (1). Under the Texas statute, other crimes constitute grounds for finding the child "in need of supervision." § 51.03(b)(1). Still another means for limiting juvenile court jurisdiction is to provide, as does R.I.Gen.Laws 1971, § 14–1–3(f), that delinquency is violation of any law of the grade of felony and more than one violation of any other law. If the delinquency definition extends only to "crimes" then a child may not be found delinquent on account of conduct which violates those parts of the penal law which are denominated "violations," In re A.A., 36 A.D.2d 1001, 321 N.Y.S.2d 59 (1971) or "offenses," In re John M., 65 Misc.2d 609, 318 N.Y.S.2d 904 (1971). If, however, the same conduct would be chargeable as either a "violation" and, therefore, not within juvenile court jurisdiction, or as a crime which is the basis for delinquency, the court will consider the petition as charging a crime. In re W., 72 Misc.2d 370, 339 N.Y.S.2d 193 (1972).

A child may also be found delinquent for violating a law which applies only to children, such as one forbidding persons under the age of 16 from possessing air guns. In re Thomas A.F., 85 Misc.2d 791, 381 N.Y.S.2d 392 (1976). Curfew laws for minors can also give rise to delinquency adjudications, provided such laws are included in juvenile court jurisdiction. These laws have been attacked as unconstitutional, but usually without success. Bykofsky v. Middletown, 401 F.Supp. 1242 (M.D.Pa.1975). A curfew law that prohibits attendance at religious or school meetings and other associational activities is overbroad, however, and violates the child's First Amendment rights. Johnson v. City of Opelousas, 658 F.2d 1065 (5th Cir. 1981). But if delinquency is defined as conduct which would be a crime if it were committed by an adult, then violation of a curfew law which is expressly limited to children and, therefore, is not a crime which it is possible for adults to commit, cannot be the basis for delinquency. In re Doe, 87 N.M. 466, 535 P.2d 1092 (App.1975), reversed on other grounds 88 N.M. 137, 537 P.2d 1399.

Since much delinquent conduct appears to be undertaken in the company of other children, resort is sometimes had to those parts of the criminal law which are directed specifically at collaborative misconduct. In re D.M.L., 293 A.2d 277 (D.C.App.1972) (aiding and abetting); In re Waldron, 237 Pa.Super. 298, 353 A.2d 43 (1975) (conspiracy).

§ 12. Noncriminal Misbehavior: Status Offenders

The authority of juvenile courts over children has never been restricted to those who violate the penal laws. Juvenile misbehavior of a noncriminal type always has and continues to constitute a substantial part of the juvenile justice system's business. The Juvenile Justice Standards, Noncriminal Misbehavior, estimate that these cases comprise "no less than one-third and perhaps close to one-half the workload of America's juvenile courts."

State statutes vary in what conduct or conditions are included in the juvenile court's jurisdiction, but because the emphasis in the statutory descriptions is heavily on conditions common to childhood rather than on criminal conduct, these are often called status offenses. Most often found in the court's jurisdiction is running away from home, truanting from school and being disobedient to parents. Some statutes also extend juvenile court jurisdiction to children who are in danger of leading an idle, dissolute, lewd or immoral life, and those who are a danger to themselves or others.

In most states status offenses are part of the statutory definition of delinquency. Increasingly, however, children who come within these descriptions are described by a different statutory label, e.g., Persons in Need of Supervision (PINS), Children in Need of Supervision (CHINS), etc.

Despite the relative vagueness of the statutory descriptions as compared to the specificity normally demanded of criminal laws, appellate courts have generally upheld these acts against constitutional attack on vagueness grounds, District of Columbia v. B.J.R., 332 A.2d 58 (D.C. App.1975), although there are a few decisions striking down some of the most generally worded provisions. Gesicki v. Oswald, 336 F.Supp. 371 (S.D.N.Y.1971), affirmed Oswald v. Gesicki, 406 U.S. 913, 92 S.Ct. 1773 (1972).

The procedural requirements for adjudication of status offenses often differ from the rules applicable in delinquency cases. In about three-fourths of the states, for example, the proof must be by a preponderance of the evidence rather than by the stricter standard of beyond a reasonable doubt. The admissibility of evidence may similarly be judged by different standards. In re Spalding, 273 Md.App. 690, 332 A.2d 246 (1975) (child's statement made to police admissible in PINS case which would be inadmissible in proceeding concerning criminal violation). In some states there is no right to counsel in these cases. In re Walker, 282 N.C. 28, 191 S.E.2d 702 (1972). These looser procedural rules may explain why some cases which could not be prosecuted as law violating delinquencies are instead processed as status offenses. In re J.M., 57 N.J. 442, 273 A. 2d 355 (1971). Status offense charges may also be used when the child's conduct falls short of violating the most relevant criminal statute. In re J.P., 32 Ohio Misc. 5, 287 N.E.2d 926 (1972) (15 year old could not be guilty of statutory rape which imposed liability only on those over 18, but he was "unruly child" who had so deported himself as to injure or endanger the health or morals of himself or others); In re A., 130 N.J.Super. 138, 325 A.2d 837 (1974) (making threats with toy gun is not crime, but is deportment endangering the morals, health or general welfare of the child).

With the exception of only a few states, juvenile courts may make disposition orders concerning status offenders which are the same as those for delinquents, including commitment to secure institutions. Court decisions which restrict this usually prohibit the mixing of status offenders and delinquents, but fall short of prohibiting use of the same institution. Blondheim v. S., 84 Wn.2d 874, 529 P.2d 1096 (1975).

An exception is State ex rel. Harris v. Calendine, —— W.Va. ——, 233 S.E.2d 318 (1977) which held it to be in violation of the state constitution to commit these children "to secure, prison-like facilities which also house children guilty of criminal conduct or needlessly subject status offenders to the degradation and physical abuse of incarceration." The existence of jurisdiction over status offenders is under strong attack, with prestigious organizations such as the National Council of Crime and Delinquency, as well as the Standards, calling for statutory amendments which would eliminate jurisdiction over these cases in any court.

§ 13. Need for Treatment

Two important distinctions must be made here. The *right* to treatment which raises the question of what help and services need to be furnished a child who is in official custody is different from the allegation and proof that the child *needs* treatment which must be made in order for a delinquency or status offense finding to be made in the first place. It is only the latter which is discussed in this section. The right to treatment law is in section 56.

The second distinction relates to ways in which the need for treatment is dealt with in the juvenile court acts. Under one, the phrase has virtually no litigation meaning. The Missouri statute is illustrative; it provides that the court has jurisdiction over a child "alleged to be in need of care and treatment because:" and then follow four specific situations, including commission of a crime. Mo.Rev.Stat. § 211.031(1). Despite the word "alleged" in the law, Missouri courts have held that no such allegation is required and that no proof of a need for care and treatment need be made. The statute is read as expressing a *legislative* determination that any child who commits a crime is in need of care and treatment. A–S v. Murphy, 487 S.W.2d 589 (Mo.App.1972).

The New York Family Court Act, on the other hand, contains similar language, but with more

[45]

significance to the trial of delinquency and PINS
cases. It is required that petitions in these cases
include an allegation of misconduct *plus* an allegation that the child "requires supervision,
treatment or confinement" (§ 731(1)(c)—delinquency) or "requires supervision or treatment"
(§ 732(c)—PINS). These added allegations must
be established, however, at the disposition hearing (§ 712(g)) and a determination of delinquency or PINS is reached at the trial or fact-finding
hearing on the basis of what conduct is proved
(§ 712(f)). At the disposition hearing the
"need" must be proved by a preponderance of the
evidence (§ 745(b)) and if it is not proved, the
petition must be dismissed (§ 751). In such a case
there would seem to be required a *nunc pro tunc*
vacating of the order finding the child to be a
delinquent or a PINS. In the latter cases, the
proof or failure of proof of the status offense will
often be seen automatically to solve the need for
treatment issue as well. Thus under the Maryland definition of a Child in Need of Supervision
which includes misconduct and a need for "guidance, treatment, or rehabilitation," an appellate
court recited the misconduct and added: "Having
so deported herself it is patent that this 16 year
old, pregnant, unmarried girl required guidance
and treatment, ..." In re Smith, 16 Md.
App. 209, 214–216, 295 A.2d 238, 241 (1972).
So too, where the conduct is characterized as nor-

mal, even if it involves a 14 year old living away from home and not attending school, a dismissal of the PINS petition at the close of the fact-finding hearing for failure to prove *mis*conduct serves to anticipate a disposition finding that there is no need for supervision or treatment. In re Reynaldo R., 73 Misc.2d 390, 341 N.Y.S.2d 998 (1973).

The phrase "need for treatment" and its equivalent is not self-explanatory. Whose need is involved? the state's in order to control its children and prevent crime? the child's need in order to overcome a specific handicap, such as a learning disorder? his need to learn how to cope with poverty? Despite such problems, when the vagueness of these statutes is tested by constitutional requirements no account is taken of the fact that juvenile court judges must guess at the meaning of the phrase and that counsel for children have no clear idea of what they must contend with. District of Columbia v. B.J.R., 332 A.2d 58 (D.C. Ct.App.1975), for example discusses whether children have sufficient notice of what it means to be habitually disobedient and ungovernable but pays no attention to the vagueness of the requirement that the child "need care or rehabilitation."

When the phrase includes, as it does in New York, the need for "confinement" it becomes more clear that it is the state's need for control that is at issue since it is seldom that a child needs

—in the sense of "benefits from"—a term in the training school. This state need is still more apparent from provisions such as the Model Act's § 32(c) which provides that: "In the absence of evidence to the contrary, evidence of the commission of an act which constitutes a felony is sufficient to sustain a finding that the child is in need of care or rehabilitation."

§ 14. Traffic Offenses

The question of whether children's violation of laws relating to the use of motor vehicles should be within juvenile court jurisdiction has become a controversial one. From the perspective of a belief that all deviant behavior, or at least all criminal behavior, is a symptom of a child's need for rehabilitative treatment, there is no reason to exclude traffic offenses from juvenile court. If the specialized approach of a juvenile court is deemed appropriate for all other violations of penal law, such as the violation of prohibitions against gambling when he makes a bet with a friend about who will win the World Series, violation of the law against solicitation of criminal conduct when he tells an older brother to hit an annoying playmate, etc., then there is nothing exceptional in attributing diagnostic significance to traffic law violations. Of course, not even the hardiest supporter of the rehabilitative intervention of juvenile courts would contend that *all* vio-

lations of penal law have the same significance—
hence the well-known intake screening of cases.
This is, in fact, the view of traditional juvenile
court legislation which treats traffic offenses no
differently from other crimes.

. This view is, however, being overtaken by a
position which would make an exception for traffic offenses and leave them to the enforcement
process used for adults. Several lines of thought
support provision such as § 2(7) of the Model
Act which excludes all but a few traffic violations from juvenile court jurisdiction. A distrust
of the view that any particular crime can be a
potent indicator of a need for rehabilitation is
part of the position. The Model Act, and much
recent juvenile court legislation, do not accept
this completely for the note to § 2(7) says that
there are *some* crimes in this class "which are
likely to need the specialized handling of the juvenile court, such as the so-called negligent homicide statute sometimes appearing in traffic codes,
driving while under the influence of liquor or
narcotics, driving without or during suspension
of a driver's license, and the like."

Taking juvenile traffic offenses out of juvenile
court is also supported by the sheer volume of
cases which might inundate the court if no such
restriction were adopted. The regular traffic
court is much more geared toward an assembly-
line processing of cases, although this sort of

perfunctory justice is not ideally a child's best introduction to the legal system.

The Model Act is one sort of middle ground on the issue of including or excluding traffic offenses. Another is proposed in the Uniform Juvenile Court Act § 44 which suggests a three part classification: (1) serious traffic violations which are handled as delinquency proceedings in the juvenile court; (2) less serious violations in which the juvenile court acts "more like a well-run traffic court" rather than a juvenile court; and (3) the least serious cases which are assigned to the jurisdiction of the regular traffic court with, however, authority in that court to transfer cases to the juvenile court where "there is a more serious problem manifested by the traffic offense." Unless the traffic court judge holds only a probable cause hearing, or the case is transferred to juvenile court for disposition following a traffic court finding of guilt, however, it seems that the Double Jeopardy Clause would prohibit trials in both courts. Breed v. Jones, 421 U.S. 519, 95 S.Ct. 1779 (1975).

Even with express legislative reservation of the most serious traffic offenses for juvenile court jurisdiction, courts tend to interpret "traffic offenses" which are to be tried in the regular court as not including major felonies. Jones v. S., 163 Ind. 191, 322 N.E.2d 727 (1975) (juvenile court can hear reckless homicide case).

§ 15. Neglect and Abuse

It has been estimated that there are as many as 150,000 neglect cases each year in the nation's juvenile courts. As is true in the area of delinquency and status offenses, reformers such as the authors of the ABA/IJA Draft Standards, Abuse and Neglect, contend that the jurisdictional reach of the law is too broad. It is also sometimes claimed that administration of the neglect laws constitutes the imposition of racial and socioeconomic standards on parents which are foreign to them and which they cannot comply with. In re P., 71 Misc.2d 965, 972–973, 337 N.Y.S.2d 203, 211–12 (1972) (claim rejected on grounds that "It would require courts to sanction less protection for the children of poor, black and uneducated parents than for children of more privileged parents thus violating their constitutional right to equal protection under the law.")

One basis for the claim of discriminatory treatment lies in the great amount of discretion granted courts by the extremely general language used in defining neglect. The Illinois statute, for example, provides:

Those who are neglected include any minor under 18 years of age

(a) who is neglected as to proper or necessary support, education as required by law, or as to medical or other remedial care recognized under State law or other care necessary for his well-being, or who is abandoned by his parents, guardian or custodian; or

(b) whose environment is injurious to his welfare or whose behavior is injurious to his own welfare or that of others.

This and similar statutes are held not to be unconstitutionally vague since "Child neglect is by its very nature incapable of a precise and detailed definition and . . . the child neglect statute does not infringe on any of the basic liberties protected by the United States Constitution . . . . The state does have a compelling interest to protect children from abuse and neglect, and to narrow the statute would have the effect of diminishing the rights of children who have no other means of protecting themselves." P. v. Schoos, 15 Ill.App.3d 964, 305 N.E.2d 560, 562 (1973). Cases upholding this position are reviewed in S. v. Mills, 52 Or.App. 777, 629 P.2d 861 (1981).

Two recent federal cases hold the other way, however. Relying on their being a core of constitutionally protected family autonomy, Roe v. Conn, 417 F.Supp. 769 (M.D.Ala.1976) dealt with an Alabama law which defined neglect to include a child whose home "is an unfit or improper place" for him and held that "The Alabama statute defining 'neglected' children sweeps far past the constitutionally permissible range of interference into the sanctity of the family unit. The fact that the home is 'improper' in the eyes of the state officials does not necessarily mean that a child in that home is subject to physical or emotional harm." At 779.

Roe relied on Alsager v. District Court, 406 F.Supp. 10 (S.D.Iowa 1975), a termination of parental rights case (see § 17), which appears to have initiated the departure from the position typified by *Schoos*, supra. *Alsager* found not only that the Iowa neglect statute inhibited the exercise of the constitutionally protected substantive right to "family integrity" but also ruled that the vagueness in the statute failed to provide the parents sufficient notice of what sorts of conduct was expected of them in order to avoid having their parental rights terminated. A third ground on which the Iowa law was struck down related to the fact that subjective official judgments had to be made in each case by virtue of the vagueness of the statute and that "The termination of the parent-child relationship in any given case may thus turn upon which state officials are involved in the case, rather than upon explicit standards reflecting legislative intent. This danger is especially grave in the highly subjective context of determining an approved mode of child rearing." At 18–19. On appeal, this decision was affirmed on the ground that the state failed to prove sufficient harm to justify termination and that there was insufficient notice of the conduct that would warrant termination. The Court of Appeals agreed with the lower court's view of the vagueness issue, but did rest its affirmance on that ground. Alsager v. District Court, 545 F.2d 1137 (8th Cir. 1976).

Roe and *Alsager* are in a clear minority and state courts continue to deny that there is unconstitutional vagueness in statutes which those federal courts would certainly not accept.

Although there are cases which indicate that neglect is found on the basis of harm to the child, In re Gregory S., 85 Misc.2d 846, 380 N.Y.S.2d 620 (1976) (mother refused to permit medical or dental examination of child); In re Wachlin, 309 Minn. 370, 245 N.W.2d 183 (1976) (mother refused to cooperate in attempts to provide speech therapy to child with neurological disorder), the more common approach of courts in determining whether a child has been neglected is to focus on the conduct of the parents or the conditions of the home, with only tenuous reference to the harm suffered by the child as a consequence of the conduct or conditions. In re Naimie, 187 Neb. 494, 192 N.W.2d 137 (1971) (lewd and lascivious conduct of mother detrimental to children's morals); In re Johnson, 188 Neb. 677, 198 N.W. 2d 466 (1972) (children left unattended in filthy home, inadequately furnished due to mother's indifference). Courts have been forced, however, to emphasize the *future* harm to children when they have been faced with neglect petitions dealing with newborn infants and the allegations of neglect must necessarily relate to what sort of parental care is to be expected if the infant is allowed to stay with the parent. The cases have uniformly affirmed the possibility of finding neglect from the evidence in such circumstances, even when the applicable statute speaks only in the present tense concerning a child who *is* neglected. In re Black, 273 Pa.Super. 536, 417 A.2d 1178 (1980). It has also been held that a finding of neglect is warranted when, after the death of one child from complications of an untreated hernia, the mother declared that for religous reasons she would not seek medical help for her other children. In re Appeal in Cochise County etc., 133 Ariz. 157, 650 P.2d 459 (1982). The Arizona court also decided that although the Supreme Court has required a "clear and convincing standard of proof in order to terminate parental rights (see § 16), for neglect only a preponderance of the evidence is necessary.

Under some circumstances unexplained injuries may support a finding of neglect. See, for example, In re Cynthia V., 94 A.D.2d 773, 462 N.Y.S.2d 721 (1983) (evidence of sexual penetrations plus body bruises).

An aggravated form of neglect, usually known as "child abuse" is often the subject of separate statutory provisions, as in Article 10 of the N.Y. Family Court Act. The core of the definition involves "physical injury by other than accidental means which causes or creates a substantial risk of death, or serious or protracted disfigurement, or protracted impairment of physical or emotional health or protracted loss or impairment of the function of any bodily organ." § 1012 (e)(1). The juvenile courts have jurisdiction to protect the child in such cases not only where the parent himself inflicts the injury described, but they will also deprive a mother of custody on these grounds where she is willing to risk injury by another person. In re A.A., 533 S.W.2d 681 (Mo.App.1976) (mother permitted father, who had been convicted of killing sibling, to visit with child); In re Armentrout, 207 Kan. 366, 485 P.2d 183 (1971) (mother willing to have daughter live at home with father who had been convicted of statutory rape of daughter). Furthermore, where child abuse has been found, courts often will take jurisdiction over other children in the family in order to remove them from the danger of being subject to similar abuse. In re Edwards, 70 Misc.2d 858, 335 N.Y.S.2d 575 (1972).

In determining whether the evidence before the court constitutes neglect courts sometimes indicate that the neglect finding depends on what the consequences might be. That is, if there is an automatic termination of parental rights, (see § 17) then more by way of misconduct and harm will be required than if the parents will only be required to submit to state supervision of their parenting behavior. In re S.D., 549 P.2d 1190 (Alaska 1976).

Although procedural rights in the neglect and abuse cases have been more slow to appear than in delinquency and status offense proceedings, the trend in both case law and legislation is clearly in the direction of requiring more formality and rights for the litigant. The right of indigent parents to publicly paid counsel, for example, is frequently affirmed by appellate courts. Reist v. Bay County Circuit Judge, 396 Mich. 326, 241 N.W.2d 55 (1976) (parents also entitled to transcript at public expense). In most states the legislation is broad enough to encompass the right of the child in these cases to have counsel. See Katz, Child Neglect Laws in America, 9 Fam.L.Q. 1 (1975).

The right to appropriate notice of the procedings goes in tandem with the right to counsel. Thus, where the petition merely recites the statutory language and does not allege any facts, the juvenile court fails to acquire jurisdiction. In re Appeal in Pima Cty., Juvenile Action No. J–46735, 25 Ariz.App. 424, 544 P.2d 248 (1976). It has also been held that the state agency to which custody of the child might be given is also entitled to notice. Division of Family Services v. J.F., 327 So.2d 128 (Fla.App.1976). Where, however, immediate action is necessary to protect children, no formal notice to the parents is needed. Sedberry v. S., 286 So.2d 237 (Fla.App. 1973).

The neglect and abuse hearing has distinctly adversary features, although not all of the characteristics of a delinquency or criminal trial. The fundamental right to present evidence belongs to the parents as a matter of due process of law. In re Hanson, 51 A.D.2d 696, 379 N.Y.S.2d 415 (1976). It is also generally held that hearsay is inadmissible in these proceedings. P. ex rel. Jones v. Jones, 39 Ill.App.3d 821, 350 N.E.2d 826 (1976) (admission of hearsay harmless error in light of confrontation and cross-examination in court). The rules of evidence which apply to all civil litigation are often declared applicable in neglect cases. Daugaard v. P., 176 Colo. 38, 488 P.2d 1101 (1971) (applying rule that expert witness may not base his opinion on hearsay).

One rule, however, has been the subject of much controversy; the burden of proof which must be borne in order to establish that there is neglect. While there appears not to be any disagreement with the view that the burden of proving neglect lies on the party asserting it, McGurren v. S. T., 241 N.W. 690 (N.D.1976), the question which has divided the courts is whether the neglect may be proved by the normal civil standard of "a preponderance of the evidence" or by something more strict. The most commonly held view is that a preponderance suffices. In re S., 26 Or.App. 429, 552 P.2d 578 (1976) (rejecting claim that proof beyond a reasonable doubt is required). Some recent cases adopt the more stringent standard of proof "by clear and convincing evidence." In re Robert P., 61 Cal.App. 3d 310, 132 Cal.Rptr. 5 (1976). Since the Supreme Court mandated the latter standard when termination of parental rights is at stake (see § 17) it has often been determined by state courts that the "preponderance" test suffices for ordinary abuse and neglect where only custody is the dispositional issue. See In re Appeal in Cochise County etc., 133 Ariz. 157, 650 P.2d 459 (1982).

§ 16. Child Abuse and Neglect Reporting Laws

By statute in every state certain persons are required to report their knowledge or suspicions that a child has been abused or neglected. Named as mandatory reporters are usually physicians, nurses, teachers, social workers and law enforcement personnel. The statutes often provide for civil or criminal penalties for failure to report and a mandated reporter may be liable to a child who suffers injuries as a result of the failure to report. See Landeros v. Flood, 17 Cal.3d 399,

131 Cal.Rptr. 69, 551 P.2d 389 (1976). In addition to a class of mandated reporters, every state permits all persons to make similar reports; in a few states everyone is a mandated reporter.

The report is usually made to an official child protection agency, either at the state or local level of government. In some states the report is to a law enforcement agency as well. Persons making reports are provided statutory immunity from both criminal and civil liability based on their reporting. In addition, it has been held that the agency receiving the reports is not required by the federal constitution to disclose to the parents the identity of the person making the report. Doe v. Staples, 706 F.2d 985 (6th Cir. 1983).

The conditions required to be reported include physical or mental injury, sexual abuse, sexual exploitation and neglect (a failure to provide adequate food, clothing, shelter or medical care) by a person responsible for the child's welfare. Thus, harm by a schoolmate or a complete stranger need not be reported. There must, however, be reports of institutional abuse—harm to children in the state's care; these reports must be made to an agency independent of the government agency responsible for the care of the child. All reports must be investigated promptly.

§ 17. Termination of Parental Rights

The most drastic action a state may take as a result of the mistreatment of a child is to terminate the parental rights of the child's parents. If these rights are terminated the parent loses the right to object to the child's adoption and has no further rights or privileges—is, in effect, a stranger, in regard to the child. In light of these consequences it is not surprising that there has been both judicial and legislative development of the procedural aspects of the termination proceedings.

Two cases have reached the Supreme Court. In both Lassiter v. Department of Social Services, 452 U.S. 18, 101 S.Ct. 2153 (1981) and Santosky v. Kramer, 455 U.S. 745, 102 S.Ct. 1388 (1982) the Court affirmed that "state intervention to terminate the relationship between a [parent] and [a] child must be accomplished by procedures meeting the requisites of the Due Process Clause." *Lassiter*, 452 U.S. at 37, 101 S.Ct. at 2164–2165 (dissenting opinion). In *Lassiter* the Court concluded that Due Process did not require that the state courts always appoint counsel for an indigent parent in termination proceedings. It was left to trial courts to appoint counsel in these circumstances on a case-by-case basis. In most of the states this decision is of little effect since the right of the parent to appointed counsel is guaranteed by statute. In about half a dozen states, however, there has been a court decision imposing the obligation to appoint counsel based on constitutional considerations. It remains to be seen whether in these latter states the courts will find a basis in the state constitution for continuing to require counsel for indigent parents in termination cases.

In *Santosky* the Supreme Court considered what burden of proof rule was constitutionally required to be met by the state in termination cases. The Court chose a middle ground between the most strict beyond-a-reasonable-doubt standard and the least strict preponderance one and determined that the state must prove its case by at least clear and convincing evidence. It reached this conclusion by balancing the interest of the parents, child and the state in avoiding an erroneous outcome against the interests in facilitating termination in appropriate cases. As a result of this decision states are still free to impose the reasonable doubt standard, but they may no longer adhere to the preponderance one.

The grounds on which parental rights may be terminated are specified by statute, the most common one being abandonment of the child. Tennessee has recently enacted a variation of this which provides for termination of the rights of an imprisoned parent who has not met statutory responsibilities to the child for four months. Courts, on the other hand, are often reluctant to terminate parental rights merely on the parent's criminal record or imprisonment when the statute requires a finding of parental "depravity." See, for example, In the Interest of Sanders, 77 Ill.App.3d 78, 32 Ill.Dec. 847, 395 N.E.2d 1228 (1979). A second common ground for termination is the neglect or abuse of the child. In some states termination cannot be the disposition in the initial neglect or abuse proceeding; there must be a time period during which the parent has the opportunity to become a more adequate parent. Where this period is mandated there is also sometimes a statutory duty on the child protection services to provide services to the parent in order to facilitate the rehabilitation. If termination proceedings are brought following a period for rehabilitation the court will take into account whether the social services agency fulfilled its statutory mandate to foster the parent-child relationship. See, for example, In the Matter of Leon RR, 48 N.Y.2d 117, 421 N.Y.S.2d 863, 397 N.E.2d 374 (1979). The statutes also specify that mental illness of the parent may serve as a grounds for termination. Courts generally accept evidence of mental illness as a justification for termination even though it is possible that therapy and medication for the parent would bring her to the point of adequately caring for the child. See, for example, In re Guardianship of Vera T., 80 A.D.2d 511, 435 N.Y.S.2d 598 (1981). This view was expressly rejected, however, by the New York Court of Appeals which held in In the Matter of Hime Y., 52

N.Y.2d 242, 437 N.Y.S.2d 286, 418 N.E.2d 1305 (1981) that termination was not warranted in a case where the court-appointed psychiatrist had testified that the mother might be able, at some future time and as a result of therapy, to care adequately for her child.

§ 18. Concurrent or Exclusive Jurisdiction

The juvenile court may be the only tribunal which is legally empowered to hear cases within its jurisdiction. If, for example, the law required that every time a child is to be charged with violating a criminal law of the state, the charge must be laid before the juvenile court and no other court, then the juvenile court would be said to have exclusive jurisdiction over these delinquency cases. If, on the other hand, either the juvenile court *or* a criminal court could try cases of law violation by children, then each court would have concurrent jurisdiction. In some instances, the criminal court has exclusive jurisdiction and the juvenile court has no authority. This is brought about by statutes which provide that as to some crimes—often described as those punishable by death or life imprisonment—the juvenile court has no jurisdiction, leaving the trial of such cases to the regular criminal court. Even after the death penalty has been abolished, either by legislation or by a constitutional decision of a court, it has been held that there is still an exemption from juvenile court legislation which attaches to offenses which were formally punishable by death. Rhodes v. S., 91 Nev. 17, 530 P.2d 1199 (1975). The exclusive jurisdiction of the criminal court over children who commit these offenses remains. Criminal courts are also often given exclusive jurisdiction over minor offenses, such as fish and game law violations and traffic offenses (see § 14). But the criminal court has no jurisdiction in the absence of a statute expressly granting it, over *attempts* to commit crimes within its exclusive jurisdiction. Dorsey v. S., 31 Md.App. 324, 356 A.2d 290 (1976). It does not, however, require any statutory authority for a court, other than a juvenile court to punish a child for contempt. Thomas v. S., 21 Md.App. 572, 320 A.2d 538 (1974).

There are issues of allocation of jurisdiction regarding abuse and neglect cases as well. There may be exclusive jurisdiction in the juvenile court to hear these matters and to order protective measures for the child, including removal from the parental home. See § 15. There may also be exclusive jurisdiction in the criminal court to try the parents for the assault that may be involved in the abuse, or for the crime of criminal neglect or endangering the welfare of a child; the same conduct and circumstances may be involved in both the criminal and juvenile court cases. P. v. Abrams, 73 Misc.2d 534, 341

N.Y.S.2d 515 (1973). In Georgia a recent statute permits an action to terminate the parental rights of a putative father to be initiated in either the juvenile or the superior court. Ga.Code § 24A–301(a)(2)(C).

If, in the course of a criminal case, it is determined that the accused is within the exclusive jurisdiction of the juvenile court on account of his age, the case must be transferred to the juvenile court, even after a guilty finding. State ex rel. Leis v. Black, 45 Ohio App.2d 191, 341 N.E.2d 853 (1975). There is often legislative authority for a *discretionary* transfer of cases within the jurisdiction of the criminal court. Logan v. S., 291 Ala. 497, 282 So.2d 898 (1973). The procedural requirements which must be followed when transfer is in the other direction—from juvenile court to criminal court under waiver authority (see § 61), need not be followed, however, when the criminal court is deciding whether to waive to juvenile court. Vega v. Bell, 47 N.Y.2d 543, 419 N.Y.S.2d 454, 393 N.E.2d 450 (1979). A juvenile whose case is transferred to juvenile court is, however, entitled to the minutes of the grand jury that originally indicted him. In the Matter of Glenford's, 78 A.D.2d 350, 435 N.Y.S.2d 292 (1981).

Where jurisdiction is concurrent—where a case may be tried in either court—there is the crucial question of who decides which is the appropriate forum in any particular case, the juvenile court or the criminal court. In a sense, the possible waiver of a case from the criminal court to the juvenile court, and from the latter to the former, are instances of a judge, the criminal court judge or the juvenile court judge, making the decision that jurisdiction should be exercised by the other court. But the usual sense in which the term concurrent jurisdiction is used is in the context of a *prosecutorial* decision about which court is to get the case. Where there is concurrent jurisdiction it is often provided that the case may be tried in whichever court the prosecutor chooses. He may, moreover, exercise this choice without following any procedural formalities. Woodward v. Wainwright, 556 F.2d 781 (5th Cir. 1977). Or the statute may provide that the choice is to be made by a grand jury—if it indicts the child for a certain crime he is to be tried in the criminal court. If, on the other hand, the indictment is for a less serious crime, the child is to be tried in the juvenile court despite the fact that he has been indicted. Blackwell v. S., 255 Ind. 100, 262 N.E.2d 632 (1970). It is sometimes required that the grand jury return its indictment within a prescribed time period from the date the child was arrested, otherwise the juvenile court has jurisdiction. But even if the period goes by with no indictment and the child is proceeded against in the juvenile court, it has been held that the grand jury may still return an indictment which vests jurisdiction in the criminal court provided that jeopardy has not yet attached in the juvenile court proceedings. S. v. Maegher, 323 So.2d 26 (Fla.App.1975).

§ 19. Double Jeopardy

The Fifth Amendment to the United States Constitution includes the prohibition "nor shall any person be subject for the same offense to be twice put in jeopardy of life or limb . . . ." In Breed v. Jones, 421 U.S. 519, 95 S.Ct. 1779 (1975), the Supreme Court decided that this restriction applied to proceedings in juvenile courts. At issue was the California procedure whereby a juvenile court had found Jones delinquent for having violated a criminal statute and then decided that he was unfit for treatment as a juvenile and ordered him criminally prosecuted as a result. He was subsequently found guilty of robbery in a criminal court and sought habeas corpus relief in the federal courts. A denial of the writ by the District Court was reversed by the Ninth Circuit on the grounds that the Double Jeopardy Clause prohibited the robbery trial. In affirming this Court of Appeals decision, Chief Justice Burger, for a unanimous Court, noted that the Court's response to the developing belief that there is "a gap between the originally benign conception of the system and its realities

. . . has been to make applicable in juvenile proceedings constitutional guarantees associated with criminal prosecutions," with the exception of the right to a jury trial. The opinion reasoned that since the Double Jeopardy Clause prohibited the risk of more than one trial and conviction and was not limited to preventing more than one punishment, the California juvenile adjudicatory hearing was, for these purposes, a trial so that a second one, in the criminal court, was not constitutionally permitted. Constitutional jeopardy attached when the juvenile court judge began hearing evidence—the same starting point that governs adult proceedings. The Chief Justice found that the powers of a juvenile court are not meaningfully different from the authority of a sentencing judge in criminal cases and, therefore, "in terms of potential consequences, there is little to distinguish an adjudicatory hearing such as was held in this case from a traditional prosecution. For that reason, it engenders elements of 'anxiety and insecurity' in a juvenile, and imposes a 'heavy personal strain,'" indications that jeopardy has attached. The state is permitted to "vindicate the very vital interest in enforcement of criminal laws" only once, and that occurred in the juvenile court's adjudicatory hearing.

Despite this reasoning, the Court went on to indicate that if the state held the transfer hearing *before* the adjudicatory hearing, double jeopardy would not occur if a criminal trial followed. All seems to turn, therefore, on the difference between a transfer and an adjudicatory hearing, a distinction that is less than perfectly clear since the former may well entail the state producing its evidence against the child in an effort to establish probable cause and the "heavy personal strain" involved in meeting this is probably higher in the average transfer hearing than it is in the average juvenile court adjudicatory hearing. As was subsequently noted by the Massachusetts court in holding *Breed* not to be retroactive, while the decision "eliminates what might be termed the technical double jeopardy problem of subjecting a juvenile to two adjudicatory proceedings, it probably does little to alleviate the practical problem of twice subjecting a defendant to the strain of marshaling his resources against the State." Stokes v. Commonwealth, 368 Mass. 754, 336 N.E.2d 735 (1975). *Stokes* found the real benefits of the decision to lie rather in the Supreme Court's reference to increasing the fairness of the transfer hearing by removing the dilemma that if the juvenile adopts an uncooperative stance, he increases the risk of the transfer decision going against him, while if he chooses to cooperate in the transfer process "he runs the risk of prejudicing his chances in adult court if transfer is ordered." 336 N.E.2d at 742.

The implications of *Breed* for the transfer, or waiver, process are discussed below in § 64. The decision would seem to invalidate the practice in New Jersey of having an informal hearing, without counsel, for some juveniles which can result in probation but no incarceration, and then a formal hearing if probation does not work out which can result in a commitment. Since delinquency is adjudicated at both hearings and the child is subject to sanctions at both, double jeopardy appears to occur. Nonetheless, this bifurcated calendar was approved in In re J.J., 132 N.J.Super. 464, 334 A.2d 80 (1975) against a double jeopardy attack on grounds that to hold otherwise "would effectively oust the court of any meaningful jurisdiction over the child and deprive the State of any chance of helping the juvenile unless he commits another serious offense. This approach is not consistent with the historical philosophy of the juvenile court or the legislative intent." 334 A.2d at 84. The *Breed* emphasis of not repeating the trauma of repeated hearings does not, however, invalidate some state procedures which provide for initial hearings before a referee and a possible finding of delinquency by a judge after the referee finds insufficient evidence. Swisher v. Brady, 438 U.S. 204, 98 S.Ct. 2699 (1978). It has, however, been held that these circumstances violate Due Process. In the

Matter of Pima County, Juvenile Action, 129 Ariz. 371, 631 P.2d 526 (1981).

By making clear that the double jeopardy protection applies to the juvenile process, *Breed* buttresses a number of state decisions which have reached that conclusion in different parts of the process. S. v. Marshall, 503 S.W.2d 875 (Tex.Civ. App.1973) (no appeal by state from juvenile court acquittal); People ex rel. Thomas v. Judges of Family Court, 85 A.D.2d 569, 379 N.Y.S.2d 656 (1976) (no new trial following judge's sua sponte mistrial over juvenile's objection); Tolliver v. Judges of Family Court, 59 Misc.2d 104, 298 N.Y. S.2d 237 (1969) (no repeated juvenile court hearings). Similar protection may be found in state penal statutes held applicable to juvenile court proceedings. In re Benny G., 24 Cal.App.3d 371, 101 Cal.Rptr. 28 (1972) (statute forbidding multiple prosecutions arising from same act or course of conduct).

The Double Jeopardy Clause also affects the course of proceedings following a successful appellate attack by the juvenile on the juvenile court proceedings. Thus, if the juvenile court improperly found him delinquent on a charge which it— but not the appellate court—thought was included in the original charge, double jeopardy prohibits permitting a new juvenile court hearing on the original charge. In re Decoster, 23 Or.App.

179, 541 P.2d 1060 (1975) (criminal mischief not included in burglary).

§ 20. Family Courts

A court with a wider jurisdiction and powers than the traditional juvenile court has been recommended by many observers of the juvenile justice system. The ABA/IJA Juvenile Justice Standards Project is among the most recent to favor a family court which would have exclusive original jurisdiction over juvenile law violations, neglected and abused children, adoption, termination of parental rights, mental illness and retardation commitment procedures concerning adults and children, offenses against children, proceedings in regard to divorce, and related family matters. The advantages of such a court over the juvenile court lie in the opportunity for a single forum, and perhaps a single judge, to deal with the diverse legal problems which arise in a family context and which often are closely interrelated. The dual problems of fragmentation and overlap would thus be avoided.

In a few states there already exists a family court which is designed to achieve these advantages, although the jurisdiction is seldom as broad as that recommended; divorce matters are frequently omitted from family court jurisdiction. It is also true that none of the family courts have a jurisdiction wide enough to encompass *all* litigation which might affect family affairs. In the District of Columbia and in Hawaii the family court is a division of the court of general jurisdiction, while the family courts in New York, Rhode Island and Delaware are independent judicial bodies.

Even in existing family court systems, however, there are both intra-court jurisdictional issues which arise and problems of recognizing that there are not rigid lines between family court and other courts. Illustrative of the former is the matter of whether the court is to proceed in a case on the basis of delinquency or of neglect, where the facts before the court appear to support both. Under the N.Y. Family Court Act § 716, for example, the court has authority to substitute a neglect petition for a delinquency petition, on its own motion, and it has been held to be an abuse of discretion for the family court judge not to do that where the mother of a child charged with delinquency failed repeatedly to appear at the court and the judge himself observed that the failure to appear may constitute neglect. In re C., 43 A.D.2d 862, 352 N.Y.S.2d 15 (1974). The question of whether to proceed with a neglect or a delinquency case arises in a juvenile court as well.

The New York act also includes jurisdiction over some criminal offenses committed by one family member against another. In some circumstances, however, this is concurrent with the jurisdiction of the criminal court and in some circumstances the family court is empowered to transfer cases to the criminal court in a manner somewhat similar to a waiver of jurisdiction over certain children who commit serious criminal offenses. See § 1014. P. v. Kenyon, 46 A.D.2d 409, 362 N.Y.S.2d 644 (1975).

§ 21. Personal Jurisdiction and Problems of Notice

It has already been indicated that some states define delinquency to include violations of the laws of other states (§ 11). In the usual cases where this jurisdiction would be asserted, the child would be physically before the court which is enforcing the other's penal law. If the child is a citizen of the state in which the juvenile court action is initiated, it may theoretically be possible that there is a sufficiently important state interest so that the proceedings could go ahead even if the child is then absent from the state; but no juvenile court legislation undertakes to provide such a broad reach.

Unless there is physical presence, or some legal foundation such as citizenship, there is no sort of notice which will provide the basis for a juvenile court exercising jurisdiction. That is, if a child violates the law of state X while temporarily in that state and then returns to his home in state

Y, state X would be without authority to adjudicate the child delinquent even if an official of state X were sent to the home in Y to notify the child personally and to deliver a formal written notice of the prospective delinquency proceedings. If, however, the child were physically seized and brought into state X, the juvenile court of X would then be able to proceed, despite the possibility that the seizure might amount to kidnapping.

In the usual case, however, the child is within the state where the juvenile court sits. Questions then arise concerning who must be notified of the proceedings, what must be contained in the notice and what must be the time interval between this notice and the actual commencement of a court hearing. These questions are answered by both constitutional and statutory rules.

In *Gault*, the Supreme Court addressed all of these issues.

> [T]he requirements [are] that the child and his parents or guardian be notified, in writing, of the specific charge or factual allegations to be considered at the hearing, and that such written notice be given at the earliest practicable time, and in any event sufficiently in advance of the hearing to permit preparation. Due process of law requires notice of the sort we have described—

that is, notice which would be deemed adequate in a civil or criminal proceeding. 387 U.S. 1, 33 (1967).

The juvenile court statutes implement these constitutional requirements. Under these laws notice is provided following the filing of a petition. The Texas Family Code § 53.06(a), for example, directs the court to issue a summons to the child named in the petition, his parent, guardian or other custodian, the child's guardian ad litem and "any other person who appears to the court to be a proper or necessary party to the proceeding." The Model Act § 15(a), on the other hand, requires a summons for the child only if he is at least 14 years old. There may be similar statutory notice rules when a minor is prosecuted in criminal court. Williams v. S., 297 So.2d 67 (Fla.App.1974).

Compliance with such statutes presents a number of issues. A failure to provide notice, or to obtain a valid waiver of it, deprives the juvenile court of jurisdiction. In re W.W.M., 479 S.W. 2d 446 (Mo.1972). Even if there has been proper notice relating to one delinquency charge against the child, a failure to give the requisite notice on another charge tried simultaneously with the first has been held to run afoul of the *Gault* requirements. Commonwealth v. Roskov, 224 Pa. Super. 393, 307 A.2d 63 (1973). Similar rulings appear in the neglect cases where, for example, it has been decided that the parent is entitled to notice of the particular statutory ground which is relied on as the basis for the alleged neglect. In re Meyer, 204 N.W.2d 625 (Iowa 1973).

Some statutes go further than the constitutional requirement and mandate an in-court notice by the judge of the details of the case, as well as the prior written notice. In re D.L.E. v. S., 531 S.W. 2d 196 (Tex.Civ.App.1975).

The right to prior written notice may be waived by the parents by their voluntary appearance at the juvenile court hearing. In re G.A.T., 183 Colo. 111, 515 P.2d 104 (1973). A parent who is entitled to this notice does not waive his right, however, if he merely appears as a witness in the case. If a parent fails to receive the required notice the lack of jurisdiction in the court may be raised by the delinquent child. In the Interest of R.P., 97 Ill.App.3d 889, 53 Ill.Dec. 251, 423 N.E. 2d 920 (1981). In re Herron, 212 N.W.2d 474 (Iowa 1973). Where a government agency, such as a social service department, must be notified of particular juvenile court proceedings, it too is taken to waive formal notice when it appears generally at the hearing. In re Murcray, 45 A.D. 2d 906, 357 N.Y.S.2d 918 (1974).

Some courts will find a waiver of the child's right to notice in his appearance at the hearing, Bailey v. Commonwealth, 468 S.W.2d 304 (Ky.

1971) while others declare that the waiver rule is different when it is the child's notice and not his parents' that is involved, In re Edwards, 298 So.2d 703 (Miss.1974), even if the child is represented by an attorney at the hearing. Reed v. S., 125 Ga.App. 568, 188 S.E.2d 392 (1972) (right to notice that hearing will deal with waiver to criminal court).

Juvenile court acts often require that the notice of the hearing, in the form of a summons to appear, be accompanied by a copy of the petition. The need for information concerning the charges is based on the need for an intelligent understanding of what the proceedings are about in order to prepare any defense the child may have to the charges. These same considerations underly statutory and constitutional rules concerning the timing of the notice. The Model Act § 16(a), for example, provides that where he can be found within the state, the summons must be personally served on a party at least 24 hours before the hearing; the Texas Family Code § 53.07(a) provides only a bit more time to prepare (2 days). Depending on the complexity of the case, this interval may be entirely inadequate for a reasonable preparation.

CHAPTER III

THE ROLES OF LAW ENFORCE-
MENT AGENTS

§ 22. Surveillance of Juveniles and Parents

Enforcement of juvenile court legislation normally begins with a citizen's complaint to some official agency, such as the police or a child protection agency, that the law has been violated, or that conditions exist which justify juvenile court action. In this case of child abuse and neglect reporting the mistreatment is a legal duty (see § 16). It is only infrequently that law enforcement agents themselves initiate that action on the basis of their own observations. Unless a private citizen demands that the police "do something" or that a child be rescued from his parents it is improbable that a child will be taken into custody and official proceedings begun, even when the child commits a fairly serious offense. See Davis, Police Discretion 1–12 (1975).

As to the police, it seems that relatively little of their time is spent on this sort of formal enforcement of the criminal law. A far more common police function is "peacekeeping"—responding to amorphous sets of circumstances such as a gathering of youth that is loud, but questionably illegal, for example—in which people "call the cops" but which are not cases the police pass on to prosecutors and courts. Private and public child welfare agencies similarly take few of their child protection cases to court and seek to alleviate problems in a consensual way. A recent observation concerning police peacekeeping appears applicable to these latter agencies as well. "[W]hat seems to unite all the situations with which police officers are required to deal—regardless whether they involve illness, discord, fun, or ceremony—is that someone thought that emergency help was necessary to ward off the risk of injury, loss, or harm, or to ward off the proliferation of danger, disorder or inconvenience. It is, of course, not totally unheard of for police officers to locate occasions of intervention on their own, but the vastly preponderant majority are solicited by citizens." ABA/IJA Standards, *Police* 31.

There is no reliable way of estimating the number of juvenile peacekeeping cases the police deal with which do not involve breaches of the law. It is similarly an unknown figure how many police encounters with juveniles result in a formal arrest, although it has been suggested that there is only one arrest for every five situations in which the police in façt do have legal grounds for arrest. Morris and Hawkins, The Honest

Politician's Guide to Crime Control 91 (1970). It also appears to be the case that the method of selecting that one case in five has more to do with the deference and respect the child shows the police than anything else.   See ABA/IJA Standards, *Police* 22; Piliavin and Briar, *Police Encounters with Juveniles*, 70 Am.J.Sociol. 206 (1964).   Among those youth whom the police do arrest, it is usually accepted that only about half of them are sent on by the police for official juvenile court processing.   There is, however, reason to suspect that even the arrest records may be quite inaccurate by virtue of widely varying practices regarding which encounters are technically counted as arrests.   Klein, Rosenswug, and Bates, *The Ambiguous Juvenile Arrest*, 13 Criminology 78 (1975).   What law enforcement agencies are authorized to do with a child following their taking him into custody is discussed in sections 26–29.

It is highly unusual for there to be anything in the law giving guidance to the police when they choose *not* to arrest, as has been suggested they do in 4 out of 5 cases.   The Texas Family Code, however, may be a forerunner of legislative attempts to provide standards for police discretion in these matters.   Section 52.01(c) of the Code authorizes a formal written "warning notice" in lieu of arrest if it is issued pursuant to guidelines issued by a law enforcement agency and approved by the juvenile court. For a discussion of several police department regulations governing police arrest discretion see LaFave, *Arrest: The Decision to Take a Suspect into Custody* 105–108 (1965).

There are other features of the system of surveillance of juveniles for law violations that should be noted. One is that the class of officials authorized to initiate the process of enforcing juvenile court laws by taking children into custody includes more than members of a police department and the child protection service. In Illinois, for example, it includes agents of the division of youth services and of the division of family services, Ill.Juv.Ct.Act, § 39.03(e)(f). Probation officers might also have statutory power to arrest children. See e.g., Cal.Welf. & Inst.Code § 584. In Texas a child may be taken into custody by: "The sheriff and his deputees, constable, marshal or policemen of an incorporated town or city, the officers, noncommissioned officers and privates of the State Ranger Force and Department of Public Safety, law enforcement agents of the Texas Liquor Control Board and any private persons specially appointed to execute criminal process." Tex.Fam.Code § 51.02(8). To this must be added juvenile probation officers as well. In re S.E.B., 514 S.W.2d 948 (Tex.Civ.App.1974).

As has been suggested in this section, being alert for the possibility of court action against juveniles is not an exclusive police function. The scope of traditional juvenile court jurisdiction gives rise to the designation of surveillance roles for other officials as well. School authorities often have this responsibility regarding the child's attendance and behavior in class by virtue of their power to initiate juvenile court proceedings concerning any child whom they observe to fall below the required standards. See e.g., Mass. Gen.Laws, c. 119, § 39E. The U. S. Children's Bureau recommends going beyond public officials in this matter and authorizes non-criminal behavior proceedings (see § 12) at the behest of "a representative of a public or nongovernmental agency licensed or authorized to provide care or supervision of children; a representative of a public or private agency providing social services for families; a school official; or a law enforcement officer." Guide § 14(b). Probably the most familiar figure with the power to turn a child's private deviance into a court case is the child's parent who is often the prosecutor in stubbornness and disobedience cases. See e.g., In re Lavette M., 44 A.D.2d 666, 354 N.Y.S.2d 636 (1974); In re Henry G., 28 Cal.App.3d 276, 104 Cal.Rptr. 585 (1973). And where the legislation authorizes a court to take charge of a child because he "is in danger of being brought up to lead an idle, dissolute or immoral life," Wash.Rev. Code Ann. § 13.04.010, then are all invited to become guardians of children's morality and to report such breaches as their surveillance discloses. Fortunately, the invitation appears not to be that often accepted, although it does sometimes happen. See e.g., In re J.P., 32 Ohio Misc. 5, 287 N.E.2d 926 (1972) (sexual intercourse by 16 year old and 15 year old was deportment to injure or endanger the health or morals of himself or others).

It appears justified to conclude that the breadth of restrictions imposed on children by juvenile court legislation gives rise to their being subject to the surveillance of many classes of adults who have special responsibilities regarding law enforcement. The fact that children are generally accountable to the adult world for virtually everything they do and are consequently accorded little privacy, ABA/IJA Standards, *Police* 14, increases the scope of the surveillance well beyond even the broad limits of what is by law prohibited juvenile conduct.

§ 23. Arrests

Whether the action taken by the police constitutes a valid arrest is important for several reasons. If the circumstances amount to a legal arrest, the police are entitled to engage in other investigatory techniques, such as searching or interrogating, which would otherwise be denied them. If there is not a valid arrest, the police may be civilly liable for false imprisonment for depriving the child of his liberty and for an assault and battery on his person. Marschall v. City of Carson, 86 Nev. 107, 464 P.2d 494 (1970). An illegal arrest, in and of itself, does not, however, render void the subsequent court proceeding. Gerstein v. Pugh, 420 U.S. 103, 95 S.Ct. 854 (1975); In re Jackson, 46 Mich.App. 764, 208 N.W.2d 526 (1973). Although it was noted in section 22 that the practical decision to arrest a juvenile depends heavily on his attitude toward the police and whether the police can fulfill their peacekeeping role without engaging in the sort of formal law enforcement that is triggered by an arrest, this present discussion is confined to the legal aspects of the arrest.

In the typical case there is little difficulty in recognizing whether an arrest has taken place . . . the officer says: "I am placing you under arrest", and takes physical control of the child as the pair move off, on foot or in the cruiser, to the station house. But suppose the officer takes custody but does not use the magic words of arrest and no change in location has yet taken place—is there an arrest? This question is vital in light of the rule that the validity of the arrest must be tested by the circumstances existing when it was imposed, and the corollary that an arrest that is invalid because proper grounds did not exist, cannot be made valid by the dis-

covery of grounds at some later point. Henry
v. U. S., 361 U.S. 98, 80 S.Ct. 168 (1959); George
v. S., 506 S.W.2d 275 (Tex.Civ.App.1974). Thus
if an officer illegally arrests a child for stealing
something, the illegality would not be affected
by then finding a pistol in the child's pocket;
the arrest would also continue to be invalid if several minutes later the officer determined that the
child needed to be taken into a protective custody
because his parents neglect and abuse him.

In determining whether an arrest has taken
place, one central factor is that of physical control. While the child need not be placed in hand-
cuffs or in the back seat of the cruiser, there
would be no arrest unless he were not free to
leave the officer's presence. In re Appeal in Pima
County, 110 Ariz. 98, 515 P.2d 600 (1973); In re
Appeal No. 245(75), 29 Md.App. 131, 349 A.2d
434 (1975) (arrest takes place when child taken
to police car parked outside his home); In the
Matter of Martin S., 104 Misc.2d 1036, 429 N.Y.S.
2d 1009 (Fam.Ct.1980) (arrest when child stopped on street and forced into police car); Minor
v. S., 91 Nev. 456, 537 P.2d 477 (1975) (no formal announcement of arrest required). The issue of time is also involved. As section 24 points
out, there is legal authority for the police to take
temporary control of a child under circumstances
that do not require the presence of grounds for
arrest. But this authority is of a fairly short

duration, and if the control is prolonged, it may have to be tested by the law of arrest. U. S. v. Luckett, 484 F.2d 89 (9th Cir. 1973). This means, of course, that until the period of time involved has expired, it is difficult to tell whether the circumstances are detention or arrest. An additional factor relates to the reason for the exercise of custodial control over the child. If it is to initiate a prosecution then the control is strongly suggestive of an arrest; conversely, if the child is taken in tow in order to protect him—as where the police remove him from his home where he has just been beaten by a parent—the law of arrest would not apply.

The law of arrest is a pattern woven of several strands: juvenile court acts, common law and constitutional principle. They relate to each other as follows. When one turns to the juvenile court statutes there is commonly encountered a provision, such as in the new Texas act, which says: "A child may be taken into custody: . . . pursuant to the laws of arrest." Tex.Fam.Code § 52.01(a)(2); see also U.J.C.A. § 13(a)(2). In order to learn what are the components of "the laws of arrest" the rules of common law must be grasped, such as that the law for felony arrests is different from the law for misdemeanor arrests. These common law rules are, however, subject to constitutional requirements, particularly those of the Fourth and Fourteenth Amendments to the federal constitution plus, of increasing importance lately, the counterparts to these provisions in state constitutions. This importance is discussed later in this section.

Two other things need to be noted about the statutes before examining the interplay of common law and constitution. The first is that the juvenile court statute may, itself, undertake to spell out the law of arrest, rather than merely incorporate common law rules as does the Texas type provision. Thus, the California statute specifies the grounds for felony arrests of children and the grounds for making an arrest for lesser offenses. Cal.Welf. & Inst.Code § 625.1. The second feature of the juvenile arrest statutes is that most of them use the phrase "take into custody" instead of "arrest" while some go further and explicitly seek to deny that the juvenile justice process is part of the machinery for enforcing the criminal law. Illinois, for example, declares that: "The taking of minor into temporary custody under this Section is not an arrest nor does it constitute a police record." Ill.Juv.Ct.Act § 703–1(3). In this form, the denial creates serious problems, such as the extent to which the constitutional rules governing searches incident to an arrest are applicable to something that is said not to be an arrest. This problem is avoided where the denial is more circumspect, as in Texas where the statute says that the custody is not an arrest "except for the purpose of determining the validity of taking into custody or the validity of a search under the laws and constitution of this state or of the United States." Tex.Fam.Code § 52.01(b). Even without this qualification, however, it is highly doubtful that constitutional provisions that would otherwise govern an arrest situation can be made inapplicable merely by a legislative insistence that an arrest be called something else. Nor does calling it something else preclude finding that the child's violent reaction to the policeman constitutes the crime of resisting arrest. In re Hartsfield, 531 S.W.2d 149 (Tex.Civ.App.1975).

A fundamental distinction in the law of arrest is between arrests made with a judicially issued arrest warrant and those made without a warrant. A warrant is simply a written order from a court to some designated public official (see Huff v. Walker, 125 Ga.App. 251, 187 S.E.2d 343 (1972), holding that a juvenile court probation officer is not authorized to apply for a search warrant) which orders him to arrest a named person and bring him before the court. Unlike cases where the officer has authority to arrest without a warrant, the officer to whom a warrant is directed has no discretion in the matter and is in violation of his duty if he fails to arrest, or to explain to the court why the warrant was not executed, Conques v. Fuselier, 327 So.2d 180 (La.

1976). The procedure for obtaining an arrest warrant is generally governed by rules of court, or by a procedural statute. Rule 4 of the Federal Rules of Criminal Procedure is a familiar model.

Most of the law governing the issuance and execution of arrest warrants is found in court opinions interpreting the Fourth Amendment to the United States Constitution and cognate provisions in state constitutions. This Amendment provides that: "The right of the people to be secure in their persons, . . . against unreasonable . . . seizures, shall not be violated, and no Warrants shall issue, but upon probable cause, supported by Oath or affirmation, and particularly describing . . . the persons . . . to be seized."

Of central importance is the rule of "probable cause" in this provision. It means a degree of certainty that is more than just suspicion, although it need not be the certainty that a jury must have in reaching a verdict in a civil case (a preponderance of probability, more than a 50% likelihood, etc.). In the context of warrants, it also means that the probable cause belief must rest in the mind of the judicial officer issuing the warrant; the arrest under a warrant issued by a judge who did not, himself, believe there to be probable cause would be invalid, even though the policeman who applied for the warrant and who executed it well believed there to be probable cause to make the arrest. See Katz v. U. S., 389 U.S. 347, 88 S.Ct. 507 (1967). The policeman must present the facts to the judge so that the latter can make the crucial probable cause decision. In speaking of the duties of a judge in this respect, the Supreme Court has noted that he "must judge for himself the persuasiveness of the facts relied on by a complaining officer to show probable cause. He should not accept without question the complainant's mere conclusion that the person whose arrest is sought has committed a crime." Giordenello v. U. S., 357 U.S. 480, 78 S.Ct. 1245 (1958).

It is not unusual for authority to issue a warrant or a summons to be vested in a court official who is not a judge. In re Dell, 56 Misc.2d 1017, 290 N.Y.S.2d 287 (1968) (summons by clerk of family court). The Supreme Court has held that a clerk may also issue arrest warrants. Shadwick v. City of Tampa, 407 U.S. 345, 92 S.Ct. 2119 (1972). It is, however, required that the official "be neutral and detached, and he must be capable of determining whether probable cause exists for the requested arrest or search." 407 U.S. at 350.

Statutes which authorize a court to issue arrest warrants against children often do not explicitly repeat the requirement that probable cause ex-

ist. See, for example, Cal.Welf. & Inst.Code §
663; Fla.Stat.Ann. § 39.03(1)(a); U.J.C.A. §
22(c); Guide § 21(c). Such laws would, however,
be interpreted to require a showing of probable
cause in order for a warrant to be granted. The
probable cause belief on which an arrest warrant
rests is that the person named in the warrant has
committed a crime.

Most arrests of children (and of adults, as well)
are made without a warrant. In these cases the
common law which is incorporated by juvenile
court statutes authorizing children to be taken
into custody pursuant to the laws of arrest, grants
police a broader authority in felony cases than it
does for misdemeanors. An officer is entitled to
arrest in the former cases if he has reasonable
grounds (probable cause) to believe that a felony
has been committed and that the person he arrests has committed it. LaFave, *Arrest, The Decision to Take a Suspect into Custody* 244 (1965).
Note that the officer need not be factually correct
in holding either of these beliefs: it may turn
out that, in fact, no felony was committed, or that
the arrested person did not commit it. The arrest
is still legal so long as his belief was based on
probable cause. "The test of probable cause is
whether a reasonable and prudent man in possession of the knowledge of the arresting officer
would believe that the person to be arrested is
guilty of a crime." In re Tucker, 20 Ill.App.3d

377, 379–380, 314 N.E.2d 276, 278 (1974); Minor Boy v. S., 91 Nev. 456, 537 P.2d 477 (1975) (to an experienced officer the smell of marijuana is probable cause).

As to misdemeanors, it was concluded in 1965 that: "While the early common law view with respect to misdemeanors was that arrest without warrant was proper only for breaches of the peace occurring in the presence of the arresting officer, the trend in more recent years, through either legislation or judicial declaration, has been to expand this power to allow arrest without warrant for all misdemeanors occurring in the presence." LaFave, supra at p. 231. This expansion continues and the American Law Institute is presently recommending that warrantless misdemeanor arrests be permitted, even if the misdemeanor was not committed in his presence, when the officer has reasonable cause to believe that no arrest will be possible unless it is immediately made, or that the person to be arrested "may cause injury to himself or others or damage to property unless immediately arrested." Model Code of Pre-Arraignment Procedures § 120.1.(b) (1975).

The relationship between common law and constitution has recently been litigated in the Supreme Court. In upholding a warrantless felony arrest on probable cause against the claim that a warrant should have been procured since there was time to get one, Justice White wrote: "The cases construing the Fourth Amendment thus reflect the ancient common-law rule that a peace officer was permitted to arrest without a warrant for a misdemeanor or felony committed in his presence as well as for a felony not committed in his presence if there was reasonable grounds for making the arrest." U. S. v. Watson, 423 U.S. 411, 96 S.Ct. 820 (1976). The *Watson* facts involved a felony and the declared congruence between the Fourth Amendment and the misdemeanor in-presence rule is, therefore dictum. The Model Code of Pre-Arraignment Procedures, however, seems to assume that the expansion of misdemeanor warrantless arrest authority is in no constitutional jeopardy since its commentary to this point of section 120.1 contains no reference to Fourth Amendment issues. See pp. 289–90 of the Model Code. At least one court agrees. U. S. v. Grosso, 225 F.Supp. 161 (W.D.Pa.1964).

Where juvenile court statutes do not simply incorporate this common law and constitutional rule by making reference to the law of arrest, they may spell out the rule in the statute itself, as is done in Cal.Welf. & Inst.Code § 625.1(c). Courts seem, automatically and without doctrinal discussion, to test the validity of the arrests of children for felonies by the same standard of probable cause. S. v. Eastmond, 28 Utah 2d 129,

499 P.2d 276 (1972). It has been suggested, however, by the Arizona Supreme Court that "It would do violence to the concept of equal protection of the law to allow a juvenile to be taken into custody under [the juvenile arrest statute] without the standard being probable cause." In re Appeal in Pima County, 110 Ariz. 98, 103, 515 P.2d 600, 605 (1973). It should also be pointed out that when a court finds an arrest to be illegal due to a lack of probable cause or otherwise, that does not necessarily mean it will decide the juvenile was wrongly arrested since authority to arrest children for conduct such as "idly roaming the streets", In re J.B. Jr., 131 N.J.Super. 6, 328 A.2d 46 (1976) or "being in such surroundings as to endanger his welfare", In re James L., 194 N.E.2d 797 (Ohio 1963) is a fall-back justification a court might use to justify the arrest.

Warrantless arrests of minors for violations of penal law which are misdemeanors rather than felonies are a bit more complicated. Where the applicable juvenile court statute authorizes taking the child into custody "pursuant to the laws of arrest" the more restricted authority which requires the offense to be committed in the officer's presence would apply where the child is taken into custody for a misdemeanor, In re J.B. Jr., supra. If, for example, a state with such a juvenile court act arrest provision were to adopt the American Law Institute proposal described above in this section, a child could be arrested without a warrant for a misdemeanor committed out of the officer's presence only if the two factors relating to an immediate need for arrest were satisfied. Where, however, the juvenile court act declares that the child may be arrested if the officer reasonably believes he is a delinquent child, then the requirement of an offense in the officer's presence or other requirements relating to misdemeanors such as those included by the American Law Institute, would not be applicable since a reasonable relief that a child is delinquent is, by virtue of the definition of delinquency (see § 11), the same thing as a reasonable belief that the child has committed a felony *or* a misdemeanor. In re Williams, 30 Ill.App.3d 1025, 333 N.E.2d 674 (1975).

Whether there is probable cause in any case depends on the particular facts and circumstances that are present. But in view of the common experience that children often commit offenses together with other children it is useful to keep in mind that it may be important that the facts in group crime cases may or may not include something of a description of the individual children involved. Thus, if there is probable cause to believe that a burglary has been committed, and that a particular automobile was used to transport the burglars to and from the scene, a warrantless arrest of children in a vehicle that fit the description of the car would be without probable cause, at least when the arrest is made the day after the offense and the police are not in hot pursuit. Smith v. S., 525 P.2d 1251 (Okl.Cr. 1975). There is no probable cause to believe that any particular child is guilty. As the Oklahoma court noted, "Guilt by association has never been an acceptable rationale and it does not constitute probable cause to arrest." At p. 1253. Hot pursuit does make a difference, however. In re Lynette G., 54 Cal.App.3d 1087, 126 Cal.Rptr. 898 (1976) (fourth girl legally apprehended when found with three others 15 minutes after robbery in which witnesses could describe the other three but not the fourth).

It was mentioned earlier in this section that state court decisions interpreting state constitutional provisions, have become quite important in recent years. The basis for this is two-fold. The first stems from the current inclination of the Supreme Court to decide that the federal constitution permits certain police and prosecutorial practices, for example, that an arrest for a traffic offense authorizes the police to make a full body search of the arrested person. U. S. v. Robinson, 414 U.S. 218, 94 S.Ct. 467 (1973); Gustafson v. Florida, 414 U.S. 260, 94 S.Ct. 488 (1973). These cases say that it is constitutionally *permissible* for the police to do this *if* the particular jurisdiction (the District of Columbia and the state of Florida, in the cases cited) authorizes it. The Supreme Court cases in no way *require* any state to authorize this police authority.

The second development is that several state supreme courts have decided, on the basis of their own state constitutional provisions, that a particular police practice is *not* acceptable, despite the Supreme Court saying that the federal constitution would permit it. Thus, the supreme court of California has decided that its state constitution poses a "more exacting standard" and has refused to allow a body search of a traffic offender. P. v. Brisendine, 13 Cal.3d 528, 119 Cal.Rptr. 315, 531 P.2d 1099 (1975). The California court has also ruled it to be a violation of the *state* constitution for police to make a probable cause warrantless arrest in a person's home in the absence of exigent circumstances. P. v. Ramey, 16 Cal.3d 263, 127 Cal.Rptr. 629, 545 P. 2d 1333 (1976). Justice Marshall indicates in his dissent in *Watson* that the Supreme Court has impliedly decided that issue the other way. 423 U.S. at 433, 96 S.Ct. at 832. Even if he is correct, the *Ramey* decision would still forbid California police from entering a person's home without a warrant to arrest him.

§ 24. Detention for Investigation

As part of both their law enforcement and peacekeeping duties the police often have occasion to make inquiries about suspicious appearing circumstances and persons well before there are legal grounds or practical reasons for making an arrest. See LaFave, *"Street Encounters" and the Constitution*, 67 Mich.L.Rev. 40 (1968). As indicated in § 22, children are particularly subject to this sort of inquiry about what they are doing. But until 1968 when the Supreme Court first addressed the issue of the scope of police power in these circumstances, it was not clear that the constitution permitted any restrictions on liberty short of an arrest on probable cause. In that year, Terry v. Ohio, 392 U.S. 1, 88 S.Ct. 1868 (1968) indicated that there were circumstances in which a seizure of the person was allowable, even if there were not grounds for arrest. The significance of this almost always lies in the admissibility of things found as a result of a search undertaken in consequence of the "stop", as this temporary detention on less than probable cause had come to be called. This admissibility issue is discussed in section 28; the admissibility of statements obtained as a result of a stop is examined in section 27.2. At this point we are concerned only with the issue of when the police are authorized to detain children in the absence of authority to arrest.

Terry does not provide a rule for identifying the circumstances which justify the stop. Justice Harlan's concurring opinion criticizes the Court for not making clear that before an officer can undertake even a limited search of outer clothing for weapons (a "frisk"), as was involved in the case, there must be a legal right to make the original stop. Two considerations appear to be important: there must be a belief that "criminal activity may be afoot" which need not be as certain as a probable cause belief—suspicion will do, and second, the facts and circumstances giving rise to the belief must be of an objective nature— a policeman's mere hunch will not do. In re Harvey, 222 Pa.Super. 222, 295 A.2d 93 (1972). The Supreme Court has not indicated whether the right to make an investigatory stop extends to all crimes, although Justice Brennan's dissent in Adams v. Williams, 407 U.S. 143, 151, 92 S.Ct. 1921, 1925–1926 (1972) objected to use of the doctrine for possessory offenses.

The authority to stop a suspicious person is of relatively short temporal duration. The American Law Institute suggests that it last no longer than 20 minutes. Model Code of Pre-Arraignment Procedures § 110.2(1). In holding that police authority to stop a person who reasonably appeared to be a juvenile runaway lapsed into an illegal detention upon the person establishing that he was over eighteen, a California court noted:

> No hard and fast rule can be formulated for determining the reasonableness of the period

of time elapsing during a detention. The dynamic of the detention-for-questioning situation may justify further detentions, further investigation, search, or arrest. The significance of the events, discoveries, and perceptions that follow an officer's first sighting of a candidate for detention will vary from case to case. Nevertheless, in determining the reasonableness of further detention, favorable answers, observations, or perceptions must be regarded by the detaining officer as suspicion-allaying, rather than suspicion-heightening.

Pendergraft v. Superior Court, 15 Cal.App.3d 237, 93 Cal.Rptr. 155 (1971).

Police authority under this doctrine to stop juveniles and detain them for investigation on less than probable cause is established by case law. In re Lynette G., 54 Cal.App.3d 1087, 126 Cal.Rptr. 898 (1976); S. v. O'Neill, 299 Minn. 60, 216 N.W.2d 822 (1974); In re Harvey, 222 Pa.Super. 222, 295 A.2d 93 (1972). Some states have had "stop and frisk" statutes since before the Supreme Court's approval of such law enforcement action and investigation of juveniles has been upheld during the pre-*Terry* period. In re Lang, 44 Misc.2d 900, 255 N.Y.S.2d 987 (1965) (without relying on the N. Y. statute). Present statutes are collected in Appendix IX of the

Model Code of Pre-Arraignment Procedures. There is nothing in their terms which precludes their application to investigatory detention of juveniles. It is curious, however, that the model juvenile court statutes do not contain any express provisions for detention of children suspected of crime on less than probable cause. The issue is similarly ignored in both the Uniform Act, the Model Act and the Children's Bureau Guide. The Juvenile Justice Police Standards recommend that children in these circumstances be accorded at least the same constitutional and statutory protections as are granted adults.

In light of the greater vulnerability of children to all sorts of adult surveillance, especially by the police, it is undesirable to say the least, that this aspect of law enforcement activity go completely uncontrolled by statutory guidelines. Even the American Law Institute formulation of authority to stop, as carefully and narrowly drawn as it is, would need to be modified in those sections which authorize police to seek voluntary cooperation from any person—including a voluntary appearance at the station house. As is true of all encounters between officials and children, special care needs to be taken that volunteering and waiver of rights to withhold cooperation are not accepted without some opportunity for an adult to discuss the situation with the child. Before any child should be allowed to volunteer to go to the police station, the police should be obliged to get in touch with the child's parents and permit them to advise their child or to consult an attorney.

Another aspect of investigative stops plus consent has been the subject of a line of cases which, unfortunately make no distinction between the effect of a police request for cooperation in children and the effect on adults. California holds that when a lawful stop of a juvenile and a solicitation of consent to a search (Okay, boys, why don't you empty your pockets on the car?") produces flight, the police have probable cause to arrest the fleeing juveniles. In re Michael V., 10 Cal.App.3d 676, 111 Cal.Rptr. 681, 517 P.2d 1145 (1974). The dissent disagrees that the quoted interrogatory was anything but an order. 517 P.2d at 1150. Flight from a police encounter ("How are you doing?") however, does not provide grounds for arrest, although it does authorize a stop and frisk. In re M., 43 A.D.2d 92, 349 N.Y.S.2d 728 (1973).

§ 25. Entrapment

There is a point at which police surveillance develops into an active relationship with juveniles which may give rise to a legal defense for the child. This is the defense of entrapment which seems to have originated in Saunders v. P., 38 Mich. 218 (1878) and is now recognized in the federal courts and in all of the states. Starrs, Comment on Entrapment, in I Working Papers of the National Commission on Reform of Federal Criminal Laws 303, 312–13 (1970). Although it appears that entrapment may be raised in a delinquency proceeding, U. S. v. Miller, 483 F.2d 61 (5th Cir. 1973), and in a criminal trial resulting from waiver of juvenile court jurisdiction, Walls v. S., 326 So.2d 322 (Miss.1976), there is no reason why the policy underlying the defense would not apply as well to juvenile court prosecutions for prohibited, but non-criminal, conduct. That policy, deeming it unfair to convict a person for conduct which was caused by the action of government agents, is most often invoked in cases involving drug sales, gambling or consensual sexual conduct where there is no unwilling victim and the police seek to obtain evidence by posing as a victim. Cases involving curfew violations or truancy, for example, involve an equal degree of unfairness when the conduct is enticed by a government agent.

Although entrapment is a generally recognized defense in criminal cases, the Supreme Court has not found it to be a requirement of the constitution; it has, however, indicated that if the police conduct in inducing the crime were to be "outrageous", due process principles may prevent a conviction. U. S. v. Russell, 411 U.S. 423, 93 S. Ct. 1637 (1973). Procedurally, the accused person has the burden of producing some evidence that the police persuaded (more than a mere request) him to commit the drug sale or other crime; then the government must prove beyond a reasonable doubt that the action of the police was not, in fact, the cause of the crime and that the defendant was willing to commit the offense to start with.   U. S. v. Braver, 450 F.2d 799 (2d Cir. 1971).   In meeting its burden under this subjective test, the government may introduce the accused's prior convictions and other evidence (but not in its case in chief before the accused juvenile has introduced his entrapment evidence, *Walls*, supra,) which helps to prove his criminal predisposition.   A small minority of states takes a different (objective) view which permits the defense to be established wholly on the proof of police conduct in procuring the offense and does not permit the government to use evidence of predisposition in refutation, see e.g., S. v. Mullen, 216 N.W.2d 375 (Iowa 1974); the Supreme Court has consistently refused to adopt this view of entrapment for the federal courts.   Hampton v. U. S., 425 U.S. 484, 96 S.Ct. 1646 (1976).

Entrapment ought to be more available to children than to adult accused persons by virtue of the greater suggestibility of youth and their stronger inclination to go along with what they perceive is wanted by adults.   The youthful status of the person raising the defense might also be advantageous to a young accused to the extent that the absence of a long criminal career would make it impossible for the state to use a long list of past convictions as proof of a criminal predisposition. There is, in addition, the further question of whether being found "delinquent" can be considered a prior conviction for purposes of the state defeating an entrapment defense. These issues appear not to have been dealt with by any court. The fluidity of youthful personality development, however, ought to be given dispositive weight in deciding that prior delinquencies are not to be accepted as sufficient proof of a fixed predisposition toward crime.

§ 26. Post Arrest Duties: Detention and Notice

It has already been pointed out that the police have a vast amount of discretion concerning whether to take a child into custody, and that in the majority of cases the police decide not to do so. If a child is taken into custody, however, statutes commonly address the question of what the police are next to do, and what they are not to do. The legislation frequently requires, for example, that the arrested child be taken to a juvenile facility, and not to a jail. Enforcement of these statutes has come to the attention of the courts almost entirely in proceedings (delinquency and criminal) against children wherein it has been claimed that there has been a violation of the statutory duty and that a consequence of the violation is that some piece of evidence, usually a confession offered in court by the state, is inadmissible (see § 31).

The statutes may require that the arresting officer notify a probation officer, or other official designated by the juvenile court, Tex.Fam.Code § 52.02(b)(2), although the most frequently found statutory duty requires the police promptly to notify the arrested child's parents. E. g. Md. Code 1974, Art. 3, § 814(b): "If a law enforcement officer takes a child into custody he shall immediately notify, or cause to be notified, the child's parents, guardian or custodian of the action." Do such statutes express a constitutional requirement of due process of law? No, said a recent Federal Court of Appeals decision, U. S. v. Watts, 513 F.2d 5 (10th Cir. 1975), holding that the due process standards established by In re Gault, 387 U.S. 1, 33–34, 87 S.Ct. 1428, 1446–1447 (1967), relating to notice to the child's parents, constitute merely a prophylactic rule designed to protect the child's more fundamental need to be aware of the charges against him and to have a reasonable opportunity to prepare his defense. Thus, the court suggested that, "the parents' function would seem to be similar to that of legal counsel." 513 F.2d at 8. In the absence of proof that Watts was in fact prejudiced by failure of the government to notify his parents ("the record here reveals that Watts himself had adequate written notice of the precise charges against him well in advance of the hearing and was at all material times represented by competent counsel." Ibid.) the court held that there was no constitutional infirmity. The court also noted that the parents were both present at the trial itself. A concurring opinion agreed with the result, but would have reached it by finding the right to parental notice to be of true constitutional dimension, not merely prophylactic, finding further, however, that violation of the right in this case was harmless beyond a reasonable doubt. 513 F.2d at 9–11.

Although the court dealt with the notice issue largely as a failure of law enforcement officers making the arrest to comply with a duty to notify parents, it should be noted in addition that there appears to have been *no* formal notice at all to the parents, even during the post-arrest federal delinquency proceedings. Thus a violation of the duty of arresting officers to notify parents, imposed by the present federal juvenile delinquency statute, Title 18 U.S.C. § 5033, as amended by the 1974 Juvenile Justice and Delinquency Prevention Act, would clearly give rise to no constitutional claim if the notice were later to be given by, for example, the federal prosecutor.

The Fifth Circuit has taken the same position and ruled summarily that violation of a state statute requiring notice to the juvenile's parents following his arrest gives rise to no denial of a federal constitutional right. Gandy v. Panama City, Florida, 505 F.2d 630 (5th Cir. 1974); Walker v. Florida, 328 F.Supp. 620 (S.D.Fla. 1971), affirmed 466 F.2d 485 (5th Cir. 1972). In a criminal case against an unmarried person under the age of 21, however, the Florida courts have held that failure to comply with a cognate statute requiring notice to parents renders the judgment of conviction void. See S. v. Whitter, 245 So.2d 913 (Fla.App.1971) (applying exception to this rule when parent has actual notice).

In addition to notice requirements, the statutes also contain directives concerning where the arrested child is to be taken. May he be taken to a jail or police station by the arresting officer? The statutes give a variety of answers. The Texas Family Code § 52.02(a) provides an essentially negative answer. It requires that "A person taking a child into custody, without unnecessary delay and without first taking the child elsewhere, shall do one of the following: (1) release the child to his parent . . . " or bring the child to a juvenile or medical facility. The issue under such a statute is whether a stopover at the stationhouse, usually in order to interrogate the child, is an "unnecessary delay." In P. v. Morris, 57 Mich.App. 573, 226 N.W.2d 565 (1975) it was held that a similar statute, requiring that the arrested child be taken "immediately" to a juvenile facility was not violated by a stop at the stationhouse in order to fill out the admission papers for the youth home; the court noted, however, that the juvenile was not placed in a cell while this was being done. Pennsylvania goes still further in permitting detours to the police station. Under a statute which directs the arresting officer to take the child to a juvenile facility "with all reasonable speed and without first taking the child elsewhere" it has been held that a two hour stop at the police station for booking and interrogation is permissible. In re Anderson, 227 Pa.Super. 439, 313 A.2d 260 (1973). The *Anderson* opinion found that the purpose of the statute was "to forbid 'forced confessions' induced by harassment," and not to forbid *all* stationhouse work.

On the other hand, some statutes expressly permit the child to be taken to the police station, as for example, Mass.Gen.Laws Ann. c. 119 § 67, while others expressly permit the police to question the child "for a reasonable period of time" in a place designated for this purpose by an appellate court. N.Y.Fam.Ct.Act § 724(b)(ii).

In light of how generally easy it is for the police to take the child to the stationhouse for interrogation under most of the juvenile court statutes it is important to note the added protection provided by section 51.09 of the Texas Family Code which forbids any waiver of the child's privilege against self-incrimination when confronted by the police unless the child has a lawyer and both the lawyer and the child agree to the waiver in writing. In re V.R.S., 512 S.W.2d 350 (Tex.Civ.App.1974).

It is not required that the police take the juvenile to any particular place and there is always discretion to release him. The most frequently found provision on this point permits release to the parents if they promise to bring him to court on the appointed day. There is no obligation on the part of the parents to do this and where the fact that the child is in trouble with the law generates sufficient anger and embarrassment, the parents may refuse to take the child back. In Boston, for example, where the juvenile court sometimes sets the child's bail at one dollar as an invitation to the parents to come forward and claim the company of their child, they often decline to do so.

The discretionary decision by the police to release the child to his parents is often governed by statutory criteria. The Model Act § 20 is illustrative. It permits detention of the child when there is no parent to take him, and when:

> (2) release of the child would present a clear and substantial threat of a serious

nature to the person or property of others where the child is alleged to be delinquent; or

(3) the release of such child would present a serious threat of substantial harm to such child; or

(4) the child has a history of a failing to appear for hearings before the court.

The Model Act is unusual, however, in its further provision that the decision to detain must be supported by "clear and convincing evidence." Juvenile court acts typically make no reference to how strong the proof must be that the detention criteria are satisfied.

These criteria, however, strongly favor keeping the child in custody in a preventive detention status. That is, these statutes authorize pretrial detention on the basis of a fear that the child will commit further crimes. It is generally thought that this cannot constitutionally be done in regard to adults charged with criminal offenses and the question arises whether such preventive detention is permissible with children. Yes, said the New York Court of Appeals in Charles L. v. Schupf, 39 N.Y.2d 682, 385 N.Y.S.2d 518, 350 N. E.2d 906 (1976). The federal Court of Appeals for the Second Circuit, however, determined that the New York statute and the practice under it did violate Due Process in that they served to impose punishment for offenses prior to any determination of guilt. The court refused to rule on the constitutionality of preventive detention, *per se*, but rather found from statistical studies submitted by the parties and from testimony by a Family Court judge that more than two-thirds of the detainees were those against whom evidence of guilt was weak, or those who were not so dangerous that they could not be released after a short period of detention and those who were deemed to have been punished enough by the detention. The court concluded that "crime prevention is not a sufficiently compelling governmental interest as to any of these detainees to justify shortcutting the fundamental procedural requirement that imprisonment follow, rather than precede, adjudication."

§ 27. Questioning the Child

As is the case in the adult criminal process, the admissibility of a child's confession is a frequently litigated issue. Since, however, this question may arise in either a juvenile court to determine delinquency or in a criminal court where a child may be prosecuted, the rules which determine admissibility may depend on which court is trying the child. Most of the rules depend upon the circumstances of the questioning which produced the child's confession. The policies underlying this body of law are designed to deter certain types of police interrogation practices, to enforce compliance with statutory duties, to insure the fairness of the court hearing and to preserve the integrity of the juvenile justice system's *parens patriae* role. Enforcement of these policies may be observed in the decisions having to do with admitting the child's confession into evidence against him.

§ 27.1 Voluntariness

The traditional test used by the Supreme Court and lower state and federal courts ruled inadmissible those confessions which were not "voluntary." This referred to a variety of considerations, including the reliability of the confession, whether the confession was a product of free will and whether the police had engaged in offensive interrogation techniques. This list is not finite and the common way of identifying the voluntariness of a confession has been to evaluate the "totality of the circumstances." These naturally included the age of the accused, a factor of central importance in Supreme Court cases holding inadmissible in criminal trials the confessions of children. Haley v. Ohio, 332 U.S. 596, 68 S.Ct. 302 (1948); Gallegos v. Colorado, 370 U.S. 49, 82 S.Ct. 1209 (1962). State courts similarly asked if, under the totality of the circumstances, the child's confession was voluntary and uncoerced. In re Carlo, 48 N.J. 224, 225

A.2d 110 (1966). The *Gault* opinion added to this that when the child's attorney is absent, "the greatest care must be taken to assure that the admission was voluntary, in the sense not only that it was not coerced or suggested, but also that it was not the product of ignorance of rights or of adolescent fantasy, fright or despair." 387 U.S. at 55, 87 S.Ct. at 1458.

Although the emphasis today is on protection of the child's privilege against self-incrimination, the issue of voluntariness still arises in juvenile law. Where coercion, physical abuse and other law enforcement misconduct produce an involuntary confession (by traditional tests) later *Miranda* warnings do not necessarily break the chain of events so that subsequent confessions by the child may be excluded as involuntary as well. In re Garth D., 55 Cal.App.3d 986, 127 Cal.Rptr. 881 (1976). In addition, even after *Miranda* rights have been given and waived, the questioning which follows the waiver is to be tested by the totality of circumstances to determine if the statement then given by the child is voluntary. U. S. v. Ramsey, 367 F.Supp. 1307, 1313 (W.D.Mo.1973). The waiver of *Miranda* rights itself needs to be voluntary. In re T., 15 Cal.App.3d 886, 893–894, 93 Cal.Rptr. 510, 514 (1971). Finally, voluntariness is important when the child becomes a witness in his own defense and the juvenile court prosecutor seeks to impeach his testimony by showing that he gave a prior inconsistent statement. If the statement was obtained in violation of the child's *Miranda* rights, it may nonetheless be used for this purpose provided it was given voluntarily. In re Michael P., 50 A.D.2d 598, 375 N.Y.S.2d 153 (1975), following Harris v. New York, 401 U.S. 222, 91 S.Ct. 643 (1971).

When a child has been interviewed by a probation officer courts have sometimes created a presumption of involuntariness of statements made during the interview. "Such interviews are infected with the inherent danger that the minor, being cognizant of the role of the probation officer in juvenile court proceedings, may feel compelled to speak about the offense in order to avoid being thought uncooperative and hence unfit for a favorable dispositional recommendation." In re Garth D., supra at 889–90.

§ 27.2 Miranda

In Miranda v. Arizona, 384 U.S. 436, 86 S.Ct. 1602 (1965) the Supreme Court held that the privilege against self-incrimination is applicable when police interrogate a person in their custody; the decision went on to provide a set of rules the police must follow in order to insure that the privilege is protected. Statements obtained in violation of the rules are inadmissible. Among these is the requirement that the person in custody be informed that: (1) he need not say anything; (2) anything he says may be used against him; (3) he has a right to consult with an attorney and to have the attorney with him during any interrogation; and (4) if he cannot afford an attorney, one will be appointed for him. Almost all courts which considered the issue have held that compliance with the *Miranda* rules is necessary in order for a child's confession to be admissible against him in juvenile court, S. v. Whatley, 320 So.2d 123 (La.1975). It has been widely assumed that this view is required by In re Gault, 387 U.S. 1, 87 S.Ct. 1428 (1967), but in 1979 the Court addressed this issue in a footnote that made the application of *Miranda* less of a certainty. The footnote remark was: "Indeed, this Court has not yet held that *Miranda* applies with full force to exclude evidence obtained in violation of its prescriptions from consideration in juvenile proceedings, which for certain purposes have been distinguished from formal criminal prosecutions. See McKeiver v. Pennsylvania, 403 U.S. 528, 91 S.Ct. 1976 (1971) [holding that jury trials are not required in juvenile courts]. We do not decide that issue today. In view of our disposition of this case, we assume without deciding that the *Miranda* principles were fully applicable to the present proceedings." Fare v. Michael C., 442 U.S. 707, n. 4 at 717, 99 S.Ct. 2560, n. 4 at 2567 (1979). Despite this uncertainty, no court seems to have withdrawn its adherence to the applicability of *Miranda*. See, for example, In the Matter of Robert O., 109 Misc. 2d 238, 439 N.Y.S.2d 994 (Fam.Ct.1981).

New Jersey courts, however, have recognized the fiction of a child making an intelligent waiver of complicated legal rights and have held that "questioning may go forward even if it is obvious the boy does not understand his rights if the questioning is conducted with the utmost fairness and in accordance with the highest standards of due process and fundamental fairness." In re S.H., 61 N.J. 108, 115–117, 293 A.2d 181, 185 (N.J.1972). Some courts have insisted that a waiver of *Miranda* rights is valid only if the warnings were given to parents or some independent adult as well as the child and he is allowed to consult with them or an attorney prior to waiver. Commonwealth v. Gaskins, 471 Pa. 238, 369 A.2d 1285 (1977); In re E.T.C., 141 Vt. 375, 449 A.2d 937 (1982) (required by state constitution); Commonwealth v. A Juvenile, 389 Mass. 128, 449 N.E.2d 654 (1983) (required if child is under 14). The majority of cases, however, have rejected such a *per se* rule. S. v. Hardy, 107 Ariz. 583, 491 P.2d 17 (1971) (overruling an earlier adopted *per se* rule); In re A.D.R., 603 S.W.2d 575 (Mo. 1980) (rejecting lower court requirement that parents be consulted). This issue may be governed by a statute which expressly renders inadmissible any statement taken in the absence of a parent, In re L.B., 33 Colo.App. 1, 513 P.2d 1069 (1973) (no compliance with statute when father present at interrogation who was himself under arrest). It may be doubtful, however, that even a trend toward involvement of parents in the interrogation process would produce a substantially more knowledgeable or frequent assertion of the child's rights. Adults, too, are intimidated by the inherently coercive atmosphere of the police station. Parents not only waive rights which are explained to them, but often put pressure on their children to tell all. Mandatory appointment of counsel, as in Texas, is a far more potent guarantee of dispassionate advice to the child.

The *Miranda* warnings must be given only if the child is in custody at the time he is questioned. In re Appeal No. 245, 29 Md.App. 131, 349 A.2d 434 (1975) (boy questioned in back seat of police car parked outside his home is in custody); In the Matter of Gage, 49 Or.App. 599, 624 P.2d 1076 (1980) (interrogation by school principal in his office is not custodial interrogation). Confessions which are spontaneously made are not, however, inadmissible, even if made by a child who is in custody. On this basis it has been held, for example, that when a boy was stopped by the police for a minor traffic violation and asked the name of the owner of the mini-bike he was riding, his reply: "I swiped it" was admissible as being "voluntary, spontaneous and unsolicited." In re T., 15 Cal.App.3d 886, 892–893, 93 Cal.Rptr. 510, 513 (1971).

At the hearing, the state must not only prove that the required warnings were given in order for the confession to be admitted, it has the burden of proving that the child's waiver of his right to remain silent and his right to an attorney was voluntarily made. In re Anthony J., 107 Cal.App. 3d 962, 166 Cal.Rptr. 238 (1980). Although in Lego v. Twomey, 404 U.S. 477, 92 S.Ct. 619 (1972) the Supreme Court held that the state need prove the voluntariness issue only by a preponderance of the evidence in order to satisfy Due Process, several states have required more and have held a child's statement inadmissible in the absence of proof beyond a reasonable doubt that he waived his rights and voluntarily confessed. In re Eduardo M., 80 Misc.2d 371, 363 N.Y.S.2d 254 (1975); S. v. Whatley, 320 So.2d 123 (La.1975). Even if the waiver of *Miranda* rights is valid, the confession still may not be admissible if it was obtained as a result of an arrest of the juvenile without probable cause. In re Appeal No. 245, 29 Md.App. 131, 349 A.2d 434 (1975), following Brown v. Illinois, 422 U.S. 590, 95 S.Ct. 2254 (1975).

In a variety of settings the juvenile may be induced to make an incriminating statement to a person who is not a law enforcement officer.

R.W. v. State, 135 Ga.App. 668, 218 S.E.2d 674
(1975) (owner of shop from which property
stolen); In re Simmons, 24 N.C.App. 28, 210 S.E.
2d 84 (1974) (person to whom obscene telephone
calls made); State v. Bolan, 27 Ohio St.2d 15,
271 N.E.2d 839 (1971) (store security officer).
In such cases there is no requirement for *Miranda*
warnings. There is either no "custody" in these
cases or compulsion by a private person does not
violate the privilege against self-incrimination.
But the confession is nonetheless inadmissible if
it is involuntary, that is, induced by threat or
promise, etc. on the part of the private party.
The use of an involuntary confession renders the
hearing unfair and a violation of Due Process
apart from any consideration of the privilege
against self-incrimination.

§ 27.3 The Role of the Attorney

The expectation of both supporters and attack-
ers of the *Miranda* doctrine was that most persons in police custody would exercise their right
to an attorney and that police interrogation would
proceed, if at all, under the watchful eye of defense counsel who would prevent abuse and coercion. It is a clear ground for reversing a delinquency finding if it is based on a confession obtained after a child's request for counsel was
ignored. In re R.A.H., 314 A.2d 133 (D.C.Ct.
App.1974). Similarly, where the parents indi-

cate that they intend to retain counsel for their child, the police are not permitted to question the child in the absence of the attorney and statements they obtain are not admissible. Arnold v. S., 265 So.2d 64 (Fla.App.1972). Interrogation is also not permitted, according to the California Supreme Court, once the child asks for his parents, since this is the equivalent of an adult asking for a lawyer. R. v. Burton, 6 Cal.3d 375, 99 Cal.Rptr. 1, 491 P.2d 793 (1971). The Supreme Court of the United States has held, however, that asking for a probation officer is neither an assertion of the privilege against self-incrimination nor is it the equivalent of asking for an attorney. Fare v. Michael C., 442 U.S. 707, 99 S.Ct. 2560 (1979). The attorney takes on central importance under the Texas statute which has been held to require that no statutory or constitutional rights—including the right to remain silent when questioned by the police—may be waived by the child unless the waiver is in writing and is made by the child *and his attorney.* In re R.E.J., 511 S.W.2d 347 (Tex.Civ.App.1974). In other words, an attorney must be appointed for a child in order to help the child decide whether to proceed without one. In New York a similar statute has been taken to apply only when the child has been brought before the court and not when he is in the custodial hands of the police. In the Matter of Roger EE, 75 A.D.2d 269, 429 N.Y.S.2d 757 (1980).

Where the child already has an attorney at the time the police question him—assigned by the juvenile court, for example, before it waives juvenile jurisdiction so as to permit a criminal trial—it has been suggested that a confession the police obtain is inadmissible unless they make reasonable efforts to notify the attorney and have him present at the interrogation. S. v. White, 494 S. W.2d 687 (Mo.1973). The source of such a rule is Massiah v. U. S., 377 U.S. 201, 84 S.Ct. 1199 (1964) although the Missouri court went further than the Supreme Court by noting that under the circumstances of "tender age" the police must, prior to any interrogation "make a reasonable effort to notify and to have present" not only the attorney, but the child's parents as well. The requirement for parents appears to be independent of the rule concerning the attorney, for the court indicates that to hold otherwise would violate the Sixth Amendment "and would contravene the basic dictates of fairness in the conduct of criminal causes and the fundamental rights of persons charged with crime." 494 S.W.2d at 692. As indicated in § 27.2, however, courts are sharply divided on a flat requirement of parental involvement in the waiver of *Miranda* rights and Missouri has recently adopted a negative view.

§ 27.4 Compliance With Statutes

Section 26 has discussed the obligations placed on the police once a juvenile has been taken into custody. Failure to comply with these statutes may have a decisive effect on the admissibility of a statement which the police obtain. Legislative requirements as to notification of parents and prompt arraignment of the arrested child may be of central importance.

As to statutes mandating notice to parents upon a child being taken into custody, the cases have held statutory violations do not, themselves, render inadmissible a confession obtained by the police, Theriault v. S., 66 Wis.2d 33, 223 N.W.2d 850 (1974). It is sometimes indicated that the failure to give notice to parents is an error which can be cured when the child waives his *Miranda rights*, P. v. Murphy, 17 Ill.App.3d 482, 308 N.E. 2d 235, although absent such a waiver the confession would be inadmissible regardless of the lack of notice to the parents.

Statutes directing the police where to take the arrested child, and when, are more significant than the parental notice statutes. Thus in Georgia it has been held that taking an arrested child directly to the police station violates a statute which says that the arresting officer must either release him to his parents or bring him to court, "without first taking the child elsewhere." M.

K.H. v. S., 135 Ga.App. 565, 218 S.E.2d 284 (1975). But since the Georgia court also found that the record did not indicate whether the child understood the *Miranda* warnings, it is not clear that the trip to the stationhouse would itself be enough to taint the confession. Usually, however, the fact that the child was taken to the police station hardly catches that attention of the courts.

Statutory requirements relating to the *speed* with which the arrested child must be taken to a juvenile court have been given more decisive effect in considering the admissibility of confessions. Under such statutes, if the child is not released to his parents, he must be delivered to juvenile authorities "without unnecessary delay" or "with all possible speed" or pursuant to some similarly phrased mandate importing haste. If the police do delay beyond what is permitted by the statute the result, according to the majority of courts that have considered the issue, is the inadmissibility of any statement the police obtain during the period of delay. U. S. v. DeMarce, 513 F.2d 755 (8th Cir. 1975). By viewing violation of such a statute to create an illegal detention, however, Illinois has held the child's confession admissible by invoking the rule that "unlawful detention will not, of itself, invalidate a confession or statement of the accused." P. v. Zepeda, 47 Ill.2d 23, 265 N.E.2d 647 (1970). As a rule based on *statutory* violation of detention requirements *Zepeda* has probably survived Brown v. Illinois, 422 U.S. 590, 95 S.Ct. 2254 (1975) which held that an *unconstitutional* detention (arrest without probable cause) leads to an inadmissible confession.

§ 27.5   Parens Patriae Interrogations

When juvenile court jurisdiction is waived and the child is tried in a criminal court, the issue of admissibility of a confession given prior to the time of the waiver has evoked a variety of responses from the law.   In some states the result may depend on who obtained the confession since a state statute may unqualifiedly prohibit criminal trial admissibility of confessions given to a juvenile officer or juvenile court personnel.   See, for example, Vernon's Ann.Mo.Stat. § 211.271(3). The same result has been reached by judicial interpretation in a few jurisdictions;   the leading case is Harling v. U. S., 295 F.2d 161 (Ct.App. D.C.1959).   The principle here asserts that while the juvenile system holds itself out as being nonpunitive and offering of help to the child, it would be fundamentally unfair for that system to use its *parens patriae* position to obtain statements which can be used for punishment through a criminal trial.

A completely contrary result is based on the view that the *parens patriae* relation exists only

between the juvenile court and the child, not between the police and the child. Therefore, so
long as the standard *Miranda* procedures are followed, it is of no legal consequence that a pre-
waiver confession is used in a criminal trial.
Mitchell v. S., 3 Tenn.Cr.App. 494, 464 S.W.2d
307 (1971).

Two intermediate positions are also discern-
able in the cases. One holds that so long as the
interrogation atmosphere is adversary and it appears from all the circumstances, such as past encounters with the law, that the child realized he
might be held criminally responsible, his confession is admissible in a criminal trial if the *Miranda* requirements are met. S. v. Wright, 515 S.W.
2d 421 (Mo.1974). No express warnings concerning the possibility of criminal punishment
must be given. It is on this issue, however, that
the other intermediate position is distinguishable,
for some courts will permit the pre-waiver confession in a criminal trial only if the child has
been clearly advised that any statement he makes
may be used against him in a criminal proceeding. S. v. Maloney, 102 Ariz. 495, 433 P.2d 625
(1966), holding child and parents must be informed of adult trial possibility; but see S. v.
Hardy, 107 Ariz. 583, 491 P.2d 17 (1971), overruling the *Maloney* rule as to *parents*.

§ 28. Searches

Juvenile law regarding searches, like its adult counterpart, is almost entirely made up of judicial opinions interpreting the Fourth Amendment to the federal constitution, in case by case determinations of whether a particular search and seizure by the police is legal. From these cases there emerge useful generalizations, such as that a search incident to an arrest does not require a search warrant, but there is almost entirely absent a detailed legislative treatment of the subject which would serve to inform both police and citizen alike of the rules which govern this sphere of law enforcement activity. The Model Act, for example, contains only one sentence on the subject, and that sentence speaks only to the remedy for violation of rules not themselves spelled out: Section 28 declares, "Evidence illegally seized or obtained shall not be received in evidence over objection to establish the allegations against him." By implication this provision would permit the use of illegally seized evidence for other purposes, such as to determine the child's custody status in a detention hearing, or to decide what should be done with him in a disposition hearing. But that is all the Model Act tells us—there is nothing by way of primary rules of behavior for the police which can be used to determine if a seizure is legal. This situation may be remedied if the American Law Institute's

Model Code of Pre-Arraignment Procedures, 1975 is adopted since the Code contains a comprehensive treatment of the rules governing search behavior, a number of which deal expressly with searches of juveniles; these are discussed in this section.

At present, however, the starting point is the core of Fourth Amendment rules which declare that a search and seizure is valid if it is authorized by a search warrant or falls within one of the recognized exceptions to the requirement that the police have a warrant. As to the warrant, it can probably be assumed that the rules relating to warrants in adult cases apply to juvenile cases as well. Thus, when the warrant in a juvenile case is based on an informer's tip the same tests for determining the validity of the warrant have been held applicable. In re M., 16 Cal.App.2d 96, 93 Cal.Rptr. 679 (1971). Furthermore, there is nothing about being a juvenile court probation officer which would permit such an official to obtain a search warrant under a statute which does not list him as among those authorized to apply for warrants. Huff v. Walker, 125 Ga.App. 251, 187 S.E.2d 343 (1972).

Application of the exceptions to the warrant requirement have been more difficult, however. In regard to the generalization that a search incident to an arrest does not require a warrant, although it seems clear that children have the benefit of the adult rule that if the arrest is illegal the fruits of the search may not be used against them, In re S., 36 A.D.2d 642, 319 N.Y. S.2d 752 (1971), the complexity of the arrest of children introduces unique questions concerning so-called incident searches. If, for example, a juvenile court act authorizes taking a child into custody "pursuant to the laws of arrest," then if the arrest is for an offense which must be committed in the presence of a law enforcement officer, an arrest of a child for such an offense which was committed *out* of the officer's presence is illegal and a search incident to it is similarly illegal. But the arrest and the search under these circumstances would both be valid if the statute authorized the officer to take the child into custody "if there are reasonable grounds to believe that the child has engaged in delinquent conduct" since this latter provision effectively removes any requirement that the delinquent conduct be in the officer's presence. In re J.B. Jr., 131 N.J.Super. 6, 328 A.2d 46 (1974). The Texas Family Code § 52.01(a) includes both sorts of arrest provisions. In a state whose arrest law includes an "in-presence" requirement for some offenses, the result of these statutory provisions is to make for legal arrests and searches of children which would be illegal in the case of adults. A similar differential result appears when account is taken of provisions which authorize children to be taken into custody on grounds which do not authorize arrest of an adult. Children may be subject to curfew restrictions, for example. Although there must be probable cause to believe that the child is violating a curfew law before he may be taken into custody, S. v. Smithers, 256 Ind. 512, 269 N.E.2d 874 (1971), once he is in lawful custody the police may search him. D.L.C. v. S., 298 So.2d 480 (Fla.App.1974) (complete search of child's person); In re B.M.C., 32 Colo. App. 79, 506 P.2d 409 (1973) (complete search on curfew arrest not authorized).

In addition to searches incident to an arrest, a search warrant is not required where the search is conducted with consent. As in the case of adults, if the child's consent is obtained by trickery, the search is invalid. In re Robert T., 8 Cal. App.3d 990, 88 Cal.Rptr. 37 (1970). In some situations it is not clear whether the police are genuinely requesting permission to search or are merely using words of request while communicating an intention to search regardless of whether permission is forthcoming. If it is the latter, the search is invalid. In making this fact determination courts do not always take account of the susceptibility of children to intimidation in the presence of police. In re Michael V., 10 Cal.3d 676, 111 Cal.Rptr. 681, 517 P.2d 1145 (1974) ("Okay boys, why don't you empty your pockets on the car?" taken to be request for permission to search). In recognition of this, the American Law Institute's Model Code of Pre-Arraignment Procedures requires that if the person searched is under the age of 16, the consent must be given by his parent or guardian. § SS 240.2(1),(a).

The issue of consent has been often litigated where the police search a juvenile's home with the consent of his parents. With but two exceptions, the parental consent has been upheld, even in cases where the child has himself refused permission to search his room. In giving the father's permission legal priority over the son's refusal a California court declared:

> In his capacity as head of a household, a father has the responsibility and authority for discipline, training, and control of his children. In the exercise of his parental authority a father has full access to the room set aside for his son for the purpose of fulfilling his right and duty to control his son's behavior and to obtain obedience. Vandenberg v. Superior Court, 8 Cal.App.3d 1048, 1055–1056, 87 Cal.Rptr. 876, 880 (1970).

In the Michigan case which constitutes the clearest exception to the judicial acceptance of parental consent, the court found it unimportant that the father owned the house and supported the child and emphasized that the question was one of the constitutional rights of a person accused of criminal conduct. P. v. Flowers, 23 Mich.App. 523, 179 N.W.2d 56 (1970). In the second case which rejects the validity of parental consent, however, the court focused on the fact that both the mother and the child were tenants or guests in the house of another. Reeves v. Warden, 346 F.2d 915 (4th Cir. 1965). The Model Code of Pre-Arraignment Procedures § SS 240.2 (1) (c) would have the result in these cases turn on whether the person giving permission to search "is apparently entitled to determine the giving or withholding of consent."

In light of the fact that a locked school locker may be the only place which a child may see as protecting his interests in privacy, the cases dealing with the authority of school officials to search students and their lockers are of major importance. Some courts provide no protection to the students. In Kansas, for example, it has been decided that: "We deem it a proper function of school authorities to inspect the lockers under their control and to prevent their use in illegal ways or for illegal purposes. We believe this right of inspection is inherent in the authority vested in the school administration and that the same must be retained and exercised in the management of our schools if their educational functions are to be maintained and the welfare of student bodies preserved." S. v. Stein, 203 Kan. 638, 640–641, 456 P.2d 1, 3 (1969). Other courts deny students Fourth Amendment protection on the ground that school officials are not the enforcement officials to whom the Amendment applies, In re Donaldson, 269 Cal.App.2d 509, 75 Cal.Rptr. 220 (1969), even if the official is a part-time juvenile police officer. In the Interest of J.A., 85 Ill.App.3d 567, 40 Ill.Dec. 755, 406 N.E. 2d 958 (1980).

More recently, however, courts appear to be recognizing a legitimate interest in privacy which needs to be protected from school officials. The New York Court of Appeals, for example, has held that "High school students are protected from unreasonable searches and seizures, even in the school, by employees of the State whether they be police officers or school teachers." P. v. Scott D., 34 N.Y.2d 483, 358 N.Y.S.2d 403, 315 N.E.2d 466 (1974). And since a school search of a student's personal effects on grounds of suspicion that he possesses something illegal does not constitute one of the recognized exceptions to the rule that the State needs a search warrant, such a search has been held illegal. S. v. Mora, 307 So.2d 317 (La.1975). On the other hand, recognition of the applicability of the Fourth Amendment does not necessarily lead to holding school officials to the same standards which govern searches by the police. Doe v. S., 88 N.M. 347, 540 P.2d 827 (1975):

> To engraft the cumbersome warrant requirement onto school searches would mean that police assistance would be required for even

the most trivial searches, e.g. for chewing gum. The normal exceptions to the warrant requirement would have little application in the school situation.

Thus, we adopt the standard that school officials may conduct a search of the student's person if they have a reasonable suspicion that a crime is being or has been committed or they have reasonable cause to believe that the search is necessary in the aid of maintaining school discipline. 540 P.2d at 832.

Where the search is illegal almost all courts apply the exclusionary rule and rule inadmissible the fruits of the search. But as is currently the case in adult proceedings, juvenile court judges, too, have strongly questioned the value of applying the rule in delinquency proceedings. In re Herman S., 79 Misc.2d 519, 521–523, 359 N.Y.S. 2d 645, 649–50 (1974). In this vein, the Supreme Court of Georgia has held that even though school officials are state agents for purposes of the Fourth Amendment, their illegal searches are not subject to the exclusionary rule. S. v. Young, 234 Ga. 488, 216 S.E.2d 586 (1975).

§ 29. Lineups and Other Identifications

The Supreme Court has decided a line of cases creating, and limiting, constitutional rights of criminal defendants relating to their identification by victims and other witnesses. Juvenile court statutes have undertaken to control the photographing and fingerprinting of juveniles but have left all other aspects of rights relating to identification procedures for resolution by the courts. The statutes say nothing, that is, about what the police may or must do when they arrange a line-up with juvenile suspects although there is often detailed statutory regulation of police procedures regarding arrest, detention, release and interrogation of children. The courts to whom the duty of shaping the law has fallen have followed the lead of the Supreme Court and applied its holdings to juvenile cases.

Thus, after the Court had decided there was a Sixth Amendment right to counsel at a line-up in U. S. v. Wade, 388 U.S. 218, 87 S.Ct. 1926 (1967) and before that right was limited to line-ups held after the commencement of adversary judicial criminal proceedings in Kirby v. Illinois, 406 U.S. 682, 92 S.Ct. 1877 (1972), state courts granted juveniles the rights they saw to flow from *Wade*. In re Holley, 107 R.I. 615, 268 A.2d 723 (1970); In re Carl T., 1 Cal.App.3d 344, 81 Cal.Rptr. 655 (1969). Following *Kirby*, it has been held that there is no right to counsel at a line-up which took place before the juvenile had been proceeded against in juvenile court. Jackson v. S., 17 Md. App. 167, 300 A.2d 430 (1973). In *Jackson* the juvenile court waived its jurisdiction and the juvenile was consequently indicted and convicted.

The pre-indictment stage of the line-up brought the case squarely within the *Kirby* rule. The Maryland court noted that these facts did not require it to decide whether formal commencement of juvenile court proceedings would be "adversary judicial criminal proceedings" so as to make the *Wade* rights applicable; no other court appears to have decided this issue. It would seem, however, that any emphasis on the "criminal" concept in the *Kirby* rule would serve to give a juvenile no rights relating to line-ups when his case is disposed of in juvenile court. Since the purpose of providing a right to counsel at the line-up stage is to assure that the in-court identification testimony is not tainted by unfairly suggestive line-ups, the generally accepted requirement of fundamental fairness in juvenile court hearings should lead to a decision that a complaint or petition filed in juvenile court is the equivalent of an indictment or other adversary judicial criminal process for purposes of rights at a line-up held subsequently.

Even if the line-up is unfairly put together, or the right to counsel had not been accorded, the in-court identification of a witness to the crime who was also present at the line-up is admissible if the testimony has a source in the witness' recollection which is independent of his viewing the accused at the line-up. This, too, has been applied to juveniles, In re Spencer, 288 Minn. 119, 179 N.W.2d 95 (1970). *Spencer* also holds that since juvenile court proceedings are held before a judge sitting without a jury, there is no necessity for a separate suppression hearing to consider the admissibility of the identification testimony.

Identifications which occur shortly after the crime and involve the police bringing the child and the victim together in a street confrontation are not subject to the right to counsel, In re Lynette G., 54 Cal.App.3d 1087, 126 Cal.Rptr. 898 (1976), while one Family Court judge held that the identification testimony would be admissible even if the police violated the child's Fourth Amendment right to be free from an unreasonable seizure when they took her into custody in order to bring her to the victim. In re Carlos B., 86 Misc.2d 160, 382 N.Y.S.2d 655 (1976). The distinction between the *Carlos B.* rule and cases such as Brown v. Illinois, 422 U.S. 590, 95 S.Ct. 2254 (1975), holding a confession obtained from a person illegally arrested is inadmissible, even if *Miranda* warnings had been given, and Davis v. Mississippi, 394 U.S. 721, 89 S.Ct. 1394 (1969), holding inadmissible fingerprints obtained from a person illegally arrested, seems to be that the identification was "occasioned by" the illegal arrest, but "was not obtained by further police action as in the instance of a search or interrogation." 382 N.Y.S.2d at 659.

In other identification issues the rules applied to juveniles also closely track the adult cases (and their reluctance to apply the exclusionary rule). When the police show a witness photographs, for example, there is no right to counsel at that time and, absent impermissible suggestiveness in the manner of the showing, the identification testimony is admissible. U. S. v. Singleton, 361 F.Supp. 346 (E.D.Pa.1973). Even if there is suggestiveness, moreover, if the witness knew the juvenile for some time prior to the showing, the testimony remains acceptable. P. v. Hutchins, 9 Ill.App.3d 447, 292 N.E.2d 494 (1972) (group picture with circle drawn around accused).

Some jurisdictions enforce a rule which, based on the *parens patriae* role of the juvenile justice system, makes inadmissible in a child's criminal trial a confession obtained from him while he was still under juvenile court authority. Where this rule has been codified, the absence of any reference in the statute to a line-up has led to the holding that line-up identifications may be used in the criminal trial, even if held before the juvenile court waived its jurisdiction. S. v. Richardson, 495 S.W.2d 435 (Mo.1974). Absent the statutory issue, there may be the same sort of distinction here as was made in *Carlos B.*, supra relating to *inaction* on the part of the police giving rise to no overreaching or breach of a parental role when all the police do is bring the accused and the witness together.

CHAPTER IV

COMMENCING THE JUDICIAL PROCESS

§ 30. Intake and Diversion

One of the traditional features of the juvenile court system is the case screening process known as "Intake." Its early history is traced in Wallace and Brennan, Intake and the Family Court, 12 Buffalo L.Rev. 442 (1963). Since the function of intake is to send cases away from the court which would be within its jurisdiction, it might more appropriately be called "out-take;" the intake function has, in fact, virtually merged with the more recently developed practice of "diversion." This latter, however, has a strong implication of directing the diverted child *into* a treatment program than does intake which emphasizes the inappropriateness of a formal court hearing in particular cases. It might be said of the screening process, therefore, that the major function of intake is to divert children.

Three developments highlight the importance of this type of screening. One is the realization that the official resources available to juvenile courts for the treatment and rehabilitation of adjudicated juveniles is largely useless for that purpose. Resort to diversion programs is a consequence of that frustration. Second, the formal hearing process is seen by many as positively harmful to young children, without regard to the further harmful effects of the corrections process. The third consideration is the increasingly disproportionate relationship between the amount of delinquent conduct and the amount of judicial resources available to deal with it. Screening is a flexible means for using these resources for the most serious sorts of cases. In so doing, it reviews the cognate decision made by law enforcement officials who also exercise an enormous amount of discretion in deciding which children to take into custody and which to refer to court. The need for juvenile courts to maintain amicable relations with police severely hampers the ability of the court screening function to exercise a completely independent judgment when the results might be seen as reversing, and, therefore, critical of the judgment made by the police. See Emerson, Judging Delinquents (1969). This problem might be avoided where the intake function is not part of the court, but is lodged in some other agency, such as the Department of Health and Rehabilitative Services in Florida. Fla.Stat. Ann. § 39.04(1). Usually, however, the intake officer is under the authority of the juvenile court judge.

The statutes often provide for a two-fold purpose for intake: to determine whether the facts of the case are such that the court could legally find that the child engaged in the forbidden conduct complained of, and whether "further proceedings in the case are in the interest of the child or the public." Tex.Fam.Code § 53.01(a)(3). There is usually no restriction on the sort of case that is subject to this determination, although New York requires that if the charge is that a serious crime was committed, the case may not be screened out without the written approval of the local director of probation. N.Y.Fam.Ct. Act § 734(a)(ii). The new Florida law provides that if the charge is *any* crime, the prosecuting official may overrule the decision of the intake officer to screen the case out and file a formal petition. Fla.Stat.Ann. § 39.04(d),(e). The Model act provides for the same sequence of decisions, but not for the mandatory review of intake set forth in the Florida law. Section 13(b) grants the person complaining about the child the right to have an adverse intake decision reviewed by the prosecutor who then has power to authorize a petition despite the intake decision. See Rubin, The Emerging Prosecutor Dominance of the Juvenile Court Intake Process, 26 Crime & Delinquency 299 (1980).

The intake official is usually required to conduct some sort of inquiry or investigation before

reaching a decision. This may include a conference with the child, his parents and the person
making the complaint in order to determine if a
result satisfactory to all the parties can be reached (the case "adjusted" in common parlance)
without a formal petition invoking the jurisdiction of the court. There may be explicit authority for using diversion programs, as in the Florida law which requires the intake officer to decide if "in his judgment the interest of the child
and the public will be served best by providing
the child care or other treatment voluntarily accepted by the child and his parents   .   .   ."
Fla.Stat.Ann. § 39.04(2)(b), although even without a statutory provision such as this, the same
decision is central to the intake function.   In
light of the fact that the choice given to the child
is either to participate in the "care or treatment"
or face a formal charge in the juvenile court, it
may be doubted that the acceptance is ever truly
voluntary. For this reason, it might be helpful
for the child to have the assistance of an attorney
at this stage of the proceedings. There does not
appear to be, however, statutory authority for
the court to appoint counsel for the child at the
intake stage and decisions concerning a constitutional right to counsel at intake have gone against
the right. In re Anthony S., 73 Misc.2d 187, 341
N.Y.S.2d 11 (1973); In re Frank H., 71 Misc.2d
1042, 337 N.Y.S.2d 118 (1972). These decisions

rely on provisions of the New York Family Court Act, also found elsewhere, which grant a degree of protection to the child by requiring that "No statement made during a preliminary conference may be admitted into evidence at a fact-finding hearing or, if the proceeding is transferred to a criminal court, at any time prior to a conviction." § 735.

This is in keeping with the otherwise voluntary nature of the participation of all parties in the intake official's inquiry. Statutes do not provide for any compulsory participation in the formal sense of being legally summoned, and often declare that "The probation service may not be authorized [in the intake process] to compel any person to appear at any conference, produce any papers, or visit any place." N.Y.Fam.Ct.Act § 734(d). As has been suggested, the compulsion on the child is hardly dissipated by such a provision. In a real sense, the victim of the child's misconduct, or other person initiating the complaint, would not have much choice in the matter either if the decision of the intake officer to refuse to file a petition ends the case. Juvenile court statutes usually do not provide for such a result, however. Illinois, for example, declares that "The probation officer may not prevent the filing of a petition by any person who wishes to file a petition under this Act." Ill.Juv.Ct.Act § 703–8(3). It has already been noted in this section that some statutes grant the complaining person a right to have the intake decision not to proceed formally with the case reviewed by the prosecutor.

Even if the child cooperates in a treatment program developed in the intake process and takes the advice of the officials seeking to divert him, there is no guarantee that a petition will not be filed against him anyway. Although the juvenile court acts frequently put time limits on the effort to "adjust" cases without the filing of a petition, six months under § 53.03(a) of the Texas Family Code; two months, extendable by the court for another 60 days under § 734(c) of the New York Family Court Act, for example, there is nothing to prevent the filing of a petition at the expiration of such periods of time unless there is an additional provision, such as is found in Florida which states that the petition "shall be dismissed with prejudice if it was not filed within 45 days from the date the child was taken into custody." Fla.Stat.Ann. § 39.05,(6). In the absence of a time limit of this sort, a petition can be filed at any time within the applicable statute of limitations, see § 39.

§ 31. Detention Hearings and the Right to Bail

After a child has been taken into custody by the police, if he is not released, he becomes involved in that part of the justice system which is increasingly specialized in juvenile affairs. The detention facility which becomes responsible for his continued custody and the court which makes decisions concerning his responsibility are, at least in theory, more committed to acting in his best interests than is the law enforcement process which first made contact with him. The descriptions of the juvenile justice system which follow in this and subsequent sections need, therefore, to be read in the context of the erosion of that theory which has been outlined in section 4.

The juvenile court legislation usually decrees that if the child is not released to his parents, the police officer is to transfer custody to a juvenile detention facility. However, this directive is typically devoid of any standards for deciding the crucial question of whether, given the choice between a parent willing to take the child and the availability of the detention institution, the police are to choose one over the other. The California law does contain a provision directed at this issue, but it raises more questions for the arresting officer than it settles. Section 626 of the Welfare and Institutions Code requires: "In determining which disposition of the minor he will make, the officer shall prefer the alternative which least restricts the minor's freedom of movement, provided such alternative is compatible with the best interests of the minor and the community." The Model Act § 20(a), while not completely devoid of the need for the exercise of some judgment by the officer, requires release to the parent "upon the ascertainment of the necessary facts," relating to the parent's being "able and willing to provide supervision and care."

It is, of course, possible for the juvenile court act to require that all arrested children be taken directly to the detention facility so that all release decisions, including those made concerning release to parents, could be reached by specialists in making judgments about the ability and willingness of parents to provide supervision and care. See S. v. Arbeiter, 449 S.W.2d 627 (Mo. 1970). This procedure has the additional advantage of permitting a release decision by juvenile authorities that does not involve review and possible reversal of the police decision to detain the child. To the extent that the need to maintain amicable relations between juvenile court authorities and police affects the decision of whether one will overrule the decision of the other—and the extent is sometimes large—it would be wise to place all interim detention decisions in the hands of those who run the detention facilities. Under Florida law the initial detention decision is to be made jointly by the intake officer and the police, with disagreements resolved by the prosecuting attorney. In California the authority to make the first detention decision is vested in the probation officer.

Time limits are usually placed on the period in which the child may be detained in the place to which the police have taken him; 72 hours is a commonly found limit. The statutes may structure these requirements either as a matter of when a petition must be filed against the child, or more commonly, when a judicial detention hearing must be held at which a decision is made by the judge whether the child is to remain in custody until the hearing of the case on the merits. The Model Act § 23 contains both sorts of provisions: a petition must be filed within 24 hours of the time the child is detained, and a detention hearing must be held within 24 hours of the time the petition is filed. Where the statutes require the court to decide whether a child is to be held beyond 24 hours from the time of the initial detention decision by the police, this review has been held to require the decision of the judge; in the absence of a statute, the authority may not be delegated to a social worker or probation officer. S. ex rel. Morrow v. Lewis, 55 Wis.2d 502, 200 N.W.2d 193 (1972).

There appears to be no constitutional requirement that any of these detention decisions—by a judge or anyone else—concern itself with releasing the child on bail. Although there are a few statutory provisions granting children in custody the right to bail, they are collected in Smith, Juvenile Right to Bail, 11 J.Fam.L. 81 (1971), most juvenile court acts contain no such provisions. Appellate courts, moreover, have interpreted both state and federal constitutional provisions relating to bail as not extending the right to juveniles. Baker v. Smith, 477 S.W.2d 149 (Ky.App.1971) (state constitutional provision that "all prisoners" are bailable not applicable); Donald R. v. Whitmer, 30 Utah 2d 206, 515 P.2d 617 (1973) (bail provision in constitution does not apply in "Juvenile Courts where incorrigible or delinquent children are being trained and their habits corrected").

What the issues are and when they must be decided in a detention hearing is, however, crucially affected by constitutional decisions concerned with the requirement that detained children be granted a prompt judicial hearing on whether there is probable cause to believe that they are guilty of the offense for which they have been arrested and detained. In Moss v. Weaver, 525 F. 2d 1258 (5th Cir. 1976) it was decided that the Supreme Court's decision in Gerstein v. Pugh, 420 U.S. 103, 95 S.Ct. 854 (1975) applied to delinquency cases. In *Gerstein* the Court held that the Fourth Amendment required a judicial determination of probable cause either before an arrest (when an arrest warrant is issued) or promptly after arrest. Since juveniles, like adults, are rarely arrested by an officer with a warrant, the *Gerstein* rule is critically important.

Moss followed *Gerstein* in holding that the procedural requirements at the hearing are not very rigorous. The probable cause hearing is not a "critically important" stage of the process and, therefore, there is no constitutionally required right to counsel at the hearing, reasoned *Gerstein*. In reaching this decision, the Supreme Court distinguished Coleman v. Alabama, 399 U. S. 1, 90 S.Ct. 1999 (1970) in which it had held that the Alabama preliminary hearing was such a stage and that counsel was accordingly required. In *Coleman*, the *Gerstein* decision noted, the preliminary hearing served to determine whether the suspected person should be charged and tried at all, not merely whether he should be held in custody; in addition, the Alabama procedure permitted confrontation and cross-examination of the prosecution witnesses, a fairly useless exercise without the assistance of counsel. But since the probable cause hearing contemplated by the Fourth Amendment does not require the production of the state's witnesses, that rationale of *Coleman* did not apply. *Coleman* is sometimes relied on by state courts in deciding that the juvenile has a right to counsel at detention hearings, P. v. Giminez, 23 Ill.App.3d 583, 319 N.E.2d 570 (1974); T.K. v. S., 126 Ga. App. 269, 190 S.E.2d 588 (1972), and it is not clear whether the Supreme Court's view of *Cole-man* in *Gerstein* will produce a change in state interpretation of state juvenile court acts dealing with the right to counsel. *Moss* found it unnecessary to decide the counsel issue since the court assumed that the past practice of representation by the public defender at detention hearings would continue.

Gerstein also reversed lower federal court rulings that "the determination of probable cause must be accompanied by the full panoply of adversary safeguards—counsel, confrontation, cross-examination, and compulsory process for witnesses." 420 U.S. at 119, 95 S.Ct. at 865–866. *Moss* followed this, noting that *Gerstein* was a Fourth Amendment case and not a due process one, and further, that the Fourth Amendment itself does not require adversary safeguards. Moss held, therefore, that none of the adversary procedural rights were necessary in juvenile probable cause hearings.

In some states the probable cause issue is part of the preliminary hearing designed to determine if there should be a hearing on the merits. P. ex rel. Guggenheim v. Mucci, 32 N.Y.2d 307, 344 N.Y.S.2d 944, 298 N.E.2d 109 (1973). Under such a system there is a right to counsel and counsel must be permitted to cross-examine the state's witnesses. P. ex rel. Lauring v. Mucci, 44 A.D.2d 479, 355 N.Y.S.2d 786 (1974).

The Fourth Amendment probable cause requirement does not mean that the juvenile court, at a detention hearing, may not take more traditional factors into account as well. *Moss* notes that a state "may properly direct its juvenile court judges to make a decision about the child's welfare when they consider whether he should be released pending his adjudicatory hearing. But if they do not find release desirable on that basis, the Fourth Amendment's principles dictate that they must not detain him unless they also find probable cause to believe him guilty."

The Rhode Island Supreme Court has recently refused to apply *Gerstein*, holding it sufficient that the Family Court judge decides whether the facts warrant the filing of a petition and that the detention decision is to be guided by statutory post-adjudication disposition criteria. It cited neither *Moss* nor *Coleman* and overlooked the inappropriateness of disposition criteria while the child is still presumed to be innocent. Morris v. D'Amario, —— R.I. ——, 416 A.2d 137 (1980).

§ 32. The Petition

If the intake and screening procedures followed when a complaint is made about a child result in a decision that a formal court hearing is necessary, that decision is reflected in the filing of a petition. This is the document which sets forth, among other things, the specific charge that a de-

linquent act has been committed or that the child
is a person in need of supervision, unruly or otherwise subject to court authority for having
violated one of the laws peculiar to children, or
that the child is mistreated. The petition is, in
other words, the counterpart to an indictment in
criminal prosecutions and to a complaint in civil
litigation. The juvenile court statutes are generally fairly specific concerning the requirements
of petitions and, because this is the document
which serves to notify the child or parent of the
claims made about his misconduct, courts have
found that constitutional provisions must be satisfied as well.

The petition itself does not cause or authorize
any change in the child's custody—it is not the
equivalent of an arrest warrant. Therefore,
there is no constitutional need for a judicial probable cause finding to precede the petition. In re
D.M.D., 54 Wis. 313, 195 N.W.2d 594 (1972).
The legislation usually does, however, impose limitations on who may sign the petition. The traditional belief that juvenile court proceedings are
a means for looking after the welfare and needs
of children is reflected in provisions such as those
in California which authorize only a probation officer to sign and file the petition. Cal.Welf. &
Inst.Code § 650. The tradition is firmly rejected by the Model Act, § 6(b) which conceives
of probation as but one part—the child-assisting

part—of the court process, and inveighs against mingling this function with the prosecutorial function by providing that "A probation officer does not have the powers of a law enforcement officer nor may he sign a petition under this (act) with respect to a person who is not on probation or otherwise under his supervision." Some statutes are far more permissive than California, such as the Illinois Juvenile Court Act § 704–1(1) which permits any adult to sign the petition against the child. Equally as restrictive as the California law, but evincing an entirely different philosophy, is the Texas Family Code § 53.04(a) which restricts the making of the petition to but one official, this time naming the prosecuting attorney. The new Florida statute similarly vests petitioning authority in the prosecutor. Fla. Stat.Ann. § 39.04(c). Consistently with its restriction on the petitioning function of probation officers, the Model Act also gives paramount importance to the prosecutor by making a distinction between who may sign a petition ("any person who has knowledge of the facts and believes that they are true" § 14(a)) and authority to file it. The latter power is vested in the prosecutor who must countersign as well as file the petition § 13(b). If the prosecutor decides *not* to file the petition, his decision in the matter is declared, moreover, to be final. § 13(a).

The law sometimes draws a distinction between beliefs that are based on personal knowledge and those that are acquired through information conveyed by others. The issue arises concerning the verification that must be made by the person signing the petition. The Illinois act, for example, provides that "The petition shall be verified but the statements made (sic) be made upon information and belief," Ill.Juv.Ct.Act § 704–1 (2), meaning that personal knowledge is not required. A New York Family Court, on the other hand, has required personal knowledge on the part of the petitioner, In re Howe, 70 Misc.2d 144, 332 N.Y.S.2d 529 (1972). The former, however, is far the more common requirement. The Texas statute has it both ways in providing that the prosecutor may make a petition either upon his own knowledge or upon information and belief. Tex.Fam.Code § 53.04(a).

Courts have sometimes been faced with the question of whether the petition must conform, in its specificity and detail, to the pleadings in criminal cases or whether the conception of juvenile justice precluding punishment and prosecution leads to the less stringent requirements of civil pleadings. When delinquency is alleged on the basis of the child having violated a criminal law, courts have declared that constitutional due process of law requires the same particularity and specificity as is needed in criminal cases. In re

D.S.H., 549 P.2d 826 (Okl.Cr.1976); In re Dennis, 291 So.2d 731 (Miss.1974). Thus, a petition is defective if it charges the child with attempting to pass a bad check, without indicating in what way the check was "bad," In re Carson, 10 Ill.App.3d 387, 294 N.E.2d 75 (1973); a charge of "auto theft on two separate occasions" is not sufficiently detailed, Berkley v. S., 473 S.W.2d 346 (Tex.Civ.App.1971); allegations of staying out all night without consent and having unlawful sexual intercourse similarly fails to charge specific criminal conduct, Sorrels v. Steele, 506 P.2d 942 (Okl.Cr.1973).

Statutes and court rules may require that the petition include a citation to the particular penal law which the child is alleged to have violated. Tex.Fam.Code § 53.04(d)(1); Md. Rules of Procedure, Rule 903(a)(2)(d). Courts have found petitions to be fatally defective if this requirement is omitted from the petition, In re Garcia, 325 So.2d 364 (La.App.1976), although if the factual allegations are sufficiently specific, a citation to the wrong statute is not grounds for invalidating a delinquency finding. P. v. Longley, 16 Ill.App.3d 405, 306 N.E.2d 527 (1973).

The need to make the charges in the petition specific and concise creates the risk that the proof adduced at the hearing may not conform exactly to the statements in the petition. In such a case, the child cannot be found delinquent by virtue of proof that he committed a crime which is not the crime that was charged against him. D.P. v. S., 129 Ga.App. 680, 200 S.E.2d 499 (1973); (burglary charged, receiving stolen property proved); In re Anthony F., 68 Misc.2d 718, 328 N.Y.S.2d 99 (1972) (theft charged, possession of stolen property proved). If, however, the crime proved is an offense included within the crime charged in the petition, that is, if proof of the latter would necessarily include proof of the former, then the variance between proof and charge is not significant. In re Whittenburg, 16 Ill.App.3d 224, 305 N.E.2d 363 (1973) (aggravated battery charged, simple battery proved); In re Maricopa County, Juvenile Action No. J–75755, 111 Ariz. 103, 523 P.2d 1304 (1974) (criminal trespass not a lesser included offense in charge of burglary).

One common way to deal with the problem of a variance between the facts that are pleaded and those that are proved is to change, or amend, the pleading—here the petition. In civil litigation there is more latitude for making these amendments, as well as amendments to supply missing allegations, than there is in the criminal process, with some states holding to a strict rule that no amendments are permissible in criminal cases. The position taken by courts that have considered the issue, however, is to permit amendments to the petition, provided that the child is not surprised by the amendment and, therefore, handicapped in making his defense to the new material. Carrillo v. S., 480 S.W.2d 612 (Tex.1972).

§ 33. The Plea

In juvenile court proceedings against children there appear to be only two affirmative responses that can be made to the charges—to admit them or to deny them. There does not seem to be any basis for admitting a third plea of *nolo contendere* as is sometimes entered in adult criminal prosecutions. Sometimes, in order to support the assertion that delinquency proceedings are different from criminal prosecutions, it is said that the child admits or denies the petition, rather than pleads guilty or not guilty; the Model Act has it both ways, speaking in section 32(c) of a "valid admission" and in section 27 of a "plea of guilty." The Texas statute may be taken as describing the common practice: "An oral or written answer to the petition may be made at or before the commencement of the hearing. If there is no answer, a general denial of the alleged conduct is assumed." Tex.Fam.Code § 53.04(e).

In the great majority of cases, children admit or plead guilty. It is rare, however, for there to be any guidance given to juvenile court judges as to the formalities which must be followed in order for the child's admission or plea to be accepted. An exception is Rule 907(b) of the Maryland

Rules of Procedure which, among other things, admonishes the judge not to encourage or discourage the child in this regard. The need for formality arises from the fact that the plea constitutes a waiver of very important rights, such as to confront and cross examine accusers, to exercise the privilege against self-incrimination, to require proof against him beyond a reasonable doubt and to present evidence in his own behalf. These rights cannot be waived by a child unless he has first been afforded the right to counsel with whom he can confer about what plea to enter. If the right to counsel, therefore, has been *ineffectively* waived, the guilty plea entered by the uncounseled child is invalid. In re Appeal No. 544, 25 Md.App. 26, 332 A.2d 680 (1975); In re Robin J., 47 A.D.2d 818, 366 N.Y.S.2d 127 (1975).

Some courts have become strict about assuring that the child's plea is made intelligently and knowingly. The Supreme Court of Appeals of West Virginia, for example, requires that the juvenile court judge first explain the nature of the charges, lesser included offenses, possible defenses and other statutory and constitutional rights, including the right to counsel which may be waived only with the advice of counsel. S. ex rel. J.M. v. Taylor, —— W.Va. ——, 276 S.E. 2d 199 (1981). See also In the Matter of John R., 71 A.D.2d 896, 419 N.Y.S.2d 625 (1979).

Even if the child is represented by counsel, the child himself must inform the judge that he desires to admit the charges; a plea entered by the attorney is insufficient. In re M.G.S., 267 Cal. App.2d 329, 72 Cal.Rptr. 808 (1968). In addition, the record of the proceedings must reflect the participation of the child himself in this process of pleading and show that he was informed of his rights by the judge, that he understood them, and that he affirmatively chose to waive them. In re Michael M., 11 Cal.App.3d 297, 89 Cal.Rptr. 718 (1970), following strictures of the Supreme Court decision in an adult criminal case, Boykin v. Alabama, 395 U.S. 238, 89 S.Ct. 1709 (1969). It has been indicated that the juvenile court judge must inquire of the child's parents, as well as the child to insure that "the waiver is voluntarily, knowingly, and intelligently given." Bridges v. S., 260 Ind. 651, 299 N.E.2d 616 (1973), In re James K., 47 A.D.2d 946, 367 N.Y.S.2d 312 (1975). A record that is silent on these matters demonstrates an invalid guilty plea. S. v. Welch, 12 Or.App. 400, 507 P.2d 401 (1973).

The consequences of a guilty plea must also be explained to the child so that he understands them. It has been held not sufficient to meet this requirement that the judge tell the child that if he admits the charges made against him that he might be committed to the juvenile corrections authority; the child must be told how many years, or until he reaches what age, the commitment may last. In re Chatman, 36 Ill.App.3d 227, 343 N.E.2d 569 (1976). The pleading rules relating to pleas in delinquency cases have been applied in "person in need of supervision" circumstances as well. In re Theodore F., 47 A.D.2d 945, 367 N.Y.S.2d 103 (1975).

§ 34. The Right to Counsel

Few of the rights granted children in the juvenile justice system would have much real meaning without an attorney to assert them, or to advise the child when it is in his best interests to waive them. The role of defense counsel is not, however, an easy one. Since most of the children who come through the system are indigent, the task of providing legal representation falls to publicly paid counsel. When, as is most often the case, the public defender is assigned this responsibility the vigor of the advocacy on the child's behalf is subject to dilution from two directions. One is the high caseload usually carried by public defenders, meaning that each case can get only a minimal amount of preparation. Although it seems clear that if the court schedules the child's hearing in disregard of the attorney's need for preparation time, this will be deemed a reversible abuse of discretion, Doe v. S., 487 P.2d 47 (Alaska 1971), there seems to be no court decision which finds a denial of the right to effective assistance to counsel in the built-in dilution of counsel's effort which arises from there being too much work.

The second source of diluting the value of the child's representation arises from the pressures—seduction may be the more accurate word—which arises from the professed dedication of everyone in the courthouse to the welfare of the client. When the judge and all his staff, plus the prosecutor, claim to be acting in the best interests of the child, the ability to oppose them by demanding respect for legal and sometimes highly technical rights, can be severely undermined. Somewhat the same inhibition concerning the invocation of procedural justice on behalf of children arises from internal sources as well, in the form of defense counsel's feelings (which he shares with almost everyone else) that there is something very wrong with a child learning that he can "manipulate" the law so as to get away with breaking it.

One way of meeting at least the problems which arise from permanent or semi-permanent assignment of public defenders to juvenile courts might be to use private attorneys on an assignment basis, with compensation for them coming from public funds. This is sometimes done in adult criminal cases, and where this is so it has been held that the court can provide the same compensation for an assigned private attorney in the juvenile court. Alexander v. Deddens, 106 Ariz. 172, 472 P.2d 41 (1971) (juvenile court can order county treasurer to pay counsel). However, if the state's scheme is that private attorneys are authorized only if the public defender refuses to accept a particular case, then there is no authority to compensate assigned counsel if there has been no such refusal. In re JGL, 43 Cal.App.3d 447, 117 Cal.Rptr. 799 (1974).

The basis of the constitutional right to counsel is In re Gault, 387 U.S. 1, 87 S.Ct. 1428 (1967) in which the Supreme Court declared that in the adjudicative stage of juvenile court proceedings which can result in the child being incarcerated in a state training school, the due process rules of the Fourteenth Amendment require that he be afforded the right to counsel. The Court attempted to confine its holdings to this, expressly professing to provide no rules for pre-adjudicative stages or dispositional matters. But, as so often happens, this attempt has come to naught and both legislatures and other courts have expanded the right to counsel beyond the narrow confines of the *Gault* language.

The Model Act § 25 makes representation by counsel mandatory.

It provides:

> (a) In delinquency cases, a child and his parents, guardian, or custodian shall be

> advised by the court or its representa-
> tive that the child shall be represented
> by counsel at all stages of the proceed-
> ings. If counsel is not retained for the
> child, or if it does not appear that coun-
> sel will be retained, counsel shall be ap-
> pointed for the child.

Despite *Gault* and the enthusiasm for counsel represented by the Model Act, there can still be found courts in which counsel is not appointed where the law clearly requires it, as was done in the juvenile court whose actions were reversed in In re Edwards, 298 So.2d 703 (Miss.1974). On the whole, however, it can fairly be said that counsel is provided children in virtually every phase of the juvenile justice process. Counsel is commonly offered during police interrogations as part of the *Miranda* rights granted children. At a preliminary hearing where there are adversary proceedings such as the presentation of the state's case through individual witnesses, counsel is provided. When the juvenile court is conduct-ing a hearing to determine if it should waive its jurisdiction and transfer the child for criminal prosecution, there is a right to counsel. In dis-position hearings and in appeals the child is usually afforded the right to counsel; in the lat-ter situation if there is a right to appeal, the right to counsel is of constitutional dimensions. Douglas v. California, 372 U.S. 353, 83 S.Ct. 814

(1963); Reed v. Duter, 416 F.2d 744 (7th Cir. 1969).

Unless there is a statute which so provides, juveniles are held not to have any greater right to counsel than adults in a similar predicament. Thus where the Supreme Court has decided that the right to counsel in probation revocation hearings is to be decided on a case-by-case basis, Gagnon v. Scarpelli, 411 U.S. 778, 93 S.Ct. 1756 (1973), it has been held that the child's right to counsel at such hearings is also to be determined on a case-by-case basis. Naves v. S., 91 Nev. 106, 531 P.2d 1360 (1975). Similarly, when an adult has no right to counsel at a probable cause hearing held following his warrantless arrest, Gerstein v. Pugh, 420 U.S. 103, 95 S.Ct. 854 (1975), a juvenile who is entitled to a probable cause hearing on the same Fourth Amendment grounds is no more entitled to counsel at the hearing. Moss v. Weaver, 525 F.2d 1258 (5th Cir. 1976). So too when the offense carries no possibility of a deprivation of liberty—there is no right to counsel. S. ex rel. Maier v. City Court, —— Mont. ——, 662 P.2d 276 (1982).

There are, of course, jurisdictional powers possessed by the juvenile court which have no adult counterpart. In regard to status offenses (see § 12) the courts are divided on whether there is a right to counsel. In re Spalding, 273 Md. 690, 332 A.2d 246 (1975) (no); S. ex rel. Wilson v.

Bambrick, 156 W.Va. 703, 195 S.E.2d 721 (1973) (yes). Statutes, however, are more agreed in providing a right to counsel in such cases.

The jurisdiction courts exercise in neglect cases also involves the right to counsel. The trend of judicial decision is in favor of providing parents with counsel in such cases, as for example in In re Myricks, 85 Wn.2d 252, 533 P.2d 841 (1975). There do not appear to be any reported cases dealing with the right of the child in neglect proceedings to be represented by counsel. The Model Act § 25(b) requires counsel "where there is an adverse interest between parent and child, or counsel is otherwise required in the interests of justice." The Abuse and Neglect Standards argue that the right to counsel enunciated in *Gault* "applies readily" to neglect cases. The Standards also report that the statutes of 35 states guarantee the right to counsel for children subject to neglect proceedings.

In some instances, counsel can waive rights on behalf of children, such as the right to object to the introduction of hearsay evidence. D.A.B. v. S., 329 So.2d 40 (Fla.App.1976) (advised judge to read psychiatric report and "take it for its weight"); or he can bind the child with stipulations and judicial admissions. Reasoner v. S., 463 S.W.2d 55 (Tex.Civ.App.1971) (counsel joined prosecutor in offering transcripts of prior hearings and dispositions). Where the right to demand a trial is at stake, however, it is held that the child himself must be personally involved and the attorney cannot plead guilty for him. See § 33. The same is true concerning the attorney's power to give up the right to a waiver hearing. Haziel v. U. S., 404 F.2d 1275 (D.C.App.1968).

Counsel for children in juvenile court do not function under any formal handicap they do not encounter in criminal proceedings. They have the right, for example, to make closing arguments before the judge reaches a decision. In re A.C., 134 Vt. 284, 357 A.2d 536 (1976); In re William F., 11 Cal.3d 249, 113 Cal.Rptr. 170, 520 P.2d 986 (1974). Because what to do with the child is of such importance in juvenile courts, counsel who fails to explore alternative courses of action to present to the court may find himself criticised for a "notable lack of zeal." Geboy v. Gray, 471 F.2d 575 (7th Cir. 1973).

Although the right to counsel is thus widespread, it is not always exercised and courts have often dealt with the question of what is required in order for there to be a valid waiver of the right. Under some statutory schemes the answer is simple. The Texas Family Code § 51.09, for example, declares that *no* statutory or constitutional rights may be waived without the written approval of the child's counsel, and this includes the right to an attorney. In re F.G., 511 S.W.2d 370 (Tex.Civ.App.1974). The New York Family

Court Act § 249–a permits a waiver of counsel only after counsel has been appointed. This same rule has been judicially imposed. See S. ex rel. J.M. v. Taylor, —— W.Va. ——, 276 S.E.2d 199 (1981). But where waivers are permitted by the child, the general rule is that they must be voluntary and that this, in turn, is to be determined by reference to the "totality of the circumstances." If there is a waiver, it must affirmatively appear on the record and will not be presumed to have taken place by an appellate court when the record is silent on the point. Rodriguez v. S., 491 S.W.2d 760 (Tex.Civ.App.1973). The right to counsel must be explained by the judge himself, Gonsalves v. Devine, 110 R.I. 515, 294 A.2d 206 (1972), and where there is a parental right to counsel in delinquency proceedings the judge must separately explain this right to the parent. In re Stanley, 17 N.C.App. 370, 194 S.E. 2d 219 (1973).

§ 35. Discovery

Implied in the tradition that juvenile court proceedings are not adversarial is the ethic that all parties cooperate by pooling their information and wisdom in determining what is best for the child. The demise of that tradition has brought juvenile justice to a confrontation with the problems of discovery—the rules defining the circumstances when one partisan is obliged to provide the other with information which may defeat the claims advocated by the providing party. The existence of the privilege against self-incrimination and the lawyer-client privilege severely restrict the ability of the state to obtain information to support its case from the defense and the problems of information exchange are, therefore, almost entirely a matter of what the child can force the state to disclose.

The death knell to the nonadversary tradition was sounded by the Supreme Court in 1966 in the context of a ruling on defense counsel's access to court records concerning the child. In Kent v. U. S., 383 U.S. 541, 563, 86 S.Ct. 1045, 1058 (1966) Justice Fortas wrote:

> We do not agree with the Court of Appeals' statement, attempting to justify denial of access to these records, that counsel's role is limited to presenting "to the court anything on behalf of the child which might help the court in arriving at a decision; it is not to denigrate the staff's submissions and recommendations." On the contrary, if the staff's submissions include materials which are susceptible to challenge or impeachment, it is precisely the role of counsel to "denigrate" such matter. There is no irrebuttable presumption of accuracy attached to staff reports.

This ruling is now commonly reflected in juvenile court acts which give the child the right to inspect court records that are relevant to his case. Ill.Juv.Ct.Act § 701–20(1); Tex.Fam.Code § 51.14(a)(2). Some statutes place the matter of disclosure of reports about the child in the discretion of the judge. N.Y.Fam.Ct.Act § 746(b). Closely related provisions of the statutes grant similar access right to records and files of law enforcement agencies which concern the child. Tex.Fam.Code § 51.14(d)(2). Access to material relied on by the juvenile court judge has also been seen as required by the constitutional right to the *effective* assistance of counsel. Baldwin v. Lewis, 300 F.Supp. 1220 (E.D.Wis.1969), reversed for failure to exhaust state remedies, 442 F.2d 29 (7th Cir. 1971).

Discovery issues go well beyond access to formally kept records. In an effort to have the results of civil litigation reflect the full facts of the controversy, state law often provides each side to the litigation broad opportunity to discover what the other side knows of the case, what witnesses it intends to call, what those witnesses are prepared to say, etc. In criminal prosecutions, on the other hand, the defendant's opportunity to obtain similar information is severely restricted, largely on the belief that " 'civil practice discovery in criminal cases would be detrimental to the administration of justice' because broadened discovery would lead to harassment and intimidation of witnesses, suppression of evidence and in [sic] increase in perjury, ..." Hanrahan v. Felt, 48 Ill.2d 171, 172–173, 269 N.E.2d 1, 2 (1971). Now that juvenile justice is suspended somewhere between civil and criminal jurisprudence, which rules of discovery are applicable in juvenile courts?

The Supreme Court of California has declared that juvenile court judges have the same degree of discretion in this regard as they have in an ordinary criminal case. In re Joe Z., 3 Cal.3d 797, 91 Cal.Rptr. 594, 478 P.2d 26 (1970). The court in Illinois, on the other hand, went further, finding first "that although a delinquency proceeding is civil in nature, it is sufficiently distinct from other civil actions to make inappropriate the automatic application of discovery provisions applicable to civil cases," but concluding that the judge could go beyond what was allowable in criminal cases and, in his discretion apply the civil discovery rules. Hanrahan, supra. When, however, the discovery is such as would ordinarily be raised in a criminal case, such as a request for a copy of the statement a victim gave to the police, the juvenile must comply with requirements in criminal cases. In re Forrest, 12 Ill.App.3d 250, 298 N.E.2d 197 (1973) (proper foundation must be laid by requesting an *in camera* inspection of police files).

Where it is not his own juvenile records which the child seeks, but those of someone else which he would like to use to impeach the credibility of that person as a witness against him, statutory provisions making such records confidential and disclosable only under particular circumstances constitute no bar to using the records for impeachment. The Supreme Court has held that the constitutional right to confront and cross-examine witnesses is to be given priority over state policies of confidentiality. Davis v. Alaska, 415 U.S. 308, 94 S.Ct. 1105 (1974). The juvenile court record may be sought, for example, in order to show that the witness was treated leniently in order to induce him to testify against the present accused. P. v. Montgomery, 19 Ill.App.3d 206, 311 N.E.2d 361 (1974).

CHAPTER V

FACT–FINDING HEARINGS

§ 36. In General

The importance of fact-finding hearings in juvenile court is a relatively recent phenomenon. There is today a strong emphasis on the disposition decision as being the significant and unique feature of the court and it was not too many years ago when that emphasis all but swallowed the fact-finding phase of the proceedings so that it was not uncommon for the case to go directly to the question of what should be done with the child before the court, with little attention to the matter of whether the facts alleged against him were true which gave the court authority to make any decision concerning him.

Since *Gault* in 1967, the law has sought sharply to reverse this tradition and to elevate the fact-finding function of the juvenile court to the status of an adversary hearing which differs from a criminal trial only in the absence of a jury from the courtroom. The Supreme Court recently has concluded on this point that "in terms of potential consequences, there is little to distinguish an adjudicatory hearing such as was held in this case from a traditional criminal prosecution." Breed

v. Jones, 421 U.S. 519, 95 S.Ct. 1779 (1975). Accordingly, one finds provisions such as in the Illinois Juvenile Court Act § 704–6 that "The standard of proof and the rules of evidence in the nature of criminal proceedings in this State are applicable to [delinquency cases]," and rulings such as that it is improper to hold a juvenile court hearing with the child in shackles pursuant to the same policies which govern imposition of similar restraints on an adult accused. In re Staley, 40 Ill.App.3d 528, 352 N.E.2d 3 (1976), and that all affirmative defenses available to an adult may be asserted in the juvenile court hearing. In re L.J., 26 Or.App. 461, 552 P.2d 1322 (1976) (insanity).

Despite this clear evolution towards a more formalized and criminalized fact-finding hearing in delinquency cases there remains unanswered the significant question concerning whether there is any constitutional option to reverse the trend and to provide for an informality and intimacy which many authorities consider valuable in dealing with children. The answer would appear to depend on a state's willingness to recognize that for a great many children—the young, minor offenders—a significant deprivation of liberty is not called for. That is, there is much language in *Gault* and its progeny to suggest that the need for criminal formalities in fact-finding hearings depends on the amount of power the state pro-

poses to exercise over the accused child. An
Oregon court has recently relied on this sort of
analysis in determining which formalities were
applicable in a case where the child could not be
committed to an institution for delinquents.

> Because the November hearing and result-
> ing judgment did not place K. in jeopardy of
> being committed to an institution with a
> " '. . . regimented routine and institu-
> tional hours . . .' [where] [i]nstead
> of mother and father and sisters and broth-
> ers and friends and classmates, his world
> [would be] peopled by guards, custodians,
> state employees, and 'delinquents' . . ."
> his reliance upon *In re Gault* and *In re
> Winship* . . . in his appeal from that
> judgment as a measure of the "rights" to
> which he was entitled is misplaced . . . . .
> In light of the limits placed upon the court's
> dispositional authority by virtue of K.'s age
> at the time of the initial hearing, we are
> satisfied that the procedures employed, and
> the rights accorded, adequately met all ap-
> plicable requirements of "due process and
> fair treatment." In re K., 26 Or.App. 451,
> 457–459, 554 P.2d 180, 184 (1976).

The most significant sort of ruling on this issue
is that, absent the possibility of a loss of liberty,
there is not a right to counsel. S. ex rel. Maier
v. City Court, —— Mont. ——, 662 P.2d 276 (1982).

If disposition authority were to be sufficiently limited by legislation then it may not be necessary or wise to continue using courts to administer a purposefully formal system for minor offenders and consideration could be given to other forms. See, for example, Fox, *Juvenile Justice Reform: Innovations in Scotland,* 12 Amer.Crim.L.Rev. 61 (1974). In Massachusetts there already is an administratively established system of Children's Hearing patterned on the Scottish system and Florida's community arbitration program, created by Fla.Stat.Ann. § 39.33 *et seq.* also bears striking resemblance to the Scottish arrangements. The aims of this latter program summarize most of the reasons for taking advantage of the views expressed in *In re K.* and *State ex rel. Maier* supra. "The purpose of this act is to provide a system by which children who commit certain minor offenses may be dealt with in a speedy and informal manner at the community or neighborhood level, in an attempt to reduce the ever-increasing instances of juvenile crime and permit the judicial system to deal effectively with cases which are of a more serious nature." Fla.Stat.Ann. § 39.33. This omits mention of the communication and participation by children and families possible under such a system. See the thorough evaluation of the Scottish Children's Hearings reported in Martin, Fox & Murray, Children Out of Court (1981). This would require, however, a legislative judgment that it is not an important function of the juvenile justice system to engage in extensive diagnosis and therapy for every child technically within its reach and recognition that many children who commit offenses can wisely be dealt with with no more power than is called for by the minor nature of their offending.

§ 37. An Impartial Judge

Since the Supreme Court has decided that the national constitution does not require a trial by jury in juvenile courts, McKeiver v. Pennsylvania, 403 U.S. 528, 91 S.Ct. 1976 (1971), it has become increasingly the province of the juvenile court judge to insure a fair trial and an impartial determination of facts.   In some important respects, these duties preclude the traditional role for the juvenile court judge whereby he became apprised in some informal and *ex parte* manner of the facts of a case, discussed the impressions he thereby gained directly with the child and then reached a decision about what is in the best interests of the child.   The evolution of the juvenile court has, by the 1980's, precluded the judge from such a paternal role and structured his function on the model of a criminal court judge trying a case in which a jury trial has been waived.   Thus, on the basis of precedents drawn mostly from criminal jurisprudence, it has been determined that even in neglect and dependency cases the judge must preserve the appearance of impartiality by not assuming a prosecutorial role in presenting the case seeking to establish the liability of the parents to the loss of their child, R. v. Superior Court, 19 Cal.App.3d 895, 97 Cal. Rptr. 158 (1971). As is true in criminal trials, however, the juvenile court judge may ask witnesses questions designed to clarify their evidence without compromising his impartiality. In re Potts, 14 N.C.App. 387, 188 S.E.2d 643 (1972). In one situation, however, there appears to be a combination of prosecutorial and judicial functions which would not likely be permitted in the criminal process. This arises in jurisdictions that have probation officers represent the interests of the state in presenting the evidence against a child as would a lawyer-prosecutor, and where, importantly, the judge is responsible for the appointment and supervision of the probation staff. In effect, therefore, one side of the case is presented to the judge by officials for whom that judge is responsible. The question of whether such a relationship is permissible was presented to the Supreme Court of Arizona which, after determining in rather wooden fashion that these circumstances did not fall within any of the traditional categories of cases where the judge had been found to be a partial fact-finder, held that the Arizona arrangements were permissible. In re Appeal in Pima County Anonymous, Juvenile Action No. J 24818–2, 110 Ariz. 98, 515 P.2d 600 (1973), certiorari denied 417 U.S. 939, 94 S.Ct. 3063 (1974). Mr. Justice Douglas dissented from the denial of certiorari, noting that when the juvenile was refused a jury trial "he was not even afforded the alternative available to an adult charged with the same offenses; trial before a judge not involved in the prosecutorial process." 417 U.S. at 941, 94 S.Ct. at 3064.

Judicial as well as prosecutorial functions may jeopardize the ability of a judge to preside at a juvenile court fact-finding hearing. Where, for example, he is made responsible for determining whether a petition should be filed against a child, one Rhode Island family court judge determined that due process considerations do not permit him to sit at the hearing of that case. In re Reis, R.I. Fam.Ct., B.N.A., 7 Cr.L. 2151 (1970) This is, however, the practice followed in Rhode Island. Statutes may also limit the propriety of the same judge handling several stages of the judicial process, as in the District of Columbia where presiding at a detention hearing precludes sitting at the adjudicatory hearing; hearing pre-trial motions to suppress, however, is outside the statutory limits and not otherwise prohibited. In re M.D.J., 346 A.2d 733 (D.C.App.1975). Restrictions such as these conflict sharply with a reform of the judicial process, designed to introduce more efficiency, which would have all stages of a case controlled by a single judge—often known as "one case, one judge." Support for this reform might lead a juvenile court judge to restrict the grounds for disqualification to cases of personal bias. In re Dianna A., 65 Misc.2d 1034, 319 N.Y.S.2d 691 (1971).

§ 38. Trial by Jury

In 1971 the Supreme Court added to its line of juvenile justice opinions by deciding that the due process clause of the Fourteenth Amendment does not require that children be accorded a jury trial in juvenile court, McKeiver v. Pennsylvania, 403 U.S. 528, 91 S.Ct. 1976 (1971). The Court noted that the great majority of states had, by statute, reached the same conclusion; these have been upheld by state courts, Robinson v. S., 123 Ga.App. 243, 180 S.E.2d 258 (1971). Since *McKeiver*, state courts have continued to deny a jury trial right, finding that it is not required by state constitutional provisions, In re Fisher, 468 S.W.2d 198 (Mo.1971); In re McCloud, 110 R.I. 431, 293 A.2d 512 (1972) (reversing Family Court decision to grant a jury trial). This view is not, however, universally held; R.L.R. v. S., 487 P.2d 27 (Alaska 1971) and some recent juvenile court statutes provide for jury trials, Tex.Fam.Code § 54.03(c). The Model Act takes the majority view and recommends against hearings before a jury, § 29(a).

In the course of his opinion for the Court in *McKeiver* Justice Blackmun stated, "There is, of course, nothing to prevent a juvenile court judge, in a particular case where he feels the need, or when the need is demonstrated, from using an advisory jury."   403 U.S. at 548, 91 S.Ct. at 1987–1988.   When a juvenile court judge in California tried this recently, however, he was first reversed by an appellate court decision to the effect that there is no such power to impanel an advisory jury, but then affirmed by the state's Supreme Court.   P. v. Superior Court, 15 Cal.3d 271, 124 Cal.Rptr. 47, 539 P.2d 807 (1975).   The California court first noted that Justice Blackmun's remark means that there is nothing in the *federal* constitution to prevent use of an advisory jury.   It then went on to hold that the California juvenile court statute granted the judge discretionary authority to impanel the advisory jury and that the discretion had not been abused in this case.   In reaching the latter conclusion, the California Supreme Court relied heavily on the facts in the record which indicated that the hearing was likely to be complicated, lengthy, involve many (up to 40) witnesses, and includes such serious and contested charges as murder and sexual abuse of a young child.   The loss of informality, in this context, was within the control of the juvenile court judge. The court emphasized that its decision was not to be read as authorizing the use of advisory juries in all delinquency hearings: "In the normal case, where the disputed jurisdictional issues are few and can be resolved with relative ease, the balance may continue to be struck in favor of an informal proceeding without the assistance of a jury. Only in the exceptional case, where the benefits to be derived from the use of an advisory jury far outweigh any benefits of informality and confidentiality which can be achieved in the circumstances, will sound judicial discretion choose to empanel an advisory jury to aid the court." 124 Cal.Rptr. at 56, 539 P.2d at 816. A contrary result has been reached in Illinois. P. ex rel. Carey v. White, 65 Ill.2d 193, 2 Ill.Dec. 345, 357 N.E.2d 512 (1976).

Federal courts have relied on the Supreme Court's interpretation of the Fourteenth Amendment in *McKeiver* in deciding that the Sixth Amendment does not afford a right to jury trial under the federal Juvenile Delinquency Act, U. S. v. King, 482 F.2d 454 (6th Cir. 1973), certiorari denied 414 U.S. 1076, 94 S.Ct. 594. Nor is there a right to a jury in proceedings under the Interstate Compact on Juveniles, even where juvenile court hearings otherwise are before a jury, Haskins v. Carter, 506 P.2d 1391 (Okl.Cr.1973).

In addition to Due Process, the Equal Protection clause of the Fourteenth Amendment has sometimes been relied on in claiming the right to a jury trial. But courts have rejected an enforced equality between juvenile court proceedings and other civil proceedings such as involuntary civil commitment of mentally ill persons, In re Clarence B., 37 Cal.App.3d 676, 112 Cal.Rptr. 474 (1974). When, however, the child reaches adulthood while in the custody of juvenile corrections authorities and the latter petition the court to continue the custody on account of the dangerousness of the adult, the analogy to the other liberty-depriving civil proceedings in which there is a right to a jury, requires that the issue of extension of custody also be tried to a jury. In re Gary W., 5 Cal.3d 296, 96 Cal.Rptr. 1, 486 P.2d 1201 (1971). The heart of the distinction is that children do not have a right to a jury, but adults do.

§ 39. Public and Speedy Trials

The Sixth Amendment to the United States Constitution declares that: "In all criminal prosecutions, the accused shall enjoy the right to a speedy and public trial." Although the Supreme Court has held these provisions applicable to state courts, In re Oliver, 333 U.S. 257, 68 S.Ct. 499, (1948) (public trial); Klopfer v. North Carolina, 386 U.S. 213, 87 S.Ct. 988 (1967) (speedy trial), it has not dealt with their impact on juvenile court proceedings. Justice Brennan, however, concurred in one of the cases decided in McKeiver v. Pennsylvania, 403 U.S. 528, 91 S.Ct. 1976 (1971), holding there to be no federally protected right to a jury trial, on the ground that under state law there was no ban on admitting the public to juvenile court and that this public exposure adequately safeguarded the same interests as did the right to a jury. 403 U.S. at 554–5, 91 S.Ct. at 1990–1991. Some states may achieve this safeguarding by an opposite set of rights, as in Texas where the public may be banned, Tex.Fam.Code § 54.08, although the juvenile has the right to a jury trial under § 54.03(c).

The Supreme Court has decided, however, that the state may not impose a criminal penalty on a newspaper for publishing the name of a juvenile offender which it obtained lawfully. Smith v. Daily Mail Publishing Co., 443 U.S. 97, 99 S.Ct. 2667 (1980). This First Amendment rule has been applied to prevent contempt actions against radio and TV media as well. State ex rel. The Times and Democrat, 276 S.C. 26, 274 S.E.2d 910 (1981). Under a state constitutional guarantee it has been held that the press does have a right to attend juvenile court and presumably under *Smith* to publish what it observes. S. ex rel. Oregonian Publishing Co. v. Deiz, 289 Or. 277, 613 P.2d 23 (1980).

Under most juvenile court acts the issue of a public trial is either a matter for judicial discretion, as in Texas, or the general public may be flatly excluded, as in Maine, M.R.S.A. Tit. 15 § 2609. Some of the acts grant the news media the right to be present and the actual presence of reporters does not violate any right of the child. In re Jones, 46 Ill.2d 506, 263 N.E.2d 863 (1970). In view of the scarcity of treatment resources, the judge might use his discretion to admit the media in a particularly appropriate case in order to publicize the problem. In the Matter of L., 24 Or.App. 257, 546 P.2d 153 (1976), Oregon and a small minority of other states give the child and his parents a statutory right to demand a public trial. It is also only a small minority of courts which, like R.L.R. v. S., 487 P.2d 27 (Alaska 1971), have found the constitution to provide a similar right; most of the courts have ruled otherwise, relying heavily on the beneficial aspects of privacy to the child. Virgin Islands v. Brodhurst, 285 F.Supp. 831 (D.C.V.I. 1968).

Although the speedy trial injunction of the Sixth Amendment has been held applicable to juvenile courts, In the Interest of C.T.F., 316 N.W. 2d 865 (Iowa 1982); Piland v. Clark County Juvenile Court, 85 Nev. 489, 457 P.2d 523 (1969) control of the timing of steps in the prosecution of juveniles is increasingly becoming a statutory matter. In federal delinquency proceedings, for example, 18 U.S.C. 5036 requires that a child in detention must be brought to trial within 30 days of the time the detention commenced. In this context "detention" does not mean free on bail, even if restrictive conditions have been imposed on the bail release. U. S. v. Cuomo, 525 F.2d 1285 (5th Cir. 1976). Violation of the 30 day limit requires dismissal of the petition unless "extraordinary circumstances" are shown. Since this speedy trial rule applies only to juveniles who are held in detention for more than 30 days, it seems there is no limit, short of the Sixth Amendment, to how long trial may be delayed so long as the detention is interrupted by release at least every 29 days. Under other statutes, detention is irrelevant and the time period runs from various fixed times, such as the filing of the complaint with the intake officer, S. v. J.H., 295 So.2d 698 (Fla.App.1974). Where a juvenile court waives its jurisdiction in order that the child may be prosecuted as an adult, the time requirements start on the date of the waiver decision. Bergman v. Nelson, 241 N.W.2d 14 (Iowa 1976). No prejudice need be shown as a result of delay in violation of the statutory period, In re Doe, 88 N.M. 644, 545 P.2d 1022 (N.M.1976), and although the statutory right may be waived, an agreement to the state's request for a continuance does not constitute a waiver. U. S. v. Gonzalez-Gonzalez, 522 F.2d 1040 (9th Cir. 1975).

§ 40. Burden of Proof

When the delinquency charged against a child is the commission of a criminal act, the state must prove every element of the crime including the mental element, or *mens rea*, In re Unsworth, 276 So.2d 337 (La.App.1973) (knowledge that stolen goods received were stolen); Alexander v. S., 284 So.2d 478 (Fla.App.1973) (intent for assault). This requirement of proving every element persists even when the conduct that is proved is as probative of a "need for treatment" as would be the complete crime, In re Pereira, 111 R.I. 712, 306 A.2d 821 (1973) (delinquency finding reversed when based on a crime of throwing object at moving vehicle; state failed to show that police car at which child threw a rock was in motion).

As in a criminal trial, the burden of proof does not shift to the child during the juvenile court hearing, even when he claims, for example, that he acted in self-defense—the state must disprove the claim beyond a reasonable doubt, S. v. Jackson, 528 P.2d 145 (Utah 1974). Although it was traditional for juvenile courts to apply a less rigorous standard of proof to delinquency proceedings, in 1970 the Supreme Court ruled that the criminal conduct itself must be proved beyond a reasonable doubt, In re Winship, 397 U.S. 358, 90 S.Ct. 1068 (1970). This requirement is also fully retroactive, Ivan V. v. New York, 407 U.S. 203, 92 S.Ct. 1951 (1972). In requiring this standard of proof, the Court restricted its ruling to delinquency based on crime, saying ". . . we intimate no view concerning the constitutionality of the New York procedures governing children 'in need of supervision.' " 397 U.S. at 359, n. 1, 90 S.Ct. at 1069–1070, n. 1. Although some state courts have tried to avoid the question of whether this non-criminal conduct must be proved beyond a reasonable doubt, P–S–M v. S., 469 S.W.2d 13 (Tex.Civ.App.1971); S. v. Turner, 107 R.I 518, 268 A.2d 732 (1970), other tribunals have addressed the issue and come out both ways, In re William D., 36 A.D.2d 970, 321 N.Y.S.2d 510 (1971) (PINS jurisdiction must be proved beyond a reasonable doubt); In re Potter, 237 N.W.2d 461 (Iowa 1976) ("clear and convincing evidence" needed to prove conduct potentially injurious to the juvenile or others). The view that coercive intervention in a child's life requires the justification and care that are demanded in criminal prosecutions is reflected in recent statutes which require that the non-criminal conduct which gives the court jurisdiction be proved beyond a reasonable doubt. Tex.Fam.Code § 54.03(f); Fla.Stat. Ann. § 39.09(b)(1). The Texas statute is unusually explicit on this, declaring that as to conduct indicating a need for supervision, "The child is presumed to be innocent of the charges against him . . . ."

On the other hand, in neglect or dependency proceedings there is a strong consensus that the proof need not be so strong as to preclude every reasonable doubt, In re Gonzalez, 51 A.D.2d 527, 379 N.Y.S.2d 87 (1976) (strong and convincing proof); In re Maricopa County Juvenile Action No. J–74449A, 20 Ariz.App. 249, 511 P.2d 693 (1973). When a child who has already been found subject to the authority of the court and placed on probation is later charged with a violation of the probation, judicial opinion is divided on the question of whether the proof at this second hearing to modify the probation order must exclude every reasonable doubt, as has been determined to be the case, for example, in California, In re Arthur N., 16 Cal.3d 226, 127 Cal. Rptr. 641, 545 P.2d 1345 (1976), or may simply be a preponderance of the evidence, as in Arizona, In re Maricopa County, Juvenile Action No. J–72918–S, 111 Ariz.App. 135, 524 P.2d 1310 (1974). The Model Act, § 39(c) recommends a standard of "clear and convincing evidence," in the context of juvenile court statutes which exhibit a variety of judgments on the question, as in the N.Y.Fam.Ct.Act § 779 (competent proof); Tex.Fam.Code § 54.05(f); Fla.Stat.Ann. § 39.11 (3)(a) (no mention of standard of proof). In proceedings to terminate parental rights the Supreme Court has mandated a standard of clear and convincing evidence. Santosky v. Kramer, 455 U.S. 745, 102 S.Ct. 1388 (1982).

§ 41. Recording the Proceedings

The importance of recording what goes on in juvenile court hearings arises when the appellate process is invoked and a transcript of the hearing is necessary as part of the record presented to a higher court. In the absence of an adequate record, especially one that does not comply with statutory requirements for including a transcript of the testimony, appeals courts have remanded juvenile cases for new hearings. In re Collins, 288 So.2d 918 (La.App.1973). Statutory requirements for recording are becoming increasingly common. The Texas Family Code § 54.09, for example, requires that, "all judicial proceedings under this chapter except detention hearings shall be recorded by stenographic notes or by electronic, mechanical, or other appropriate means. Upon request of any party, a detention hearing shall be recorded." It was the view of the Supreme Court in *Gault*, 387 U.S. 1, 59 n. 2, 87 S.Ct. 1428, 1460 n. 2, that juvenile court recording helps to create "a healthy atmosphere of accountability."

Some courts have found a constitutional requirement that a recording be made. In re Aaron, 266 So.2d 726 (La.App.1972) reasoned that although an appeal is not constitutionally required, if it is accorded adult criminals, then it must be extended to juveniles; the same constitutional compulsion which thereupon provides an indigent appellant the right to a transcript for the appeal "requires that the incidents of an effective appeal, including a record from which a transcript can be drawn, be made available to juvenile defendants." at 729. An Ohio court, on the other hand, found a constitutional right to have the proceedings recorded as "a necessary incident to the requirement of counsel because accountability is completely lost in the absence of either." S. v. Ross, 23 Ohio App.2d 215, 262 N.E.2d 427 (1970). In some states a refusal of the juvenile court judge to have the hearing recorded will not be reversed on appeal unless the juvenile can show that he was prejudiced by the refusal. In re Edwards, 18 N.C.App. 469, 197 S.E.2d 87 (1973).

§ 42. Rules of Evidence: In General

Rules of evidence, designed to promote a fair, rational and expeditious means for proving facts, are applied in juvenile courts, although there are a number of particular evidence rules which may be deemed inappropriate for some juvenile court proceedings. For example, in status offense cases it has been held that in light of the consequences for the child being substantially less serious than they are in delinquency prosecutions, the privilege against self-incrimination does not apply. In re Carter, 20 Md.App. 633, 318 A.2d 269 (1974). In all juvenile court cases, however, the fundamental rule that to be admissible the evidence must be relevant is enforced. In re McMaster, 165 Mont. 450, 529 P.2d 1391 (1974). When a jury makes the delinquency determination it is also important that the evidence not be unduly prejudicial to the child. In re J.D., 513 P.2d 654 (Alaska 1973).

Juvenile court acts may invoke the whole of the body of evidence law in a variety of ways. The Model Act, § 32(c), for example, requires that the delinquency finding be based either on a valid admission or upon "competent, material, and relevant evidence." The Texas Family Code § 54.03(d), on the other hand, provides that "Only material, relevant, and competent evidence in accordance with the requirements for the trial of civil cases may be considered in the adjudication hearing." Whether it is the civil or the criminal rules which apply may be important in determining whether the juvenile court is required to observe rules that are peculiar to criminal cases, such as that the testimony of the victim of a sex offense must be corroborated, In re Robert M., 37 A.D.2d 527, 322 N.Y.S.2d 62 (1971), or that a guilty verdict may not be based entirely on the unsworn testimony of a child under 12, In re Wade H., 41 A.D.2d 817, 342 N.Y.S.

2d 696 (1973), or on an uncorroborated confession of the accused. In re W.J., 116 N.J.Super. 462, 282 A.2d 770 (1971). The corroboration of a child's confession appears not to be constitutionally required since in *Gault* the Supreme Court required "sworn testimony subjected to the opportunity for cross-examination in accordance with constitutional principles" when there is "absent a valid confession," implying that if there is such a confession there is no further need for sworn testimony.

Rules of evidence may normally be waived by a failure to invoke them in the form of an objection when inadmissible evidence is offered. It is, of course, an absurdity to expect a child to be familiar with these rules and they can, therefore, only be invoked to his advantage when he is represented by counsel. In recognition of this the California law provides that if he has no lawyer, "it shall be deemed that objections that could have been made to the evidence were made." Cal.Welf. & Inst.Code § 701.

§ 43. Constitutional Exclusions

When there has been a violation of a child's constitutional rights in the law enforcement process it is generally required that evidence obtained as a result of the violation is not admissible against him in the juvenile court. Thus, things seized from him as a consequence of an illegal arrest, a statement obtained from him as a consequence of an illegal arrest, a statement obtained from him in violation of his privilege against self-incrimination, etc. are all subject to the so-called exclusionary rule.

It should be noted, however, that the Supreme Court has recently been restricting the scope of the exclusionary rule and that juvenile court law has followed that lead. In U. S. v. Calandra, 414 U.S. 338, 94 S.Ct. 613 (1974) the Court indicated that the exclusionary rule is a judicially created remedy and not a personal constitutional right. This has led the Supreme Court of Georgia to hold that "the expected benefits and the expected detriments of applying the exclusionary rule must be weighed to determine whether that rule may be invoked to suppress the fruits of the search." S. v. Young, 234 Ga. 488, 216 S.E.2d 586, 589 (1975). As a consequence of this weighing, *Young* decided that the exclusionary rule did not apply to illegal searches by school officials.

Similarly, the Supreme Court has held that a confession obtained from an adult in violation of his rights under *Miranda* may be used to impeach him when he testifies on his own behalf. Harris v. New York, 401 U.S. 222, 91 S.Ct. 643 (1971). When a child testifies in his delinquency hearing, a confession obtained from him which would not have been admitted to establish the delinquency, can be used as a prior inconsistent statement to impeach his credibility. In re Noble, 15 Wn.App. 51, 547 P.2d 880 (1976).

Constitutional evidence rules which remain intact, however, appear to be enforced fully in juvenile proceedings. Even where there is no jury, for example, it has been ruled to be reversible error for the juvenile court judge to take into account the fact that the child has exercised his constitutional right not to testify. In re D.A.M., 132 N.J.Super. 192, 333 A.2d 270 (1975), applying Griffin v. California, 380 U.S. 609, 85 S.Ct. 1229 (1965). And since *Gault* makes clear that the privilege against self-incrimination applies in the juvenile court hearing, the judge must affirmatively advise the child that he need not testify, In re Lee G., 46 A.D.2d 910, 363 N.Y.S.2d 9 (1974), and he may not proceed to question the child about the alleged offense without first obtaining a waiver of the privilege. Landry v. S., 504 S.W.2d 580 (Tex.Civ.App.1974). If, however, the disposition power of the court in a particular case is legislatively circumscribed so that the child cannot be committed to a secure institution for delinquents, as is often true in status offense proceedings, the privilege against self-incrimination may not be applicable at all. In re Carter, 20 Md.App. 633, 318 A.2d 269 (1974). What other constitutional rules bear this same relationship to the juvenile court's disposition power is not as yet clear. In a decision similar to *Carter* it was noted that there had been adequate notice, opportunity to prepare a defense, to cross-examine adverse witnesses and representation by counsel. In re K., 26 Or.App. 451, 554 P.2d 180 (1976). These may represent the minimal requirements of due process which will not yield to any restrictions on disposition power.

§ 44. Impeachment

There are a variety of means for showing that the testimony of a witness is not worthy of belief by the trier of fact. When the juvenile himself is a witness, for example, he may be impeached by introduction of a prior inconsistent statement, even if that statement was given to the police under circumstances which render it inadmissible for its testimonial value, that is, to prove the truth of its contents. In re Noble, 15 Wn.App. 51, 547 P.2d 880 (1976). Witnesses against the juvenile may, of course, also be impeached by prior inconsistent statements. In re Farms, 216 Pa.Super. 445, 268 A.2d 170 (1970). Testing credibility by means of a lie detector can be done in juvenile court under the same conditions that govern its use in adult proceedings. Commonwealth v. A Juvenile, 370 Mass. 450, 348 N.E.2d 760 (1976).

Most of the impeachment issues which arise in juvenile law, however, have to do with another technique, namely, the use of the witness's juvenile court record. Although there is generally no restriction on the use of an adult's record of criminal conviction to attack the credibility of that adult when he appears as a witness, the problem arises in juvenile law by virtue of commonly found statutory provisions that the juvenile court proceedings are not admissible in any other court except for purposes of sentencing proceedings in a criminal court. The Supreme Court has held, however, that such confidentiality requirements must yield before the right of an accused person to confront and cross-examine witnesses against him, so that a criminal accused is not barred by juvenile law confidentiality statutes from asking a juvenile witness against him whether he is then on probation from a juvenile court as a means of indicating his bias against the accused adult. Davis v. Alaska, 415 U.S. 308, 94 S.Ct. 1105 (1974). *Davis* has been interpreted as requiring the policy of confidentiality of juvenile records to give way before an accused's right to present evidence in his own behalf; where questions put to a defense witness would have involved disclosure by that witness of the juvenile record of a prosecution witness, it has been held error to prevent the question. S. v. Cox, 42 Ohio St.2d 200, 327 N.E.2d 639 (1975). *Davis* also means that in a criminal court a witness may be cross-examined about his testimony given in juvenile court. S. v. Parnes, 134 N.J. Super. 61, 338 A.2d 223 (1975).

But where the rights of an accused person do not conflict with the policy of confidentiality, there is nothing in *Davis* to prevent the policy from barring use of juvenile records. Thus, when a child's statement given to a police officer has become part of the juvenile court record in a delinquency proceeding against him, the confidentiality statute prevents use of that statement in a civil action for damages against him. Camp v. Howe, 132 Vt. 429, 321 A.2d 71 (1974).

It is also commonly held, pursuant to statutory provisions declaring juvenile court proceedings not to be criminal, that a juvenile court record is not a "conviction of crime" within the meaning of the rule which permits a witness to be impeached by showing that he has a criminal record, Johnson v. S., 3 Md.App. 105, 238 A.2d 286 (1967), even if the witness asserts on direct examination that he has never been convicted of a crime. S. v. Mathews, 6 Wn.App. 201, 492 P.2d 1076 (1972), or the impeachment is undertaken against a child charged with delinquency in a juvenile court and the effort is to undermine his credibility by showing previous delinquency findings against him. In re Alexander, 16 Md. App. 416, 297 A.2d 301 (1972). Where enforcement of these statutes conflicts with the effort of an accused person—child or adult—to impeach a witness against him, it seems that *Davis* would bar preventing that effort, although it might still be open for a court to determine that a delinquency record has too little probative value on the credibility issue to be used for this purpose. Admission of records of arrests, for example, juvenile or adult, has been held to be prejudicial error on account of their slight probative value and high potential for prejudice. P. v. Wasson, 31 Mich.App. 638, 188 N.W.2d 55 (1971).

§ 45. Accomplice Testimony

In a criminal prosecution it is sometimes required that a conviction may not rest entirely on the uncorroborated testimony of the accused's accomplice. The basis for this rule has been stated to be that "In essence, the uncorroborated testimony of an accomplice witness, standing alone, cannot establish the guilt of an adult beyond a reasonable doubt." In re S.J.C., 533 S.W.2d 746, 749 (Tex.1976) (dissenting opinion). Since delinquency must be established beyond a reasonable doubt (see § 40) it is not surprising that many courts have decided that the uncorroborated testimony of a child's accomplice is not sufficient to support a finding of delinquency. In re Julius S., 44 A.D.2d 826, 355 N.Y.S.2d 158 (1974). As specified by a Georgia court, in delinquency proceedings there must be shown: "(1) Corroborating facts or circumstances   .   .   .

to connect the defendant to the crime or lead to the inference that he is guilty, and, (2) the corroborating evidence must be independent of the accomplice's testimony." D.W.D. v. S., 136 Ga. App. 304, 221 S.E.2d 72, 73 (1975).

It has been contended that Equal Protection for children requires that this corroboration rule be applied in juvenile proceedings. Over strong dissent, In re S.J.C., 533 S.W.2d 746 (Tex.1976) rejected this argument and held that neither fundamental fairness nor Equal Protection imports the adult rule into the juvenile court. The majority opinion deals only with the due process issue, noting that the juvenile court judge did find the child delinquent beyond a reasonable doubt by virtue of the probative value of the accomplice's testimony; the matter of Equal Protection received no attention, except in the dissent.

Where the corroboration rule is not strictly enforced, and it is only required that accomplice testimony be viewed cautiously and with suspicion, the same requirement has been applied to delinquency cases. In re Williams, 325 So.2d 854 (La.App.1976) (holding that on the facts there was not proof beyond a reasonable doubt).

§ 46. Privileges

The most significant privilege involved in juvenile cases is the privilege against self-incrimination which *Gault* found to be required as part of due process of law. Apart from the role of the privilege in the confrontation between child and police (see § 27.2), the privilege functions to prevent the state from calling the child as a witness and to prevent the judge from questioning the child without obtaining a formal waiver of the right not to speak imparted by the privilege.

The doctor-patient privilege which permits the patient to prevent the doctor from disclosing communications made during the consultation or treatment is as available in juvenile as in other courts, and where the child is the patient a parent may not waive the privilege on behalf of the child. In re Sippy, 97 A.2d 455 (D.C.App.1953); In re M.P.S., 342 S.W.2d 277 (Mo.App.1961).

Where an adult accused has been referred to a psychiatrist for evaluation on motion of the state it has been held that the privilege against self-incrimination may be used to justify a refusal to speak to the doctor. Lee v. County Court, 27 N.Y. 432, 318 N.Y.S.2d 705, 267 N.E.2d 452 (1971) and there is no reason why a child may not similarly use the privilege. S. v. Hathaway, 211 A.2d 558 (Me.1965) (concurring opinion), for example, notes that where the child was in hospital confinement by order of the court "he had no obligation to answer the doctor's questions concerning any participation . . . in any crime." In *Hathaway* the child had been advised of his privilege both by the examining psychiatrist and an attorney. Under these circumstances neither the privilege against self-incrimination nor the doctor-patient privilege could be used to prevent the psychiatrist from testifying to the conversations he had with the child.

Recent efforts to persuade courts to recognize a new privilege which would protect communications between parent and child have been unsuccessful. In re Terry W., 59 Cal.App. 745, 130 Cal.Rptr. 913 (1976); Cissna v. S., 170 Ind. 437, 352 N.E.2d 793 (1976). Nor does any statute appear to have created such a privilege. The possibility of a judicially-created parent-child privilege is discussed (and found inapplicable) in In the Matter of Mark G., 65 A.D.2d 917, 410 N.Y.S.2d 464 (1978).

§ 47. Hearsay

One of the ways traditional juvenile courts avoided adversary formalities was to have the facts presented to the judge by the probation officer who had investigated the case. This presentation included statements made by persons who had first hand knowledge of the important events and thus was made up of substantial amounts of hearsay. That is, when a witness (the probation officer) tells the judge that another has declared fact A to be true, fact A is being proved through hearsay.

It is a general rule of evidence, applicable in both civil and criminal cases, that hearsay is incompetent evidence and is not admissible. The hearsay nature of testimony must be distinguished, however, from a witness's lack of personal knowledge. If, for example, a witness testifies that a juvenile is 16 years old, and it turns out from cross-examination that he asserts this as a fact because someone has told him this is the child's age, the proper objection is to a lack of personal knowledge, not hearsay grounds. Hughes v. S., 508 S.W.2d 167 (Tex.Civ.App.1974). If, on the other hand, the witness says, "X told me the child is 16," that would be hearsay.

The hearsay rule is applicable to juvenile court proceedings in the sense that, upon proper objection, hearsay evidence should not be admitted. But when the juvenile court judge and not a jury is the trier of fact, as is almost always the case, it is usually held that any error in the admission of hearsay was harmless on the assumption that the judge gave it no weight in reaching a decision, especially if he expressly says for the record "I recognize that this is hearsay and cannot be considered for that purpose," as happened in R.D. v. S., 138 Ga.App. 440, 226 S.E.2d 289 (1976). If, however, the appellate court concludes from the record that the hearsay in fact influenced the juvenile court judge, then a delinquency finding will be reversed. Gilbert v. Commonwealth, 214 Va. 142, 198 S.E.2d 633 (1973).

In spite of the commonly made assumption that hearsay did not influence the judge, a delinquency finding will be reversed if, apart from the hearsay, there is not sufficient competent evidence to support the finding. Rusecki v. S., 56 Wis. 299, 201 N.W.2d 832 (1972); In re Harris, 218 Kan. 625, 544 P.2d 1403 (1976) ("nonamenability" decision in waiver hearing cannot be based entirely on hearsay). And if the record is "so replete with inadmissible hearsay testimony that [the juvenile] was effectively denied his right to a fair hearing" a delinquency finding similarly cannot stand. In re Dudley, 310 So.2d 919 (Miss.1975).

The great vice of hearsay is that it precludes cross-examination of the out-of-court declarant and is, therefore, deemed too unreliable to support important decisions. The constitutional right to confrontation and cross-examination is not, however, coextensive with the hearsay prohibition, for there are exceptions to the hearsay rule which are constitutionally acceptable. Commonwealth v. Ransom, 446 Pa. 457, 288 A.2d 762 (1972). The certified report of a chemist, for example, is admissible under the "business record" exception as proof that the substance possessed by a juvenile was heroin. In re Kevin G., 80 Misc. 2d 517, 363 N.Y.S.2d 1999 (1975). So, too, is the spontaneous accusation of the victim of a theft admissible as hearsay through the testimony of one who heard the accusation, under the exception known as "res gestae." C.A.J. v. S., 127 Ga.App. 813, 195 S.E.2d 225 (1973). Where, however, a document which qualifies under the official records exception to the hearsay rule, or under the business records exception, contains hearsay, it has been held that the document, thus containing double hearsay, is inadmissible in juvenile court in as much as its use would deny the child's rights to confrontation and cross-examination. Rusecki v. S., 56 Wis. 299, 201 N.W.2d 832 (1972).

§ 48. Findings

Following the close of the evidence in a hearing the court is required to decide whether the allegations in the petition have been proved. It is sometimes provided by statute that when the juvenile court judge finds the allegations have been established he must also state the grounds for his finding. N.Y.Fam.Ct.Act §§ 752, 1051. A recitation that a child is found delinquent "under the evidence provided to the court" does not comply with such a requirement and the fact that, as a court of limited jurisdiction, the juvenile court's judgments are void unless they show on their face the facts which establish their jurisdiction, renders the noncompliance more than a mere technical error. Powell v. Greg, 118 Ga. App. 225, 163 S.E.2d 251 (1968). In cases where the child is found delinquent for committing an offense which is different from the one originally charged against him in the petition, a failure of the juvenile court judge to make formal findings of fact will cause the delinquency finding to be reversed. In re R.N., 527 P.2d 1356 (Utah 1974).

Where it is required that the petition allege that the child needs treatment (see § 13), the findings under statutes such as the N.Y.Fam.Ct. Act § 752 must include the grounds for finding the need.

Some statutes make it possible for the child to be placed under supervision without any findings being made concerning the petition's allegations. In New York there is an "adjournment in contemplation of dismissal" which the court may make for a period of six months, after which, if the child's conduct has been satisfactory, the petition is dismissed. N.Y.Fam.Ct.Act § 749(a). The California statute permits probation without a formal finding if the court is satisfied that the child comes within its jurisdiction. Cal.Welf. & Inst.Code § 725(a); the Model Act § 33 provides that prior to findings the court may "suspend the proceedings, and continue the child under supervision in his own home, under terms and conditions negotiated with probation services and agreed to by all parties affected." If the child fails to comply with the terms of this consent decree, the proceedings under the original petition resume "and the child held accountable just as if the consent decree had never been entered." § 33(d).

§ 49. Dismissing the Petition

Although the juvenile justice system provides many informal opportunities for screening cases out and for dropping charges against a child, once a petition is filed a termination of the proceedings may be neither informal nor simple. Under the District of Columbia Code, for example, the judge may not dismiss the petitions without giving the District the opportunity "to address itself to the issue whether 'social reasons' (i.e., the child's welfare and the public interest) justified the dismissals." In re R.L.R., 310 A. 2d 226, 227 (D.C.App.1973) Even without such a statutory restriction, it has been held that there is an absence of common law power in the court to dismiss the case against the child without the prosecution's consent. Ex parte S., 263 S.C. 363, 210 S.E.2d 600 (1974). There is, on the other hand, a common law power in a prosecutor to dismiss a case without leave of court at any time before a jury is impaneled and it has been held that this power may be exercised in juvenile court. Moore v. S., 186 Neb. 67, 180 N.W.2d 917 (1970).

In the absence of a statutory restriction, a juvenile court may continue the case without making formal findings and, as is possible under consent decree statutes such as the Model Act § 33, dismiss the petition if the child does not get into further trouble during the period of the continuance.

§ 50. Protective Orders

Firmly rooted in beliefs concerning the causes of juvenile delinquency is the role of family life. Defective home conditions, inadequate or malicious parents, the whole "under the roof culture," have all been cited throughout the 19th and 20th centuries as basic to the development of delinquent conduct. It is not surprising, therefore, that legislation sometimes provides authority for the juvenile court judge to issue orders controlling the conduct of the parents or guardian of a child adjudged to be delinquent; it is still more natural, of course, that similar judicial authority over parents should exist in neglect cases. In New York, for example, the provisions for an Order of Protection in delinquency and in neglect cases are nearly exact duplicates of each other, see N.Y.Fam.Ct.Act §§ 759, 1056; and the Model Act simply has one provision, § 44, for all cases.

These protective orders can only be made against persons over whom the court has obtained jurisdiction, i.e., who have properly been served with notice of the initial proceedings.

The Model Act § 44(3) additionally requires that there be separate notice and opportunity to be heard concerning the protective order. These orders concerning parents cannot be made *instead* of a disposition directed at the child since it is a prerequisite of authority under these provisions that there already be a disposition order in the case. The relationship of the protective order to the disposition is most apparent in the Model Act which requires a finding "that the person's conduct is or may be detrimental or harmful to the child, and will tend to defeat the execution of the order of disposition made." § 44(2). The court is, therefore, authorized to "restrain the conduct" of that person in the protective order. Under both the New York and Model formulations, the protective order impliedly may not last beyond the period of the disposition order. Violation of protective orders are punishable as contempt.

In the absence of specific legislative authority, a juvenile court has no power to order a parent to do any affirmative act, such as to cooperate with a rehabilitative program to which the child has been ordered. S. v. S.M.G., 313 So.2d 761 (Fla.App.1975). The *S.M.G.* court also made clear that even if the juvenile court is a division of a court of general jurisdiction which has broad contempt powers, the lack of authority to make the underlying order against the parent precludes resort to those powers to enforce the order.

CHAPTER VI

DISPOSITIONS

§ 51. Separate From Jurisdictional Findings

The *Gault* opinion included a footnote which declared that: "The problems of preadjudication treatment of juveniles and of postadjudication disposition are unique to the juvenile process; hence, what we hold in this opinion with regard to the procedural requirements at the adjudicatory stage has no necessary applicability to other steps of the juvenile process." 387 U.S. 1 at 31, n. 48, 87 S.Ct. 1428 at 1445–1446, n. 48. None of the other Supreme Court opinions which have been so influential in shaping modern juvenile law directs itself to the disposition phase of juvenile court hearings either. Nonetheless, despite the total absence of any direct intervention by the Supreme Court, one of the most fundamental changes in juvenile court procedures of the present era is the insistence that the question of what disposition is to be made of a given child must be separated from the question of whether facts exist which bring him within the court's jurisdiction. The so-called "bifurcated hearing" which requires that disposition issues not be reached until and unless there has been a finding of delinquency began to appear in the

law, in fact, several years before the Supreme
Court first entered the field. See, for example,
section 746 of the New York Family Court Act
and section 702 of the California Juvenile Court
Law, Welf. & Inst.Code, both of which require
the disposition hearing to follow upon completion
of the adjudication of delinquency and which
were enacted in the early 1960's. The new Texas
statute is emphatic. "The disposition hearing
shall be separate, distinct, and subsequent to the
adjudication hearing." Tex.Fam.Code § 54.04
(a).

This relatively early requirement that the
judge not deal with the question of what to do
with the child until there has been a jurisdictional finding was aimed at "purifying" the fact-
finding functions of the court and did not, consequently, concern itself with the means by which
the disposition decision was reached. It has been
recently noted in this regard that: "Whether our
focus is on legislation, judicial opinions, existing
proposals for reform, or scholarly writing, we
encounter either silence or concern for only one
or two aspects of dispositional procedure." ABA/
IJA Standards, Dispositional Procedures 1.

One indication of the great significance of the
separate disposition hearing is In re Celia R.,
36 N.Y. 317, 367 N.Y.S.2d 770, 327 N.E.2d 812
(1975) which held that it violated a child's due
process rights to hold the hearing in her absence

under circumstances where she might have contributed to the accuracy of the facts taken into consideration and to the choice of disposition which the judge was considering. It is also wrong for the juvenile court judge not to hold a disposition hearing at all and to render a disposition order at the same time that he finds the child delinquent. In re Wooten, 13 Md.App. 521, 284 A.2d 32 (1971). The juvenile court abuses its discretion, according to the Rhode Island Supreme Court, if it fails to provide the child or his attorney a right to allocution. In re Wilkinson, 116 R.I. 163, 353 A.2d 199 (1976). On the other hand, the child does not have a right to insist on such an immediate disposition and the court may choose to postpone the disposition hearing in order to acquire relevant information, P. v. Cato, 4 Ill.App. 1093, 283 N.E.2d 259 (1972).

Although some statutes, such as the above cited California provision and the Model Act § 32(d), require that the disposition hearing in neglect cases be separate from the fact-finding hearing, much of the evidence which establishes the neglect, unlike the evidence which normally proves the delinquency, is strongly probative of what the disposition should be. Thus, it has been held that a unitary hearing in a neglect case is permissible, Johnson v. P., 170 Colo. 137, 459 P.2d 579 (1969), although it has also been decided that the notice of the proceedings in such a hearing must include information concerning what dispositions the court might make. S. v. Jamison, 251 Or. 114, 444 P.2d 15 (1968).

§ 52. Disposition Authority

Juvenile court statutes commonly grant a relatively limited range of options: the basic choices are probation, commitment to an institution or placing the child in the custody of a relative, foster home or a child care agency. Recently, restitution has been added to many statutes. The dispositions for status offense children might differ only in that they may not be committed to the public juvenile corrections agency which receives those found to be delinquent. But this is not always the case and both classes of children are often found in the same institutions. See § 12.

Whatever disposition the juvenile court orders must be authorized by the statute. In re A.F., 37 Colo.App. 185, 546 P.2d 972 (1975) (statute does not authorize "split sentence" whereby child serves jail sentence on weekends as a condition of probation); In re M.L., 65 N.J. 438, 317 A.2d 65 (1974) (juvenile court not authorized to impose fine on delinquent child); In re A— N—, 500 S.W.2d 284 (Mo.App.1973) (no suspended commitment). In the Matter of J.J., 431 A.2d 587 (D.C.App.1981) (court may not order corrections agency to pay for services without granting custody to agency).

The statutory relationships between the juvenile court and the juvenile corrections agency may involve further restrictions on the juvenile court's disposition authority. Thus, where the statute limits the court's commitment powers to a commitment to that agency, the court may have no further power to direct that the child be placed by the agency in a particular facility such as the state training school, as was decided to be the Arizona law in H.M.L. v. State, 131 Ariz. 385, 641 P.2d 873 (App.1981). Several states grant such exclusive discretionary control to the corrections agency. Not only may direct commitment to a reform school be unauthorized by statute, but the juvenile court may similarly lack power to commit a delinquent child to a mental hospital. In re M.J.E., 43 Cal.App.3d 792, 118 Cal.Rptr. 398 (1974).

Some juvenile court acts are less restrictive than the holdings of the above cited cases would indicate. Florida's § 39.11(f), for example, authorizes the juvenile court to require the child to render a public service in a public service program. In Ohio the parents may be required to make restitution for the damage their child has caused.

Two statutory provisions are fairly unique. One is the Model Act's § 34(a)(4) which permits the juvenile court, in the case of a child who is at least 14 years old, to excuse him from "any legal requirement of compulsory school attendance" and to authorize him to be employed in any position which is not hazardous for children under 18. This power is conditioned, however, on the court first finding that "school officials have made a diligent effort to meet the child's educational needs, and after study, the court further finds that the child is not able to benefit appreciably from further schooling."

The second provision goes well beyond the Model Act and provides the juvenile court with unprecedented power to require services for juveniles. The New York Family Court Act § 255 declares:

> It is hereby made the duty of, and the family court or a judge thereof may order, any state, county and municipal officer and employee to render such assistance and cooperation as shall be within his legal authority, as may be required, to further the objects of this act.

This provision has been put to a wide variety of uses. In re Edward M., 84 Misc.2d 363, 373 N.Y.S.2d 739 (1975) (county commissioner of social services to provide foster homes); In re James B., 75 Misc.2d 1012, 349 N.Y.S.2d 492 (1973) (special education programs); In re Terrance J., 78 Misc.2d 437, 353 N.Y.S.2d 695 (1974) (police ordered to expunge records); In re Carlos P., 78 Misc.2d 851, 358 N.Y.S.2d 608 (1974) (school board ordered to admit juvenile to vocational school). It appears to grant N.Y. Family Court judges power to require any public agency to carry out its statutory duties regarding children over whom the court has authority, and in this sense the law creates a judicial ombudsman on behalf of juvenile court children.

§ 53. Right to Counsel

It would be the rare case in which a child were represented at a fact-finding but not at the disposition hearing. In light of the fact that most cases do not involve a contest over whether the child has committed an offense or is otherwise within the jurisdiction of the court, the appointment of counsel is almost automatically the equivalent of providing the child a lawyer for the disposition hearing. In some states there is an express statutory right to counsel for the disposition, e.g. N.Y.Fam.Ct.Act § 741, while other statutes are in broad terms which include this right at the disposition hearing, e.g. Model Act § 25.

An analysis of the child's constitutional right to counsel would rely on the "critical" nature of the disposition hearing being analogous to the "critical" nature of the waiver hearing that was involved in Kent v. U. S., 383 U.S. 541, 86 S.Ct. 1045 (1966), and on the equal protection argument arising from the adult's right to counsel guaranteed by Mempa v. Rhay, 389 U.S. 128, 88 S.Ct. 254 (1967).

Because both the statutory provisions and the constitutional basis appear so firm, the question does not appear in any reported decision in which a juvenile court refused to provide counsel at a disposition. Where, however, a juvenile court interfered with counsel's ability to function effectively at the disposition hearing, this has been held to be reversible error. In re A.H., 115 N.J. Super. 268, 279 A.2d 133 (1971).

§ 54. Procedural Requirements

The law relating to the procedures which must be followed at a disposition hearing is traditionally made up of bits and pieces and, except for the ABA/IJA, Dispositional Procedures Standards and a few of the new statutes is rarely comprehensively dealt with. The 1978 Florida revision contains several procedural innovations, including notice to the victim, a required discussion with the child concerning his feelings and a set of criteria for making a disposition choice. Fla. Stat.Ann. § 39.09.

Among the more commonly found statutory provisions governing disposition procedures is the one which declares that evidence at the disposition hearing must be "relevant and material," omitting the additional requirement for evidence at the adjudication hearing that it be "competent." The impact of this omission is to make admissible hearsay proof, the most important example of which is the predisposition study in which informants (out-of-court-declarants, in hearsay terms) provide the judge with information relevant to the disposition choice. Cases upholding the use of hearsay evidence at the disposition hearing have emphasized that the due process principles announced in *Gault* and other Supreme Court decisions in this field have no application at the disposition hearing. Tyler v. S., 512 S.W.2d 46 (Tex.Civ.App.1974); In re Meek, 236 N.W.2d 284 (Iowa 1975).

The exclusionary rule which makes inadmissible evidence obtained in violation of the child's constitutional rights is generally assumed to be inapplicable. The Model Act § 28, for example, declares the rule applicable at the adjudicatory hearing, implying that such evidence may properly be used for disposition purposes. In re A.A.A., 528 S.W.2d 337 (Tex.Civ.App.1975) contains similar implications. Whether the child may be questioned at the disposition hearing, without the formalities that must be observed in obtaining a waiver of his privilege against self-incrimination as is required at the adjudicatory hearing, is similarly unclear. In In re Smith, 33 Ill.App. 354, 337 N.E.2d 209 (1975) the judge advised the child at the disposition hearing that

he had to decide what was best for the child, and
added:

> Maybe one of the things that is going to help
> me decide what really is best for you in the
> long run is the knowledge of where the hell
> that gun is. You don't have to tell me any-
> thing. But I am just telling you, it may help
> you. Where is the gun? At 211.

This was upheld as a proper exercise of discretion, with no reference to the Fifth Amendment.

Conversely, it has been held error to *prevent*
the child and his parent from testifying at the
disposition hearing. In re Michael C., 50 A.D.
2d 757, 376 N.Y.S.2d 167 (1975). Under the
Florida statute above—cited all parties must be
given the opportunity to comment on the disposition issue; there does not appear to be any right
to cross-examine, however.

§ 55. The Social Study

Individualized justice is often taken to be the
most salient characteristic of juvenile court dispositions. In order to have the disposition conform to this ideal, the juvenile court judge requires information about each particular child.
This is usually provided by an investigation, usually performed by a member of the probation
staff, and a report, known as the social study or
disposition report. Others who work in the court
—psychiatrists or social workers—may also con-

tribute to the information before the judge; thus the Texas Family Code § 54.04(b) provides that "At the disposition hearing, the juvenile court may consider written reports from probation officers, professional court employees, or professional consultants in addition to the testimony of witnesses." Some statutes make the study mandatory, as the New York Family Court Act provisions dealing with children found to have committed serious offenses ("designated felony act"). Section 750(s), added by 1976 amendments to the Family Court Act, illustrates the scope of these reports.

> Following a determination that a respondent has committed a designated felony act and prior to the initial dispositional hearing, the judge shall order a probation investigation and diagnostic assessment. The probation investigation shall include, but not be limited to, the history of the juvenile including previous conduct, the family situation, any previous psychological and psychiatric reports, school adjustment, previous social assistance provided by voluntary or public agencies and the response of the juvenile to such assistance. The diagnostic assessment shall include, but not be limited to, psychological tests and psychiatric interviews to determine mental capacity and achievement, emotional stability and mental disabilities. It shall in-

clude a clinical assessment of the nature
and intensity of impulses and controls of the
juvenile, and of the situational factors that
may have contributed to the act or acts.
When feasible, expert opinion shall be ren-
dered as to the risk presented by the juvenile to others or himself, with a recommendation as to the need for a restrictive
placement.

If the statute does require a social study, it is
prejudicial error for the juvenile court not to
order one. Strode v. Brorby, 478 P.2d 608 (Wyo.
1970). The juvenile court acts do not normally
specify when the investigation is to be made and
general practice appears to be to accumulate the
data before there has been any formal delinquency finding. This has the advantage of permitting
the disposition hearing to go forward without
delay, but the disadvantage of broadcasting to
sources, such as school officials, from whom the
information is sought that the child is in trouble
with the law. Current practice in this respect
also creates an undue risk that disposition information will reach the judge prior to a decision in the adjudicatory phase. The ABA/IJA,
Dispositional Procedures Standards 2.2 recommends that the investigation not be undertaken
until after there has been a finding.

Juvenile court statutes may prohibit the judge
from seeing any predisposition study before the

finding of delinquency has been made. The New York law, for example, provides in regard to this information: "Such reports of memoranda shall not be furnished to the court prior to the completion of the fact-finding hearing and the making of an order . . ., and may be used in a dispositional hearing and only therein." Section 750(1), added by 1976 amendments to the Family Court Act. It is reversible error if the juvenile court judge circumvents the bifurcated hearing statute by obtaining the report prior to making a jurisdictional finding. In re R., 1 Cal.3d 855, 83 Cal.Rptr. 671, 464 P.2d 127 (1970) (law violation); In re D.J.B., 18 Cal.App.3d 782, 96 Cal. Rptr. 146 (1971) (status offense).

The child and his attorney are granted varying degrees of access to the social study. In this respect, Kent v. U. S., 383 U.S. 541, 86 S.Ct. 1045 (1966) is important. There, in the context of the question of what the role of counsel is in regard to a social study relevant to whether the child should be waived for a criminal trial, the Supreme Court was presented with the view that "counsel's role is limited to presenting 'to the court anything on behalf of the child which might help the court in arriving at a decision; it is not to denigrate the staff's submissions and recommendations.'" The Court strongly disagreed. Justice Fortas replied: "on the contrary, if the staff's submissions include materials which are susceptible to challenge or impeachment, it is precisely the role of counsel to 'denigrate' such matter. There is no irrebuttable presumption of accuracy attaching to staff reports." Although it is not made clear in *Kent*, denial of access to these materials may constitute a denial of the right to the effective assistance of counsel and, therefore, be a mistake of constitutional dimensions. Traditional juvenile court statutes do not deal with the issue of the right to see the social study, although more recent enactments do grant a limited right. The Texas Family Code § 54.04 (b) is illustrative.

> Prior to the disposition hearing, the court shall provide the attorney for the child with access to all written matter to be considered by the court in disposition. The court may order counsel not to reveal items to the child or his parent, guardian, or guardian ad litem if such disclosure would materially harm the treatment and rehabilitation of the child or would substantially decrease the likelihood of receiving information from the same or similar sources in the future.

The Florida statute has no such limitations and provides that the report "shall be made available to the child's legal counsel." Fla.Stat.Ann. § 39.09(j). The report may be oral, but it must be disclosed a reasonable time prior to the disposition hearing. J.B. v. S., 418 So.2d 423 (Fla. App.1982).

§ 56. Probation

All the juvenile court acts provide for probation as a permissible disposition of delinquents and children determined to have committed "status offenses." Even in light of a growing concern over violent behavior, New York has enacted legislation which permits the court to use probation in the case of serious violent delinquency, although the new law also gives the court authority to sentence the child to a secure institution for a minimum of one year. N.Y.Fam. Ct.Act § 753–a.

On the other hand, probation is not unqualifiedly *required* by any of the juvenile court acts. It is presumptively required under the new Washington statute for minor and first offenders. Wash.Rev.Stat. § 13.40.160(2). There does not seem to be any other statute which mandates probation or any other minimally restrictive result for misconduct that is only a *de minimus* violation of the law. The general absence of any mandatory legislation of this sort is probably attributable to a reluctance on the part of lawmakers and others to give up the view that even the smallest delinquency might be a "call for help" or otherwise symptomatic of a need for official intervention.

In its earliest historic development, probation meant that the probationer continued to live at home, but was required to accept the counseling and supervision of a probation officer. For the bulk of juvenile probationers, this is still the case as a matter of court practice. But the statutes governing juvenile probation may go beyond the tradition by authorizing the juvenile court to require the child to reside out of his home as one of the conditions of probation. The Texas Family Code § 54.05(d), for example, permits the court to place the child on probation ". . . in his own home or in the custody of a relative or other fit person . . . in a suitable foster home; or in a suitable public or private institution or agency, except the Texas Youth Council." The only placement thus excluded is the state's official juvenile corrections agency. Even without such specific statutory authority, California courts have approved probation conditions which have included the requirement of weekends in a "training academy," In re Preston B., 273 Cal.App.2d 607, 78 Cal.Rptr. 436 (1969), and not less than five nor more than twenty days in a juvenile correctional facility. In re Ricardo M., 52 Cal.App. 744, 125 Cal.Rptr. 291 (1975).

These California cases were decided under a statute which permits the juvenile court to "impose and require any and all reasonable conditions that it may determine fitting and proper to the end that justice may be done and the reformation and rehabilitation of the ward enhanced." Cal.Welf. and Inst.Code § 730. More common, however, is a statute which simply authorizes the court to make "reasonable conditions" of probation. In light of the virtual absence of any consensus about what "justice" means in this context and an equivalent lack of knowledge concerning what will promote "reformation and rehabilitation," both statutory forms amount to a grant of complete discretion to juvenile court judges to do as their own personal judgment dictates.

When the probation conditions require that the child leave his home, the question of how long the period of probation may be is particularly important. Many statutes provide that probation may continue for the whole of the child's minority; some put this until the 21st birthday, despite other provisions of law which terminate minority at 18. New York, on the other hand, is an example of some sense of proportionality in juvenile court dispositions; section 757(b) of its Family Court Act limits probation for delinquents to a maximum of two years and one year for persons in need of supervision. If, however, there are "exceptional circumstances" each period may be extended for an additional year. The New York judge may make the probation order for less than these maxima; the Florida statute, on the other hand, mandates that probation last no longer than could a term of commitment. The Model Act combines features of both approaches by providing for an initial probation of one year, renewable in one year doses until the child reaches 19 if the court finds each renewal "is necessary to protect the community or to safeguard the welfare of the child." § 37(b)(2)(c).

Whether a court may make restitution to the victim of the child's offense a probation condition has been a difficult issue in light of the common view that fines may not be imposed on delinquent children. E.P. v. State, 130 Ga.App. 512, 203 S.E. 757 (1973). Although the legality of such a condition was sometimes questioned, Bordone v. F., 33 A.D.2d 890, 307 N.Y.S.2d 527 (1969), it now seems acceptable, both by statutory amendments, N.Y.Fam.Ct.Act § 757(c)(1), and judicial opinion that restitution has a rehabilitative effect which fines do not. P.R. v. S., 133 Ga.App. 346, 210 S.E.2d 839 (1974).

The supervision which a child receives on probation can vary from intense personal contact with the probation officer to mere perfunctory reporting by telephone or even by mail. Theoretically, the relationship is precisely what the individual child requires. As a practical matter, it has more to do with the size of the caseload each probation officer is responsible for and the "success" or "failure" of the juvenile has at least as much to do with such extraneous factors as it does with the willingness or the capacity of the child to conform his behavior to the requirements of the probation order. Nonetheless, as far as the statutes are concerned, the violation of probation conditions is entirely the responsibility of the juvenile and the law makes no explicit provision for balancing his efforts against the magnitude of the task set before him in the decision whether his failure to comply with probation conditions should lead to an escalation of the sanctions imposed on him, usually in the form of a commitment to the state corrections agency. As is true elsewhere, the result of probation violation is made a matter of judicial discretion.

When there has been a violation of probation, it is often the child's probation officer himself who takes the child into custody to answer the violation charge since statutes commonly give probation officers arrest authority, at least as to their own probationers. The statutes also require that there be probable cause before such an arrest can be made. There has been some dissent from this combination of law enforcement and supervision roles in probation—see, for example, the Uniform Juvenile Court Act § 7(5) —but even the Model Act, § 6(b) permits not only probation officers but social service workers as well, to arrest children under their supervision.

Even before the Supreme Court declared that proceedings to revoke the probation of an adult probationer must comply with due process standards, Gagnon v. Scurpelli, 411 U.S. 778, 93 S.Ct. 1756 (1973), state courts had invoked due process in juvenile cases and invalidated summary revocations. Keller v. S. ex rel. Epperson, 265 So.2d 497 (Fla.App.1972). The importance of *Gagnon* is exemplified by the view of an Arizona court that "Although adult and juvenile probation are governed by different statutes, the due process and fair play concepts apply to both . . . ." In re Maricopa County Juvenile Action No. J–77286, 25 Ariz.App. 563, 545 P.2d 74 (1976), although statutes may require proof beyond a reasonable doubt. Finch v. S., 506 S.W. 2d 749 (Tex.Civ.App.1974).

Sometimes the procedural rights in juvenile revocation proceedings are analogized, not to adult revocations, but to juvenile adjudicatory hearings to declare the child delinquent initially. Franks v. S., 498 S.W.2d 516 (Tex.Civ.App.1973). This is the approach taken by the Model Act § 39 which requires that petitions to revoke probation be subject to the same rules as govern the original petitions and that, except for the burden of proof rule being "clear and convincing evidence" rather than proof beyond a reasonable doubt, "proceedings to revoke probation shall be governed by procedures, safeguards and rights and duties applicable to delinquency and neglect cases contained in this (act)."

If the court determines that a condition has been violated, the consequences are a matter of judicial discretion. The probation need not be revoked, but may be continued, or another disposition can be made. Where the court originally committed the child and suspended it in order to put the child on probation, the suspension can be revoked and the commitment put in effect. In making this choice, it has been held that no separate disposition hearing need be held. In re B.L.M., 31 Colo.App. 106, 500 P.2d 146 (1972).

§ 57. Institutions

The most severe disposition a juvenile court can itself make is to commit the juvenile to the state's juvenile corrections system. In some states the juvenile court can commit the child to a particular institution in the system, while other states permit only a commitment to the state's juvenile corrections agency (the Texas Youth Council, the California Youth Authority, the Massachusetts Department of Youth Services, etc.).

Despite the fact that most of what is conceived as outright abuse and cruelty occurs in the juvenile training schools or reform schools, the juvenile court judge has relatively little statutory power of a supervisory nature. In Florida it has been held that the judge has no authority to require periodic reports from the Division of Youth Services. Department of Health and Rehabilitative Services v. Crowell, 327 So.2d 115 (Fla.App. 1976). The Minnesota Supreme Court has ruled that the judge cannot review decisions to release children. In re M.D.A., 306 Minn. 390, 237 N. W.2d 827 (1975). In California the juvenile court cannot recall its commitment to the Youth Authority, limit the period of commitment nor can it order a child placed in a specific facility. P. v. Getty, 50 Cal.App.3d 101, 123 Cal.Rptr. 704 (1975). In Oregon, however, as a result of an appellate decision holding that the juvenile court had no control over parents' rights to visit committed children, the legislature added a provision to the juvenile court laws declaring: "Commitment of a child to the Children's Services Division does not terminate the court's continuing jurisdiction to protect the rights of the child or his parents or guardians." This amendment is sufficient authority to vest control over visitation. In re Richardson, 267 Or. 374, 517 P.2d 270 (1973). Juvenile courts do not usually have jurisdiction to hear habeas corpus actions, with the result that judicial power to declare that the conditions in juvenile institutions constitute unconstitutional cruel and unusual punishment is usually exercised by a federal district court, as in the leading case of Morales v. Turman, 383 F. Supp. 53 (E.D.Tex.1974).

The statutes of most states permit status offenders to be committed to the same institutions which house delinquents and it is rarely required that they be kept separated from the delinquents. Blondheim v. S., 84 Wn.2d 874, 529 P.2d 1096 (1975) (association with delinquents prohibited). Still more rare are decisions such as In re Ellery C., 32 N.Y.2d 588, 347 N.Y.S.2d 51, 300 N.E.2d 424 (1974) forbidding a status offender commitment to a delinquent training school. Even if a status offender is in a non-secure facility, if he escapes from it he may be adjudicated delinquent on the basis of the escape and then be subject to all powers of the court in dealing with delinquents. In re M.S., 139 N.J.Super. 503, 354 A.2d 646 (1976).

A few juvenile court acts permit the juvenile court to commit a delinquent child directly to a correctional facility which also houses adult prisoners. This power has been upheld by federal courts. U. S. ex rel. Murray v. Owens, 465 F.2d 289 (2d Cir. 1972) (15 year old to Elmira Reformatory). Where a federal court finds that the conditions in the adult facility are so bad as to constitute cruel and unusual punishment in violation of the Eighth Amendment, short term commitments for "shock treatment" have been enjoined. Baker v. Hamilton, 345 F.Supp. 345 (W.D.Ky.1972).

A more common means whereby a delinquent child may end up in an adult penal institution is via an administrative or judicial decision transferring him from the juvenile corrections system to the adult one. Boone v. Danforth, 463 S.W.2d 825 (Mo.1971), finding an administrative transfer to violate due process and equal protection requirements, discusses the division of opinion among state and federal courts on this issue. The Missouri Supreme Court relied on the fact that the juvenile court could not have committed the child directly to the adult prison and that there was no notice or hearing at the administrative level. Where, however, the transfer results from a judicial hearing on the issue at which the juvenile is accorded all the procedural rights applicable to an adjudicatory hearing, including the right to counsel, the transfer has been found to comport with constitutional requirements. Moore v. Haugh, 341 F.Supp. 1263 (N.D.Ia.1972), affirmed 409 U.S. 809, 93 S.Ct. 204. The Model Act § 34(d) prohibits either commitment or transfer "to a penal institution or other facility used for the execution of sentences of persons convicted of a crime."

Whether commitment to a juvenile correctional agency or institution is the appropriate disposition is usually left by the statutes in the uncontrolled discretion of the juvenile court judge. Under the Washington statute a serious offender is subject to a presumptive commitment. There are, however, cases of an appellate court finding an abuse of the discretion and refusing to accept the commitment. In re Appeal No. 179, 23 Md.App. 496, 327 A.2d 793 (1974) (record contained judge's remarks indicating he was seeking to deter others and did not show that "the separation of the child from his parents is in 'his welfare or in the interest of public safety'," at 795.) Courts may also find an abuse of discretion if they are not satisfied that the juvenile court has sufficiently explored alternative dispositions. In re Arlene H., 38 A.D.2d 570, 328 N.Y.S.2d 251 (1971). This ruling might be supported further by a statute which places conditions on use of the commitment power. In California, for example, where the juvenile court law provides, "No ward of the juvenile court shall be committed to the Youth Authority unless the judge of the court is fully satisfied that the mental and physical condition and qualifications of the ward are such as to render it probable that he will be benefited by the reformatory educational discipline or other treatment provided by the Youth Authority.", it has been held error to commit a child to the Authority on the sole grounds that suitable alternatives do not exist. In re Aline D., 14 Cal.3d 557, 121 Cal.Rptr. 816,

536 P.2d 65 (1975). The dissent in *Aline D.*
would read the statute as requiring only that the
CYA commitment be the most beneficial one
available to the court, at 567, 121 Cal.Rptr. at
822–823, 536 P.2d at 70–71. The ABA/IJA
Standards, Juvenile Delinquency and Sanctions
would permit discretion to sentence to a secure
facility only if the juvenile is found to have committed an offense which is in one of the three
highest classes of seriousness or is in the fourth
class provided the juvenile has a prior record.
Whether the juvenile court judge should use this
power is governed by the Standards, Dispositions, which directs that:

> In choosing among statutorily permissible
> dispositions, the court should employ the
> least drastic category and duration of dispo-
> sition that is appropriate to the seriousness
> of the offense, as modified by the degree of
> culpability indicated by the circumstances of
> the particular case, and by the age and prior
> record of the juvenile.

The general rule found among juvenile court
statutes is that when a commitment is made, it
may last until the juvenile reaches his majority.
The effect on this rule of statutes which lower
the age of majority from 21 to 18 has produced
disparate results in courts which have been asked
whether juvenile court commitments automatically terminate at 18. In re Bartley, 338 A.2d

137 (Del.Super.1975) (custody terminates at 18); U. S. v. Shaver, 506 F.2d 699 (4th Cir. 1974) (lowering of voting age does not lower custody time); S. ex rel. Johnson v. Hershman, 55 Wis.2d 499, 200 N.W.2d 65 (1972) (custody terminates at 18, but corrections agency can request extension from court).

A frequently litigated issue concerning the duration of the juvenile court commitment relates to the fact that the term of years until majority is often longer than any prison term to which an adult could be sentenced who had been convicted of violating the same law. Does that violate the child's right to Equal Protection of the laws? The judicial opinion is unanimously no, even where the claim for equality was made in a case involving a child being found delinquent on grounds that he stole a bag of potato chips and was committed for a term that could be as long as eight years. In re Blakes, 4 Ill.App. 567, 281 N.E.2d 454 (1972). Such results are sustained by invoking the litany that the juvenile's commitment is not punishment and is for his own good. In re J.K., 68 Wis.2d 426, 228 N.W.2d 713 (1975).

Legislatures have more recently taken a slightly different view. In Connecticut, for example, the traditional indeterminate commitment to age 21 has been changed to a maximum of two years. Conn.Gen.Stat.Ann. § 17–69. In New York, the period generally applicable for commitment of delinquents is 18 months; recent amendments to the Family Court Act, however, have created a new category of "designated felony acts" comprised of more than a dozen of the most serious offenses in the penal code, and within this category, "designated class A felony acts" which are defined as violations of the laws defining murder in the first or second degrees, kidnapping in the first degree and arson in the first degree. A child found delinquent on grounds of having committed a class A felony act is subject to a "restrictive placement" for a period of five years, the first one of which must be served in a secure residential facility while the second year of the term must be served in a nonsecure residential facility. There are also minimum terms for designated felony acts which are not class A felony acts. None of the sentences may last beyond the juvenile's twenty first birthday, however. N.Y. Fam.Ct.Act, § 753–a, added by the Juvenile Justice Reform Act of 1976.

In many states it is possible for the original commitment period to be extended upon application by the custodian agency to the court. The statutes which authorize this usually limit the period of any extension to the child's twenty-first birthday; in California it may extend indefinitely through continuous two year extensions. Cal. Welf. & Inst.Code § 1802. The procedural rules

in these extension hearings are generally those
which apply at an adjudicatory hearing except
for the burden of proof which must be sustained
in establishing that the extension is necessary.
The New Mexico statute, for example, provides
that "All of the procedural safeguards and the
basic rights contained in the Children's Code
shall apply to the hearing and proceeding in con-
nection with [the extension hearing]. If the
court finds on the basis of clear and convincing
evidence, competent, material and relevant in nature, that the child is in need of further care and
rehabilitation, it may extend the agency's legal
custody to a date not extending beyond the
child's twenty-first birthday." N.Mex.1953
Comp.Laws (Supp.1973) § 13–14–35(H). The
procedural requirements usually include proper
notice of the application for the extension to both
the child and his parents. P. ex rel. Arthur F.
v. Hill, 36 A.D.2d 42, 319 N.Y.S.2d 961 (1971),
affirmed 29 N.Y.2d 17, 323 N.Y.S.2d 426, 271
N.E.2d 911.

It is seldom that a child spends the entire authorized time of the commitment in an institution and in the usual case he is released under a
parole supervision after a few months. Should
the supervising authority decide that the child
has engaged in some sort of misconduct, either
a new act of delinquency or a violation of one of
the conditions of his release, the child may be

subject to being returned to the institution to serve out the remainder of his commitment. As was the tradition in cases of adult parole revocation proceedings under such circumstances, the child was entitled to virtually no procedural protections when the decision was made to revoke the parole.

In the adult situation, however, Morrissey v. Brewer, 408 U.S. 471, 92 S.Ct. 2593 (1972) decreed that parole could not be revoked without according the parolee certain procedural rights. Although the Court did not provide a right to counsel in these proceedings, it did hold that there had to be a fair opportunity to meet the charge of misconduct and to address the issue of whether the parole should be revoked even if the misconduct is proved. Thus, there has to be notice of the charges, opportunity to know the case against him and the chance to present favorable evidence. The right to confront witnesses established by *Morrissey* was, however, qualified by the Court and is not necessary where the hearing officer finds "for good cause" that confrontation should not be required. *Morrissey* has generally been followed in decisions determining the rights of juvenile parolees, although the results are sometimes more and sometimes less than *Morrissey* provides. For example, P. ex rel. Silbert v. Cohen, 29 N.Y.2d 12, 323 N.Y.S. 2d 422, 271 N.E.2d 908 (1971) includes the right

to counsel; In re Morgan, 35 Ill.App. 10, 341 N.
E.2d 19 (1975) holds that the *Morrissey* and
Gagnon (Gagnon v. Scarpelli, 411 U.S. 778, 93 S.
Ct. 1756 (1973) applying the parole rules to probation revocation proceedings) cases do not
make it necessary for there to be a separate dispositional hearing after the violation of parole
has been established.

§ 58. Cruel and Unusual Punishment and the Right to Treatment

The genesis of the right to treatment is often
traced to the field of mental health and to its
exposition in Birnbaum, The Right to Treatment,
46 A.B.A.J. 499 (1960). The medical model of
juvenile justice which posits delinquency as a
symptom and corrections as treatment is fertile
soil for assertion of a similar right, although the
parens patriae idea which goes back at least to
Ex parte Crouse, 4 Whart. 9 (Pa.1838) and its
rejection of punishment as a feature of juvenile
corrections, provides a child-oriented doctrinal
base for a right to treatment for adjudicated delinquents. It is not surprising, therefore, to find
a New Jersey juvenile court approaching issues
of statutory and constitutional interpretation
with, "The Juvenile and Domestic Relations
Court, by virtue of its *parens patriae* responsibility, has not only the right but indeed a solemn
duty to exercise its statutory and inherent pow-

ers in obtaining effective treatment for adjudicated delinquents. This duty cannot and will not be delegated to an agency with powers much more strictly delimited than those of the court." In re D.F., 138 N.J.Super. 383, 391–392, 351 A.2d 43, 48 (1975) (ordering state corrections agency to place child in private hospital for psychiatric treatment).

Several features of right to treatment suits may be noted. One is that despite widespread agreement that treatment, where it is thought to have any positive effect, is more effectively accomplished in a more natural community setting rather than in an isolated institution, the right to treatment litigation appears to have been entirely on behalf of incarcerated juveniles. That is, the absence of case law on behalf of probationers suggests that children on probation or otherwise in a community program have not made the same demand for a right to treatment as their fellows in the training schools, Nelson v. Heynes, 491 F.2d 352 (7th Cir. 1974), or the detention centers, Martarella v. Kelley, 359 F. Supp. 478 (S.D.N.Y.1973). The reasons for this undoubtedly relate to the fact that claims of a right to treatment are joined with claims that there are violations of the juveniles' right to be free from cruel and unusual punishment in the programs (use of tranquilizing drugs in *Nelson,* for example) or disciplinary procedures of institutions (the beatings and useless, strenuous and degrading exercises in Morales v. Turman, 383 F.Supp. 53 (E.D.Tex.1974), for example). Perhaps another reason for the limited focus of right to treatment suits may be found in the doctrines next outlined. *Morales* was reversed in Morales v. Turman, 535 F.2d 864 (5th Cir. 1976). The opinion of the District Court is discussed in this section, therefore, as an indication of the scope of the concept "right to treatment," not as a matter of current law.

The second feature of these cases is the variety of constitutional theories on which they may be seen to rest. Provisions mandating due process of law, equal protection of the laws, freedom from cruel and unusual punishments, in both state and federal constitutions, have been invoked in a panoply of parallel and overlapping claims. Due process violations, for example, arise from a failure to provide the treatment which is the *quid pro quo* for adjudicating children in a procedure which contains less than the full protections of the criminal process. The right to treatment may also be viewed as a substantive right embodied in due process law. The due process requirement for "fundamental fairness" has similarly been invoked as a standard to which correctional experiences of juveniles must comply. Since the traditional period of commitment—to age of majority—is often longer for delinquents than would be the sentence legally possible for an adult convicted for the same crime, there may be a denial of equal protection of the laws unless this longer period in state control can fairly be characterized as a time of treatment.

In reliance on Robinson v. California, 370 U.S. 660, 82 S.Ct. 1417 (1962) in which the Supreme Court found it to be cruel and unusual punishment to impose criminal penalties on the status of being a drug addict, a similar argument can be constructed against imposing severe restrictions on the liberty of a person in the status of being a delinquent. The strength of this diminishes, of course, as it becomes more clear that delinquency is a finding which rests on what the child did, not on who he is. Another form of this prong of the claim for treatment is that in light of the lack of criminal responsibility of children, there is no justification for incarcerating them unless they are provided treatment, a claim which sounds in both fundamental fairness and cruel and unusual punishment terms. Finally, it may be noted that since dispositions have no legislatively mandated relationship to the gravity of the delinquent conduct which underlies them, the failure thus to observe the fundamental principle of proportionality can be justified only if the disposition entails treatment.

A third feature of the right to treatment litigation is that it includes demands for one or more forms of relief. There may be, for example, a demand that the absence of treatment entitles the juvenile to release from the institution, a claim made in the form of a petition for the writ of habeas corpus. The federal Civil Rights Statutes, furthermore, provide the basis for claiming declaratory relief or monetary damages, as well as affirmative ("provide treatment") and negative ("stop using drugs on the inmates") orders of an injunctive nature. A court may also be asked to order an institution simply to be closed on grounds that it is inherently incapable of providing treatment, a position which would derive support from a showing of how easily and consistently, on the other hand, the institution has delivered cruel and unusual punishment.

A somewhat overlapping feature, but of central importance, is that the suits bring a confrontation between judges who are asked to require that treatment facilities, programs and personnel be provided, and executive agents of the government who are, by law, the ones who must come up with what is ordered. The confrontation usually takes the form of the defendants pleading that the legislature has not appropriated sufficient funds for them to buy the things the court is ordering. The right to treatment cases are thus the vehicle for alleviating the chronic shortage of resources in the juvenile justice system. In *Morales*, supra, for example, the court noted at the outset that the defendants had argued "that execution of the relief requested by the plaintiffs, the United States, and the *amici* will necessitate the expenditure of state funds and thus constitute, in their words, a 'raid on the treasury' of the state." 383 F.Supp. at 59–60. The court concluded, however, that enforcement of constitutional rights may indeed cost the state something, but that is no reason to stay the enforcement. Consequently, the *Morales* opinion constitutes the most extensive and detailed "shopping list" for what must be provided by the Texas correction authorities. This rested in large part on the view "that the Texas Youth Council cannot constitutionally continue to incarcerate all or almost all of the children committed to its care. An important incident of the right to treatment is the right of each individual to the least restrictive alternative treatment that is consistent with the purpose of his custody." 383 F.Supp. at 124. A major segment of the court's order, therefore, was that "Within a reasonable period, making allowance for careful planning but not for foot-dragging, the defendants must cease to institutionalize any juveniles except those who are found by a responsible professional assessment to be unsuited for any less restrictive, alternative form of rehabilitative treatment. Additionally, the defendants must within the same period create or discover a system of community-based treatment alternatives adequate to serve the needs of those juveniles for whom the institution is not appropriate." 383 F.Supp. at 125.

A partly unresolved characteristic of the right to treatment relates to what is meant by "treatment." Wald & Schwartz, *Trying a Juvenile Right to Treatment Suit*, 12 Am.Crim.L.Rev. 125, 126–134 (1974) makes clear that far more than psychological therapy for mental illness is involved in the concept of treatment in this setting. It includes, for example, the development of social, educational, vocational and communication skills. Yet there remains the unanswered question of, whatever it includes, is "treatment" something which the child (or his attorney or his guardian *ad litem* or his parents, or all of these collectively) says he wants, on the one hand, or is it something which some officials decide he "needs" on the other? What element of consent is involved? Is there at stake a child's right to receive the treatment he wants or the state's right to impose the treatment it deems best? As far as case law is concerned, it is fairly clear that it is the latter. The ABA/IJA Juvenile Justice Standards, Dispositions, on the other hand, would make all "treatment" voluntary with virtually the only exceptions being made relating to programs, such as education, which *all* children are required to participate in, and medical treatment directly aimed at preserving the delinquent's health. The three-judge federal court which reconsiders the *Morales* orders will have the opportunity to deal with the voluntariness element of the right to treatment in a detailed way since the Court of Appeals has indicated that the record "amassed" by the District Court may be used in the three-judge court's disposition of the case. 535 F.2d at 874.

CHAPTER VII

WAIVER FOR CRIMINAL TRIAL

§ 59. In General

Even if the relevant statutes give the juvenile court *exclusive* jurisdiction over children who are accused of committing criminal acts, it is still possible for some children to be tried in a criminal court. In all but two states (NY and Vt.) the juvenile court is authorized to decide not to keep the child within its jurisdiction and have him tried in the regular criminal court. This process, variously known as waiver, transfer, certification, etc., has been a feature of the juvenile court system since 1899 when the first juvenile court was established in Illinois. A few juvenile court acts give the juvenile an option to seek a criminal trial, P. v. Thomas, 34 Ill.App.3d 1002, 341 N.E.2d 178 (1976). When a child has been thus waived for a criminal trial, the consequences of conviction may be as severe as they might be for an adult convicted of the same crime, S. v. Anthony, 239 N.W.2d 850 (Iowa 1976) (sentenced to 50 years) with two possible exceptions which should be noted. In some states the use of the death penalty is restricted to persons over a certain age, so that the child convicted of a capital crime following juvenile court waiver may not be sentenced to death. Second, it is possible in some states for the sentencing judge to have authority to sentence the child in the same manner which the juvenile court could have done if jurisdiction had not been waived. That is, upon conviction in the adult court the child might be committed to the juvenile corrections system, or placed under the supervision of the juvenile probation staff. There cannot, of course, be any waiver of a child who is within the juvenile court's jurisdiction on grounds other than criminal conduct.

Where the juvenile court's jurisdiction is *concurrent* with the criminal court (see § 16) the waiver process is less significant since the decision to proceed in the criminal court and to prosecute the child initially removes from the juvenile court a sizeable number of children who would otherwise be considered for waiver to the adult court.

The waiver process is a statutory one, with the requirement of eligibility for waiver and the procedures to be followed spelled out in the juvenile court legislation. Eligibility has traditionally been restricted to older juveniles who are charged with very serious crimes, although recent statutory amendments have tended to lower the age and to broaden the qualifying offenses. See § 58. The Supreme Court has had two occasions to review the waiver process, Kent v. U. S., 383 U.S. 541, 86 S.Ct. 1045 (1966) and Breed

v. Jones, 421 U.S. 519, 95 S.Ct. 1779 (1975).
Since the *Kent* case arose under the statutes for
the District of Columbia, a few courts have taken
it as an instance of the Court's interpretation of
the District's governing legislation, and not as
laying down constitutional rules, Commonwealth
v. Martin, 355 Mass. 296, 244 N.E.2d 303 (1969),
although the great majority has read the *Kent*
rules, discussed below, as constitutional requirements. *Breed* is clearly constitutionally binding
on all jurisdictions.

§ 60. Age and Offense

Under the majority of waiver statutes only
children who are in the upper age range of the
juvenile court's jurisdiction may be waived. A
frequently used cut-off for this purpose is 15,
although it may go as low as 13. Where there is
such a provision restricting waiver to the more
mature juveniles, it is the age at the time the alleged offense took place which is important. Tex.
Fam.Code § 54.02(a)(2). On the other hand,
in a recently increasing number of states *any*
child may be sent for a criminal trial, regardless
of his age at the time of the crime.

The nature of the offense similarly has a variety of impacts on the waiver process. In a few
states there is no limit of this sort and the child
may be waived for a criminal trial on even the
most minor charges. More commonly, however,

the juvenile court acts require that the child be charged with a serious offense, usually one that is a felony. Where the criminal statute gives the sentencing judge authority to impose less than a felony sentence (county jail confinement rather than a state prison sentence), the statute restricting waivers to felony offenses is satisfied even if the criminal court judge sentences the juvenile to the county jail. It is the *possible* penalty which determines the grade of the offense for waiver purposes. Hernandez v. S., 90 Nev. 65, 519 P.2d 107 (1974). If the crime for which the child is waived has a minimum age requirement, the criminal trial must be on a charge which encompasses the child's actual age. Thus waiver of a 17 year old on a charge of first degree rape, an offense which by statute can not be committed by a male under the age of 18, can result only in a criminal trial for second degree rape, as to which there is no such age restriction. King v. S., 518 P.2d 889 (Okl.Cr.App.1974).

§ 61. The Hearing

The first case in which the Supreme Court reviewed the work of a juvenile court was Kent v. U. S., 383 U.S. 541, 86 S.Ct. 1045 (1966). The Court reversed the waiver decision of the juvenile court of the District of Columbia and ruled that in light of the critical nature of the waiver decision, "there is no place in our system of law for reaching a result of such tremendous consequences without ceremony—without hearing, without effective assistance of counsel, without a statement of reasons." *Kent* laid down several requirements for the waiver process: (1) the child is entitled to counsel; (2) there must be a hearing on the waiver question; (3) the attorney must be given access to the court's records and reports which are taken into account in the waiver decision; and (4) the juvenile court judge must give his reasons for waiving his jurisdiction. As to the hearing, Justice Fortas indicated that it need not "conform with all the requirements of a criminal trial or even of the usual administrative hearing; but we do hold that the hearing must measure up to the essentials of due process and fair treatment."

Although *Kent* came up on issues of statutory interpretation, and the Court's language concerning the impact of the constitution is not perfectly clear, most state and lower federal courts which have reviewed juvenile court waiver cases have held that the *Kent* requirements are of constitutional dimensions, especially when that case is considered in the light of *Gault* which was decided one year later. U. S. ex rel. Turner v. Rundle, 438 F.2d 839 (3d Cir. 1971). A few state courts insist that only an interpretation of the District of Columbia statute was at stake and have held that *Kent* does not, therefore, apply to state procedures. In re Bullard, 22 N.C.App. 245, 206 S.E.2d 305 (1974), appeal dismissed 285 N.C. 758, 209 S.E.2d 279. Nonetheless, the right to appointed counsel appears to be recognized even in states where *Kent* is deemed not controlling. Commonwealth v. Roberts, 362 Mass. 357, 285 N.E.2d 919 (1972). When there is concurrent jurisdiction over the child's crime and the criminal court has discretionary authority to waive criminal jurisdiction in favor of juvenile court processing, it has been held that the criminal court need not comply with *Kent* in refusing to exercise that authority, Vega v. Bell, 47 N.Y. 2d 543, 419 N.Y.S.2d 454, 393 N.E.2d 450 (1979); Huffman v. Missouri, 399 F.Supp. 1196 (W.D.Mo. 1975), affirmed 527 F.2d 899 (8th Cir. 1976), and that the juvenile has the burden of persuading the criminal court judge to waive criminal jurisdiction. Commonwealth v. Pyle, 462 Pa. 613, 342 A.2d 101 (1975).

Under either view of *Kent*, courts have held that the juvenile is entitled to notice that the hearing in juvenile court will be concerned with waiver. The requirement of notice, however, is often not very strictly enforced. Turner v. Commonwealth, 216 Va. 666, 222 S.E.2d 517, (1976) (need not be in writing and is waived if no objection raised); Commonwealth v. Franklin, 366 Mass. 284, 318 N.E.2d 469 (1974) (fact that statute authorizes waiver is sufficient notice to child's attorney); S. v. Halverson, 192 N.W.2d 765 (Iowa 1971) (notice timely if court announces waiver will be considered before defense counsel makes opening statement).

The traditional rule on the burden of proof would require that the state persuade the judge that the child should be waived, according to the relevant statutory criteria. S. v. Carmichael, 35 Ohio St.2d 1, 298 N.E.2d 568 (1973) ("reasonable grounds" to believe waiver criteria satisfied). As a result of 1976 amendments to § 707 (b) of the California Welfare and Institutions Code, however, if the child is alleged to have committed designated serious offenses, the juvenile court is required to waive jurisdiction "unless it concludes that the minor would be amenable to the care, treatment and training program available through the facilities of the juvenile court based upon an evaluation of [the same statutory criteria which govern all other waiver decisions]." This provision seems to create a presumption of waiver which arises from the fact of certain allegations being made in the petition and to shift the burden of persuasion to the child on the issue of amenability. In Breed v. Jones, 421 U.S. 519, 95 S.Ct. 1779 (1975) the Supreme Court noted that it has "never attempted to prescribe the criteria for, or the nature and quantum of evidence that must support a decision to transfer a juvenile for trial in an adult court." State courts have upheld waiver where the judge is convinced that the criteria are satisfied by a preponderance of the evidence. In re Murphy, 15 Md.App. 434, 291 A.2d 867 (1972).

Even when the burden is on the state, the child must be permitted to participate in the hearing by putting in his own evidence on the waiver question. In re Doe, 86 N.M. 37, 519 P.2d 133 (1974). The state's case may be based upon the uncorroborated testimony of the juvenile's accomplice, Kern v. S., 522 P.2d 644 (Okl.Cr.App. 1974), and the juvenile court judge may consider hearsay evidence, Clemons v. S., 162 Ind.App. 50, 317 N.E.2d 859 (1974), although the waiver decision is invalid if the juvenile court heard *no* competent evidence at all. Leach v. Superior Court, 98 Cal.Rptr. 687 (Cal.App.1972).

The right to a hearing on the waiver issue may be given up by the child and, considering the view the Supreme Court has taken of the critical importance of the juvenile court's decision to retain or give up jurisdiction, the question arises whether formalities similar to those applicable to the taking of a guilty plea must be followed before a child can be taken to have validly waived his right to a hearing. In Haziel v. U. S., 131 U.S. App.D.C. 298, 404 F.2d 1275 (1968) it was held, on analogy to the guilty plea rules, that the juvenile court judge must address the child personally to determine that he understands the consequences of his choice. On the other hand, in In re Maricopa County, Juvenile Action No. J–73355, 111 Ariz. 37, 523 P.2d 65 (1974) the Supreme Court of Arizona held that the warnings and explanations constitutionally mandated by Boykin v. Alabama, 395 U.S. 238, 89 S.Ct. 1709 (1969) for guilty pleas are not required in the child's waiver of a finding of probable cause.

§ 62. Criteria for Waiver

Since waiver is a statutory procedure, the criteria which govern the waiver decision are found in the juvenile court acts. These are sometimes put in very general terms, authorizing, for example, waiver when required by "the interests of the public" or "the best interest of [the] child or of the public." Claims that these statutes are unconstitutionally vague have been rejected by appellate courts, In re F.R.W., 61 Wis.2d 193, 212 N.W.2d 130 (1973). The broadness of waiver statutes has also been seen as a positive virtue in light of the individualizing concept implicit in juvenile law since "any attempt to explicate the standards with greater particularity appears not merely unnecessary but undesirable as likely to set up mechanical categories which the spirit of the law forbids." L. v. Superior Court, 7 Cal. 3d 592, 601–602, 102 Cal.Rptr. 850, 856, 498 P. 2d 1098, 1104 (1972).

Where the criteria are spelled out in the statute, they often are heavily weighed toward providing protection of the public from the child via an adult trial. For example, the Texas Family Code § 54.02(f) requires the juvenile court to consider:

(1) whether the alleged offense was against person or property, with greater weight in favor of transfer given to offenses against the person;

(2) whether the alleged offense was committed in an aggressive and premeditated manner;

(3) whether there is evidence on which a grand jury may be expected to return an indictment;

(4) the sophistication and maturity of the child;

(5) the record and previous history of the child; and

(6) the prospects of adequate protection of the public and the likelihood of the rehabilitation of the child by use of procedures, services, and facilities currently available to the juvenile court.

Under such a statute, ability of the corrections system to provide a long-term and secure program which will keep the child from committing further crimes is of paramount importance and the policy appears to be that if juvenile corrections cannot come up with facilities of this sort then the child should be sent to the criminal system where lengthy sentences and secure penal institutions are available. Even where the statute has a more general criterion, such as that the child would not be amenable to a program available through the juvenile court, it has been held proper for the court to take into account the length of time needed for confinement. P. v. Browning, 45 Cal.App. 125, 119 Cal.Rptr. 420 (1975), overruled on other grounds in P. v. Williams, 16 Cal.3d 663, 128 Cal.Rptr. 888, 547 P.2d 1000 (1976). Five years confinement in juvenile corrections may not be enough to persuade the juvenile court to retain the child. In re Appeal in Pima County, 22 Ariz.App. 327, 527 P.2d 104 (1974). The prediction about how long a child might need to be confined before his behavior became more law abiding is often made by an "expert," but such testimony is not a requirement.

Although it is apparent both from the terms of the waiver statutes and from the factors which courts take into account in making waiver decisions that the welfare of the child is of secondary importance at best, courts can sometimes even be found indulging the view that the child's best chance for rehabilitation is in the adult penal system and therefore "it was to his best interest to be certified." In re Salas, 520 P.2d 874, 875 (Utah 1974). But this appears to be little more than a pro forma compliance with the requirement that the waiver be in the child's interest.

Not all courts have treated the waiver issue as a permissible resort to the adult system when there has been experience, or a prediction, that juvenile corrections is incapable of changing the particular child's criminal behavior. In In re J.E. C., 302 Minn. 387, 225 N.W.2d 245 (1975) the Supreme Court of Minnesota reviewed a case in which the juvenile had been waived because "no program exists or has been designed which can rehabilitate [the juvenile], with adequate protection for the public, prior to his twenty-first birthday." The realities of the dilemma faced by the juvenile court judge were clear: "It appears that the juvenile court has under these circumstances only two alternatives, namely, to retain jurisdiction over him as a juvenile, with the knowledge that no matter what action is taken the offender will soon again be turned loose on society to continue his depredations, or to refer him as an adult prosecution and probably subject him to a lengthy sentence with doubtful rehabilitative sources available." Despite this, the court refused to affirm the waiver. Implicitly relying on the view that somewhere, somehow, there is the right treatment program for every offender, the court characterized the case as one where "the finding of lack of amenability to treatment or danger to the public is based upon the correctional authority's failure to provide favorable treatment facilities." The court went on to remand the case to the juvenile court so that a more active role could be taken by the juvenile court judge in finding out why there were not more alternatives. "We think the judge of the juvenile court should inquire into (1) whether there is presently any program available for treatment for this and other similar juveniles; (2) if no program is available, whether it is feasible and possible to put together an effective program which could treat this and similar juveniles; (3) if so, why has the Department of Corrections failed to make such a program available?" Presumably, these three factors must now be taken into account in waiver decisions by Minnesota juvenile court judges.

§ 63. Statement of Reasons for Waiver

One of the central holdings of *Kent* is that "Meaningful review requires that the reviewing court should review. It should not be remitted to assumptions. It must have before it a statement of the reasons motivating the waiver including, of course, a statement of the relevant facts. It may not 'assume' that there are adequate reasons nor may it merely assume that 'full investigation' has been made. Accordingly, we hold that it is incumbent upon the Juvenile Court to accompany its waiver order with a statement of the reasons or considerations therefore."

State courts which have found that *Kent* is not constitutionally controlling have most often taken this position on the issue of the requirement of a statement of reasons, upholding waivers in the absence of any such statement by the juvenile court. Commonwealth v. Roberts, 362 Mass. 357, 285 N.E.2d 919 (1972). When there is no appellate review of the waiver order it has similarly been held that the constitution does not require a statement of reasons. U. S. ex. rel. Bombacino v. Bensinger, 498 F.2d 875 (7th Cir. 1974). *Kent* has also been seen as merely laying down a requirement that there be a hearing before waiver is made; the rule concerning "a statement of the relevant facts" is not a constitutional one. In re Slack, 17 Or.App. 57, 520 P.2d 905 (1974).

In general, however, state courts have held that due process requires findings, Mathews v. Commonwealth, 216 Va. 358, 218 S.E.2d 538 (1975), and a statement of reasons. S. ex rel. T.J.H. v. Bills, 504 S.W.2d 76 (Mo.1974). This is not satisfied by a waiver order which recites the language of the statute as a statement of reasons. Risner v. Commonwealth, 508 S.W.2d 775 (Ky.1974). An oral statement by the judge which is reflected in the record will suffice, however. In re Salas, 520 P.2d 874 (Utah 1974).

State statutes commonly require that a background investigation of the child, his record and family circumstances be made. In addition to the seriousness of the offense, it is the content of this report which provides the factual basis of the waiver decision. Where the record does not show that such an investigation was made and considered, the waiver will not be upheld. P. v. Bowers, 54 Mich.App. 565, 221 N.W.2d 472 (1974).

§ 64. Proof of Delinquency

There is a constitutional distinction between a waiver hearing and an adjudicatory hearing in juvenile court. If the court holds an adjudicatory hearing, Breed v. Jones, 95 S.Ct. 1779, 421 U.S. 519 (1975) prohibits subsequent waiver and criminal trial on the grounds that the criminal trial violates the child's right to protection of the Double Jeopardy Clause of the Fifth Amendment. For these purposes, an adjudicatory hearing is one which can result in a finding that the child "has violated the criminal law and in a substantial deprivation of liberty." In some states this may be called a "hearing on the merits" or a "fact finding hearing."

This recent requirement that the waiver hearing must precede the adjudicatory hearing makes no change in most states where the waiver hearing either includes no inquiry at all into whether the child committed the act charged against him, or where the waiver decision must be based on a finding of *probable cause* concerning the crime, In re R.J.C., 520 P.2d 806 (Alaska 1974). The child is not constitutionally entitled to a probable cause finding. U. S. ex rel. Bombacino v. Bensinger, 498 F.2d 875 (7th Cir. 1974). The finding of probable cause may be waived by the child. S. v. Thompson, 113 Ariz. 1, 545 P.2d 925 (1976). *Breed* does, however, say that waiver may not be included as a dispositional option following a finding of delinquency.

It is not clear that *Breed* forbids a waiver procedure which includes a positive finding by the judge that the child violated the law. So long as the outcome of such a procedure is only a decision to waive or not waive, and does not permit a disposition such as commitment or probation—a "substantial deprivation of liberty"—the case can proceed to either an adjudicatory hearing in juvenile court if the decision is against waiver, or to a criminal trial if there is a waiver. The problem created by the former alternative relates to the propriety of the same judge first making a finding as to the law violation in the waiver hearing and then making the same finding at the delinquency hearing. *Breed* provides no hint whether there is any constitutional infirmity in having the same judge pass on the question twice. The opinion rather deals with this issue as a matter of the additional burden on juvenile court resources which is posed, and in this context finds the burden not to be substantial in light of the likelihood that the child might well waive what right he might have to a second judge in order to have his delinquency hearing before a judge who has already demonstrated a certain sympathy for him by not waiving jurisdiction.

§ 65. Appeal From Waiver

In most states a child may appeal from the juvenile court's waiver decision, In re Doe II, 86 N.M. 37, 519 P.2d 133 (1974), although courts which hold the decision not to be a final order and, therefore, not appealable, point out that to allow waiver to be appealed at that point would make for a great delay in the final disposition of juvenile cases. In re Watkins, Miss., 324 So.2d 232 (1975). If the juvenile court act does permit such an appeal the juvenile must pursue that course or he may find that in a later appeal from his criminal conviction he is foreclosed from raising the illegality of the waiver. S. v. Shepherd, 213 Kan. 498, 516 P.2d 945 (1973). Even if he merely waits until he can move in the criminal court to dismiss the indictment prior to trial on grounds that the waiver was defective, he may find that it is too late. S. v. Evangelista, 134 N.J.Super. 64, 338 A.2d 224 (1975). Similarly, when the waiver decision is directly appealable, it has been held that the child may not seek an extraordinary writ to prevent the waiver. Graham v. Ridge, 107 Ariz. 387, 489 P.2d 24 (1971).

In contrast to these exclusive remedies, P. v. Allgood, 54 Cal.App. 434, 126 Cal.Rptr. 666 (1976) indicates that in California it is possible to attack the waiver order either by direct appeal, or by habeas corpus, or by an extraordinary writ or by appeal from the criminal conviction. A different Court of Appeal, however, has held that the appeal of a conviction may not be used to question the validity of the juvenile court's waiver. P. v. Rising Sun, 55 Cal.App.3d 1024, 128 Cal.Rptr. 281 (1976). Like alternatives may be available in other states as well. Hamilton v. Commonwealth, 534 S.W.2d 802 (Ky.1976). Where a collateral attack is made on the waiver order following a criminal conviction, courts hold that if the conviction was on a guilty plea, the plea serves to waive any defect in the waiver process. S. v. LePage, 536 S.W.2d 834 (Mo.App.1976).

When the waiver order is reviewed, the decision of the juvenile court judge is given great respect. It will be overturned, for example, only if there is a "gross abuse of broad discretion", or is "contrary to the great weight of the evidence and is palpably wrong." Steele v. S., 289 Ala. 186, 266 So.2d 746 (1972).

If the juvenile court refuses to waive its jurisdiction it is generally held that the state has no standing to appeal that decision. In re Waterman, 212 Kan. 826, 512 P.2d 466 (1973). Whether the state may go ahead with the criminal trial while the child's appeal from a waiver decision is pending has been answered in opposing ways. Moreno v. S., 511 S.W.2d 273 (Tex.Cr.App.1974) (it may); Aye v. S., 17 Md.App. 32, 299 A.2d 513 (1973) (it may not).

CHAPTER VIII

APPEALS

§ 66. The Right to Appeal

In *Gault* the Supreme Court was presented with an appeal raising the issue of whether appeals from juvenile court decisions were constitutionally required. The Court refused, however, to rule on the validity of the Arizona system which made no provision for appeals. Since then, however, Arizona has amended its statute to provide for an appeal from juvenile court and similar statutes are found in all other jurisdictions as well. Even in the absence of specific statutory authority granting the juvenile a right to appeal, it has been held that Equal Protection requires that he have the same opportunity to appeal as does an adult faced with a criminal conviction. In re Brown, 439 F.2d 47 (3d Cir. 1971). The Equal Protection requirement has also been held to necessitate according the juvenile the same right to notice of his rights to appeal, information about what steps need be taken in order to appeal, the time limits in which the appeals right must be exercised and of his right to appellate counsel, as is done in criminal cases. In re N., 36 Cal.App. 935, 112 Cal.Rptr. 89 (1974). There is, however, no consensus that juvenile appeals must be governed by the same rules which apply to criminal appeals. It has been held, for example, that there is no right to an interlocutory appeal such as is available in criminal cases, People v. P.L.V., 172 Colo. 269, 472 P.2d 127 (1970), and that the right to bail on appeal from a conviction does not apply to juvenile appeals. In re Appeal for Montgomery County, 29 Md.App. 701, 351 A.2d 164 (1976).

There may also be a statutory right to a redetermination of the case in the juvenile court itself. Commonwealth v. Croft, 445 Pa. 579, 285 A.2d 118 (1971). When a rehearing is at the option of the child, he must be informed of that right. In re Drexel F., 58 Cal.App. 801, 130 Cal. Rptr. 253 (1976) (rehearing of case decided by referee before juvenile court judge).

§ 67. Final Orders

Juvenile court statutes normally restrict appeals to cases where the appellant seeks review of a "final order" or a "final judgment". This is in order to prevent piece-meal review of a case in which the resources of appellate procedure might be used on issues that turn out to be not important to the final posture of the case. This restriction also serves to avoid delaying the final disposition of cases. For this reason it is generally held that no appeal lies from an adjudication of delinquency; the child must wait until a disposition has been made before he can claim a "final order" on which to appeal. B.F. v. State, 550 P.2d 991 (Okl.Cr.App.1976). Statutes sometimes permit appeals at either time. Mass.Gen. Laws Ann. c. 119, § 56. Where there is a disposition, the right to appeal is not frustrated by inserting the word "temporary" in the disposition order. Sanchez v. Department of Family and Children Services, 235 Ga. 817, 221 S.E.2d 589 (1976) (temporary custody); In re Belding, 190 Neb. 646, 211 N.W.2d 715 (1973) (temporary probation). But a commitment for diagnostic study, following a delinquency finding, is not an appealable order. In re Bolden, 37 Ohio App. 7, 306 N.E.2d 166 (1973).

§ 68. The Record on Appeal

The requirements as to form and contents of the record which is presented to the appellate court are usually found in court rules. Since there are normally rules for criminal appeals which are different from rules governing appeals from civil judgments, the question arises as to whether delinquency appeals must conform to one or the other. Courts have decided the issue both ways. In re D.J., 330 So.2d 34 (Fla.App.1975) (record to be prepared as in criminal appeal); In re Appeal for Montgomery County, 29 Md.App. 701, 351 A.2d 164 (1976) (criminal appellate rules relating to release on bail pending appeal held not applicable).

Regardless of the question of which rules govern the appeal, the child needs at least the transcript of the juvenile court proceedings to present to the appellate court, unless the appeal is *de novo*, in which case the *de novo* trial proceeds as if there had been no original proceeding. If he cannot afford to pay for the transcript, one will be furnished him at public expense. J. v. Superior Court, 4 Cal.3d 836, 94 Cal.Rptr. 619, 484 P.2d 595 (1971). Where the juvenile has ability to earn money, however, the court may require that he do so and pay for the transcript in installments. In re DiIorio, 112 R.I. 443, 311 A.2d 566 (1973). Indigent parents are entitled, as well, to a free transcript in order to pursue their appeal. In re Appeal in Pima County, 112 Ariz. 170, 540 P.2d 642 (1975).

Absent any excuse such as indigency, the failure of the juvenile to present the appellate court with a record of the juvenile court hearing from which there can be seen the actions which are claimed to be reversible error, will result in his losing the appeal. As one court has put it: "All reasonable presumptions are in favor of the judgment of the trial court on appeal, and it is appellant's burden to overcome these presumptions by affirmatively showing the errors charged."

In re Burke, 37 Ill.App.3d 790, 347 N.E.2d 23 (1976).

§ 69. Notice and Timing

It is usually required by statute that the party desiring to appeal give written notice of his intentions within a certain period of time. The Model Act, for example, uses a limit of 30 days. The intention to appeal may be communicated orally, however, provided the record of the case indicates that this was done. Reasoner v. S., 463 S.W.2d 55 (Tex.Civ.App.1971). The time for these purposes generally runs from the date of the disposition or other final order. In re Williams, 267 So.2d 918 (La.App.1972). Unless the notice of appeal is given within the required time, the appellate court lacks jurisdiction to hear the case, In re Donald R., 56 Cal.App. 850, 129 Cal.Rptr. 26 (1976), and the issue may be raised by the court itself in the absence of a challenge by a party to the timeliness of the appeal. In re R.L. P., 536 S.W.2d 41 (Mo.App.1976). There is evidence of some flexibility in administering these deadlines, at least where the failure to meet them is not the fault of the appellant. For example, in In re T.A.F., 252 So.2d 255 (Fla.App.1971), the late filing of the appeal was excused where the parents had been erroneously advised by the juvenile court that the period ran from the time they received a copy of the order instead of from the day the order was entered.

The timing of notice of appeal is only one of the timing issues in the appellate process. There are also time limits for providing the court the transcript and record and for filing briefs in the appellate court. Failure to "perfect" the appeal by complying with these rules may result in dismissal of the appeal. L__ B__ v. S., 513 S.W.2d 303 (Tex.Civ.App.1974).

*

INDEX

References are to Pages

ACCOMPLICE TESTIMONY
Corroboration of, 200–201

ADULT SYSTEM
See also Waiver for Criminal Trial
Differences from, 7–8
Houses of Refuge as separation from, 13
Incompleteness in separation from, 12–13
Juvenile courts as separation from, 12–13
Separation from, generally, 3–4

APPEAL
Bail pending, 270–271
Equal protection, 268
Final order, requirement for, 269–270
Informing juvenile of right to, 268
Notice of intention to, 272–273
Record for, 270–272
Right to, 268–269
Rules governing, 270–271
Time limits, 273
Transcript, see Transcript
Type of, 6–7, 270–271

ARREST
Common law,
Felony, 93–94
Misdemeanor, 94
Confessions, see Confessions
Consequences of illegality, 85–86
Constitutional rules for, 91–92, 94–95, 98–99

ARREST—Continued
Criteria for, 86–88
Guidance for police, 82–83
Investigations authorized by, 85–86
Number of, 81–82
Persons authorized to effect, 83
Post-arrest duties, importance of, 107–108
Probable cause, 91–92, 95–98
Statutory provisions, 88–90, 95–97
Time for determining legality, 86–88
Warrants, 90–91

BAIL
Appeal, see Appeal
Detention hearing, see Detention Hearing

BURDEN OF PROOF
Beyond a reasonable doubt, 188–189
Neglected children, 58–59, 190–191
Probation revocation, 190
Status offenders, 188–189

CHILD ABUSE
Neglected children, see Neglected Children

CHILD WELFARE
Philosophy, see Philosophy

COERCION
See also Philosophy
Limited need for, 19–20

CONCURRENT JURISDICTION
See also Jurisdiction
Choice,
By grand jury, 67–68
By prosecutor, 67
Meaning of, 64
Waiver for criminal trial, see Waiver for Criminal Trial

INDEX

References are to Pages

CONFESSIONS
Authorized place of detention, 110–111, 125–126
Corroboration, 193–194
Criminal court admissibility, 127–128
Delay in release or arraignment, 126–127
Due process, denial of, 122
Illegal arrest, 126–127
Interrogation by private persons, 121–122
Miranda warnings,
    Contents of, 117–118
    Custody requirement, 120, 122
    Illegal arrest, 121
    Impeachment, see Impeachment
    Necessity for, 118–119
    Parents, 119–120
    Spontaneous statements, 120–121
    Waiver of, 116, 121
        Burden of proof, 121
Notice to attorney and parents, 124–125
Parents, request for, 123
Policies of admissibility rules, 114–115
Probation officer, interrogation by, 117
Right to counsel, 122–123
Voluntariness,
    Absence of attorney, 116
    Affected by Miranda warnings, 116
    Traditional test, 115

COUNSEL
    See also Right to Counsel
Absence, effect of, 116, 124, 194
Access to court records, 170–171
Functions of, 168
Interrogation abuse prevented by, 122
Lawyer-client privilege, 170
Need to pay for, 18
Notice to, prior to interrogation, 124

COURTHOUSE
Varieties of, 3–4

CRIMINAL CAPACITY

Common law presumption against, 30–33
Proof of in juvenile court, 31–32

CRIMINAL LAW

See also Mens Rea; Status Offenders
Applicable only to children, 40–41
Collaborative misconduct, 41
Delinquency as violation of, 37–41
Exceptions to jurisdiction, 39–40
Federal and state law, 38–39
Vindication of, 28
Violation of as symptom, 38–39

CRUEL AND UNUSUAL PUNISHMENT

Adult facility, 233–234
Habeas corpus authority, 232–233
Right to treatment, see Right to Treatment

DETENTION FOLLOWING ARREST

Confessions, see Confessions
Place of, 110–112
Release or detention decision, 147–148
Time limits, 149

DETENTION FOR INVESTIGATION

Constitutionality of, 100
Guidelines, need for, 103–104
Justification for, 100–101
Significance of, 100
"Stop and frisk" statutes, 102–103
Time limits, 101–102
Voluntary cooperation in, 104

DETENTION HEARING

Bail, right to, 149–150
Probable cause determination, 150–151, 152
Right to counsel, 150–151
Time for, 149

DISCOVERY

Based on partisan procedures, 169–170

Civil and criminal rules of, 171–172

Impeachment of witness, 173

Records, inspection of, 170–171

DISCRETION

    See also Intake

Commitment to institution, 234–236

Criticism of, 16–17

Defining neglected children, 51–52

Neglect petition substituted for delinquency, 74

Police decision to arrest, 81–82

Post-arrest release, 112–113

Public trial, 185–186

Reports, disclosure of, 171

Transfer from criminal court, 66

Venue,

    Choice of, 25–26

    Transfer of, 25

DISPOSITION AUTHORITY

Compulsory education, excusing from, 215–216

Corrections agencies, control by, 215

Court's power and procedural rules, 196–197

Ideal of individualization, 220

Limited by statute, 214

Public agencies, court power over, 216–217

Range of options, 214

DISPOSITION HEARING

Absence of child, 212–213

Allocution, right to, 213

Exclusionary rule, 219

Hearsay, admissibility of, 218–219

Necessity for, 213

Neglect cases, 213–214

Privilege against self-incrimination, see Privilege Against
    Self-incrimination

Procedural requirements, 218–220

INDEX

DISPOSITION HEARING—Continued
Right to counsel, see Right to Counsel
Separate from fact-finding, 211–212
Social study,
    Access to, 222–225
    Consideration of, 220–221
    Contents of, 221–222
    Necessity for, 221
    Timing of, 222–223

DIVERSION
Intake, see Intake
Petition, see Petition

DOUBLE JEOPARDY
Appeal, 72
Applicable in juvenile courts, 68
Informal hearings, 71
Mistrial, 72
Multiple prosecutions, 72
Retrial on included offense, 72–73
Waiver for criminal trial, see Waiver for Criminal Trial

ENTRAPMENT
Juvenile court, relevance to, 105
Nonconstitutional basis of, 105
Policy behind, 105
Recognition of, 104–105
Vulnerability of children, 106–107

EQUAL PROTECTION
Age limits for males and females, 34–35
Appeal, see Appeal
Arbitrary age lines, 34
Corroboration of accomplice testimony, 201
Denied by geographic distinctions, 12
Duration of commitment, 237

EVIDENCE RULES
Generally, 192–194
Statutory provisions, 193
Waiver of, 194

INDEX

References are to Pages

EXCLUSIONARY RULE
Disposition hearing, see Disposition Hearing
Restriction of, 195
Searches, see Searches
Statement of, 194

EXCLUSIVE JURISDICTION
See also Jurisdiction
Attempted crimes, 65
Capital cases, 64–65
Criminal court, 64
Delinquency in juvenile court, 64
Neglect and abuse cases, 65–66
Transfer to juvenile court, 66

EXPERT TESTIMONY
Hearsay basis in neglect cases, 58

FACT–FINDING HEARING
Criminal trial, similarity to, 174–175
Informality, opportunity for, 175–178
Recent significance of, 174

FAMILY COURTS
Advantages of, 73
Criminal offenses, 74–75
Judicial specialization in, 11
Jurisdiction,
    Omissions from, 73–74
    Scope of, 22–23, 73
Type of cases heard, 11

FINDINGS
Necessity for, 206–207
Supervision in absence of, 207–208

HEARSAY
Disposition hearing, see Disposition Hearing
Harmless error in admission of, 204
Lack of personal knowledge distinguished, 204
Neglect cases, 58

HEARSAY—Continued
Reversible error, 205
Traditional admission of, 203

HISTORY OF JUVENILE COURT
Changes in, 2–3
Founding first court, 5
Traditional image, 1–2

IDENTIFICATION PROCEDURES
Criminal trial, 139–140
Illegal arrest, 139
Independent source rule, 138
Photographic identification, 140
Right to counsel 137–138
Statutory rules, 136–137
Street confrontations, 139

IMPEACHMENT
Arrest record, 200
Juvenile court record, 197–199
Lie detector, 197
Prior inconsistent statement, 197
Statement violating Miranda rules, 195–196, 116–117

INSTITUTIONS
See also Philosophy
Adults, commitment with, 233–234
Authority to commit to, 231
Criteria for commitment, 234–236
Duration of commitment, 236–239
Extension of commitment period, 238–239
Judicial supervision of, 231–233
Non-punitive, 13
Status offenders, see Status Offenders

INTAKE
Diversion, 144, 146
Function of, 141
Investigation, 143–146
Screening, 141–142

INTAKE—Continued
Statements at, admissibility of, 144–145
Statutory purposes, 143

JAILS
Children in, 4, 15–16

JUDGE
Interrogation of witnesses, 179
Judicial functions, combination of, 180–181
Juvenile specialist, 8–9
Model for, 1–2, 178–179
Opposition to status offender proposals, 19–20
Prosecutorial role, 179–180
Right not to testify, consideration of, 196
Rotating assignments, 9
Specialist in full time court, 11
Time devoted to juvenile cases,
    General jurisdiction court, 10–11
    Limited jurisdiction court, 10–11

JUDICIAL SYSTEM
Full time juvenile court, 9–10
General jurisdiction courts, 8–9
Juvenile court in, 6
Limited jurisdiction courts, juveniles in, 8–10
Number of juvenile courts, 8
Type of court trying juveniles, 8–10

JURISDICTION
    See also Concurrent Jurisdiction; Exclusive Jurisdiction: Family Courts; Jurisdictional Age
Appellate, 22
Contempt, 65
Error as voiding, 23
Established for adjudicatory hearing, 21
Family courts, see Family Courts
Geographic, 7, 11, 21
Notice, 21–22
Original, 22
Personal jurisdiction, see Personal Jurisdiction

INDEX

JURISDICTION—Continued
Subject matter, 7
Traffic offenses, see Traffic Offenses
Varied meaning of, 21–23

JURISDICTIONAL AGE
See also Equal Protection
Criminal responsibility, age of, 29
Immunity under age seven, 29
Lower limits,
Absence of for neglect, 27–28
Emergence of, 29–30
Maximum limits,
Common law age rule, 33
Delayed prosecution, 36–37
Fixed by statute, 33–37
Need for proof of, 33–34
Time of offense, 33
Status offenses, 30

JURY
Absence of, 7–8
Advisory, authority for, 182–183
Constitution, not required by, 181, 183–184
Statutory authorization for, 181

LAW ENFORCEMENT
Attitude toward delinquency, 5
Interaction with, 5
Peace keeping role of police, 80–82
Surveillance of juveniles, 80–85

MENS REA
Proof of in juvenile court, 32–33, 188

NEED FOR TREATMENT
See also Treatment
Allegation of, 45–46
Ambiguity of, 47
Distinguished from right to treatment, 45
Evidence establishing, 46–47, 188

NEED FOR TREATMENT—Continued
Litigation meaning of, 45–46
Necessity for proof of, 46, 207

NEGLECTED CHILDREN
    See also Exclusive Jurisdiction ; Jurisdictional Age
Burden of proof, see Burden of Proof
Child abuse, 56
Disposition hearing, see Disposition Hearing
Institutional confinement with delinquents, 14
Judicial interpretations, 54–55
Number of in court, 51
Procedural rights, 57–59
Statutory definition of, 51–52

NOTICE
Constitutional requirements, 76–77
Failure to provide, 77–78
Personal jurisdiction, see Personal Jurisdiction
Persons to receive, 77
Petition, see Petition
Provided in court, 78–79
Right to in neglect cases, 57–58
Timing of, 79
To parents following arrest, 108–110
Waiver of, 78–79

PARENT–CHILD PRIVILEGE
Assertion of, 203

PAROLE
Frequency of, 239
Revocation of, 239–241

PERSONAL JURISDICTION
    See also Notice
Foreign state law violations, 75–76
Protective orders, see Protective Orders

PETITION
Amendment to, 158–159
Citation to statute, 157

PETITION—Continued
Dismissal of, 208
Diversion, filing following, 146
Factual allegations in neglect cases, 57
Filing of, 155
Notice function of, 153–154
Probable cause for, 154
Refusal to file, 145
Signing of, 155
Specificity of, 156–157
Variance in proof, 158–159
Verification of, 156

PHILOSOPHY
See also Institutions; Punishment, Treatment
Assertion of rights inhibited by, 18–19
Child welfare in, 13–14
Compromise of adversary process, 19
Conflicting views, 6
Constitutional law in, 15, 17
Continuity of, 12–14
Criminal jurisprudence in juvenile courts, 17–20
Criminal law in, 15, 17
Discretion as basic feature of, 14
Education programs in institutions, 13
Ethical aspects, 14
Ethics of new technologies, 15
Incomplete separation from adult system, 15–16
Nonpunitive nature of institutions, 13–14
Punishment, disclaimer of, 13–14
Purposes of juvenile court, 8
Retribution, sparing children from, 14
Separation from adults, 12–13
Sources for change in, 14–15

PLEA
Form of, 159
Formalities for, 151–152
Guilty pleas, preponderance of, 7

PLEA—Continued
Information for making, 152
Number of, 150
Parental participation in, 152
Right, to counsel at, 151

PREVENTIVE DETENTION
Constitutionality of, 113–114

PRIVILEGE AGAINST SELF–INCRIMINATION
See also Confessions
Disposition hearing, 219–220
Function of, 201–202
Judge's duties concerning, 196
Psychiatric examination, 202–203
Right to counsel, see Right to Counsel
Status offenders, see Status Offenders

PROBATION
Conditions of, 226–227, 228
Duration of, 227–228
Permissible disposition, 225
Revocation, 229–231
Supervision, nature of, 228–229

PROTECTIVE ORDERS
Enforced through contempt power, 210
Personal jurisdiction, necessity for, 209
Statutory authority for, 209

PUBLIC TRIAL
News media, presence of, 186
Right to, 186
Supreme Court views on, 184–185

PUNISHMENT
See also Philosophy
Coerced treatment as, 16, 19
Separation from adults negates, 13–14

REHABILITATION
See Treatment

[*287*]

INDEX

REPORTING LAWS
Identity of reporter, disclosure of, 60
Immunity of reporters, 60
Mandatory reporters, 59
Penalties for failure to report, 19–60
Reportable conditions, 60

RIGHT TO COUNSEL
Adults, comparison with, 166–167
Confessions, see Confessions
Constitutional course of, 164
Detention hearing, see Detention Hearing
Dilution of effectiveness, 162–163
Disposition hearing, 217–218
Intake, 144–145
Neglect cases, 157–158, 57, 167
Phases of process, 165–166
Plea, see Plea
Private attorneys, use of, 163–164
Privilege against self-incrimination, waiver of, 104
Status offenders, 166–167
Unwaivable, 155, 159, 123, 164–165, 168
Waiver for criminal trial, see Waiver for Criminal Trial
Waiver of, 169

RIGHT TO TREATMENT
Constitutional theories, variety of, 243–244
Cruel and unusual punishment, relation to, 242–243
Doctrinal source of, 241–242
Financial costs, 245–246
Institutionalized juveniles, claim for, 242
Least restrictive alternative, 246
Relief, forms of, 245
Treatment, see Treatment

SCOTLAND
Lay justice system, 7, 177–178

SEARCHES
Consent, 132–134

SEARCHES—Continued
Exclusionary rule, 129–136
Incident to arrest, 129, 130–132
School searches, 134–136
Statutory omissions, 129
Warrant rules, 130

SOCIAL STUDY
See Disposition Hearing

SPEEDY TRIAL
Constitutional right to, 186
Statutory requirements, 186–187

STATUS OFFENDERS
Generally, 41–44
Attack on jurisdiction over, 44
Burden of proof, see Burden of Proof
Conduct and conditions constituting, 42
Defined as delinquents, 42
Disposition of, 44, 233
Misconduct short of criminal violation, 43–44
Number of, 41–42
Privilege against self-incrimination, 192–193, 196
Procedural requirements for trial, 43
Removal from court jurisdiction, 19–20
Right to counsel, 166–167

TERMINATION OF PARENTAL RIGHTS
Generally, 61–64
Burden of proof, 62
Consequences of, 61
Counsel, parents' right to, 61–62
Grounds for, 62–63
Mental illness of parent, 63–64
Services, duty to provide, 63

TRAFFIC OFFENSES
Justification for including in jurisdiction, 48–49

References are to Pages

TRAFFIC OFFENSES—Continued
Minor, not within jurisdiction, 39
Selective exclusion from jurisdiction, 49–50

TRANSCRIPT
Appeal, needed for, 191
Constitutional right to, 54, 179–180, 256, 57, 191–192, 271

TREATMENT
    See also Diversion; Intake; Philosophy
Ambigious meaning of, 247–248
Empty promise of, 19
Individualized, 14
Individualized incomplete, 17
Need for treatment, see Need for Treatment
Punishment in coercion for, 16

VENUE
    See also Discretion
Choice of, 25–26
Definition of, 23
Determination of,
    Constitutional requirements, 26–27
    Place of offense, 24, 25–26
    Residence of juvenile, 24, 25–26
Transfer of, 25
Waiver of jurisdiction, 26

WAIVER FOR CRIMINAL TRIAL
    See also Double Jeopardy
Age of juvenile, 251
Appeal from, 265–267
Burden of proof, 255–256
Concurrent jurisdiction, relationship to, 250, 254
Criminal offense, requirements for, 251–252
Criteria for, 257–261
Delinquency, proof of, 263–265
Double jeopardy in, 60–63, 240–251, 68–70, 263–264
Findings of fact, requirement for, 262
Hearing, requirements for, 252–257

INDEX

References are to Pages

WAIVER FOR CRIMINAL TRIAL—Continued

Investigation, requirement of, 263
Notice of, 254–255
Reasons, statement of, 261–262
Right to a hearing, waiver of, 256–257
Right to counsel, 253–254
Sentencing consequences of, 249–250
States permitting, 249
Statutory basis for, 250

†